The Influencer Industry

The Influencer Industry

The Quest for Authenticity on Social Media

Emily Hund

PRINCETON UNIVERSITY PRESS

PRINCETON AND OXFORD

Published by Princeton University Press
41 William Street, Princeton, New Jersey 08540
99 Banbury Road, Oxford OX2 6JX

press.princeton.edu

ISBN 978-0-691-23102-0
ISBN (e-book) 978-0-691-23407-6

British Library Cataloging-in-Publication Data is available

Editorial: Meagan Levinson and Jacqueline Delaney
Production Editorial: Jill Harris
Text Design: Heather Hansen
Jacket Design: Heather Hansen
Production: Erin Suydam
Publicity: Maria Whelan and Kathryn Stevens
Copyeditor: Leah Caldwell

Jacket illustration: Calathea plant botanical illustration by Aum / rawpixel

This book has been composed in Arno Pro with Neue Haas Grotesk Display Pro

Printed on acid-free paper. ∞

Printed in Canada

10 9 8 7 6 5 4 3 2 1

For my family

Contents

Illustrations

Acknowledgments

There are few things more overwhelming than pausing to consider the many people and events that made the completion of a book possible, especially when that book, from seed of an idea to finished manuscript, took the better part of a decade.

All of the formal work for this manuscript occurred while I have been a part of the Annenberg School for Communication at the University of Pennsylvania, first as a doctoral student and then as a fellow and affiliate at the Center on Digital Culture and Society. The support of ASC's faculty and staff has been instrumental to the book's journey, as well as mine. My PhD adviser Joseph Turow has been a dependable source of encouragement, thoughtful questions, and puns, fundamentally shaping my thinking along the way. Feedback from Barbie Zelizer and Victor Pickard gave me the perspective I needed to imagine what this book project could be. Guobin Yang and CDCS pulled me out of a postpartum pandemic fog and provided the financial and moral support to write this manuscript. I cannot thank them all enough.

Over the years I have been lucky to collaborate on other research projects with brilliant and kind people from whom I have learned so much. Brooke Duffy took a chance on me when I was a first-year student and she was a new professor. We were complete strangers—albeit strangers whose educational and professional trajectories had uncanny similarities—but immediately got to work. Without her tremendous generosity as a collaborator, mentor, and friend, I would not be where I am today. In separate projects, Caitlin Petre and Lee McGuigan widened my perspective in important ways—with the added bonus of having fun working together.

My deepest thanks to the bloggers, influencers, and content creators who shared your stories, goals, and challenges with me, and to the marketers, brand representatives, talent managers, trend forecasters, and other influencer industry professionals who offered your expertise, reflections, and questions. I am so grateful to each one of you for your time and your willingness to help analyze this world as you navigated it yourselves. Thanks especially to Sharon McMahon, Blair Eadie, Darby Cisneros, and the Museum of Ice Cream for allowing me to use your Instagram images in this book.

Meagan Levinson and the team at Princeton University Press have been enthusiastic, thoughtful, and supportive from our first email exchange, and I am so glad to have worked with them to bring this book to the world. I sincerely appreciate the anonymous reviewers who provided insightful and good-faith feedback on the proposal and first draft of the manuscript. Laura Portwood-Stacer provided vital advice about the publishing process and helped me get started on this path.

A wise person once said that behind every successful woman is a group text hyping her up, and I would like to confirm here that this is true—perhaps more than ever during a pandemic. The in-person and digital support of the Hive Mind—Elena Maris, Rosie Clark-Parsons, and my office mate of six years Samantha Oliver—has been essential in confronting the idiosyncrasies, struggles, and excitement of pursuing this work. I also rely on the support and laughs provided by the PSU Besties—Ashley, Christa, Elyse, Emily, Steph—and my oldest friend Amy. I am lucky to have friends who are truly the "realest."

This book is ultimately for, and made possible by, my family. For my husband Henry, first and foremost, who has supported me unconditionally since we were teenagers and is the most involved and devoted father and partner one could ask for. For our sons, whose births brought highs and lows we did not know were possible and put everything in perspective. For my parents and in-laws, who have helped with childcare and provided moral support throughout. My mom, in particular, encouraged (some might say nagged) me to pursue graduate education when I wasn't sure if it was time to make the leap, and has provided piles of relevant magazine and newspaper clippings over the years. For my sisters, sisters-in-law, and brothers-in-law, whose support and pride I deeply appreciate. For all four of my grandparents, whose amazing and steadfast presence in my life has shaped it profoundly, and my great-grandparents, whose immense sacrifices and extremely limited access to, in some cases, even the most basic education, I carry with me always. For these reasons and many more, I hope to always be a steward of the wonderful opportunities I have.

Introduction

Staring out from the cover of *New York* magazine's September 2019 issue was a close-up of a young woman's face, wide-eyed with a resigned "can you believe this?" expression, covered in red rubber darts. The cover line read, "What Instagram did to me." Readers familiar with the fashion blogosphere of the 2000s or New York City's arts or media scenes in the 2010s would recognize the face as that of Tavi Gevinson, who first made a name for herself in the late 2000s as a preteen style blogger. Her rise had been nervously and obsessively tracked by blog readers, journalists, and industry insiders. In the span of a few short years, Gevinson reaped enormous rewards from being an early entrant into the world of social media self-branding: from taking selfies to being photographed by Annie Leibovitz; from attending middle school to sitting front row at Fashion Week (and famously pissing off a *Grazia* editor by blocking the view with an enormous hair bow); from hanging out in the comments section of her blog to running her own digital teen magazine with the blessing of legendary editor Jane Pratt and radio producer Ira Glass. But by the time of this 2019 cover story, Gevinson, then aged twenty-three, had also been through the wringer. She had been a test case, patient zero, for the influencer industrial ethos: the idea that anyone can cultivate a loyal audience by providing consistent and relatable content on social media, and then use that audience's likes, follows, and other engagement metrics as evidence of "influence" to be leveraged for a range of social and economic rewards—many of them accessible through partnering with commercial brands to entwine their messages with one's own.

The notion that rewards await those who craft an authentic-seeming public image has existed for centuries, and it has been particularly salient in American entrepreneurial culture. As media historian Jefferson Pooley has pointed out, American literature of the early 1900s encapsulated a "core contradiction" of American culture then and now: "Be true to yourself, it is to your strategic advantage."[1] Given fertile ground by the technological and socioeconomic conditions of the 2000s, this concept has grown wildly in the twenty-first century, powering a multibillion-dollar industrial machine that has reshaped the creation and flows of culture, ideas about who and what is powerful, and technologies and social norms of communication. This is the influencer industry. And Gevinson was finding the whole thing a bit existentially troubling.

In the accompanying essay for *New York*, Gevinson wrote about how her experience growing up online shaped her sense of self and her experience of the world, in ways that are both obvious and unknowable. The audience she cultivated through her blog and grew exponentially through Instagram provided her with job opportunities on stage, film, and high-end ad campaigns, as well as with friends, entrée to elite events, and an identity. It gave her an income, and even a home in a luxury apartment building where she lived rent-free for a year in exchange for posting about the experience. "I can try to imagine an alternate universe where I've always roamed free and Instagram-less in pastures untouched by the algorithm. But I can't imagine who that person is inside," she wrote. Gevinson is acutely aware that it was her seemingly effortless ability to be herself that spawned this existence, but she admitted to doing "rapid-fire stage-mom math" to keep her digital persona in line with others' expectations. "Somewhere along the line, I think I came to see my shareable self as the authentic one and buried any tendencies that might threaten her likability so deep down I forgot they even existed," she wrote. Among the many reasons to distrust Instagram—not least of which is its exploitation of leisure time with constant data collection and ad-targeting—she continued, "most unnerving are the ways in which it has led me to distrust myself . . . I think I am a writer and an actor and an artist. But I haven't believed the purity of my own intentions ever since I became my own salesperson, too."[2]

ʘʃ

Ten years before this cover hit newsstands, in the summer of 2009, I was an eager new college graduate with a longtime vision of working in magazines. I went to New York two weeks after graduation to start an internship in the features department of a storied fashion title. This was the exact sort of position in which I had dreamed I would land—aside, of course, from the lack of pay and stability. Another intern and I shared the job of department assistant, answering phones, scheduling, pulling products for front-of-book pages, and generally pitching in on whatever projects needed it. I was also continuing my paid job as a contributing writer at my hometown newspaper and relying on a loan from my parents, who had agreed to help with rent for two months. If I had not found a way to support myself fully by the time it ran out, my time in New York would be over. I knew the multidimensional absurdity of this situation, but I had accepted the toxic narrative that working for free was the only way "in" to a paying job at a major media company, and since no one in my life had ever pursued this type of path, that narrative was all I had. I was young and not ready to let reality get in the way of my ambitions.

On my first day, what struck me most was the emptiness and quiet of the offices. My desk was on the edge of the area where the staff sat; my view was of rows of empty white workstations. I swallowed my uncertainty and acted as though everything was normal, and that I belonged. But despite its seemingly impenetrable glamour, the Hearst Tower was not immune to the economic realities that seemed to be swallowing the world whole. Less than a year prior, the United States' housing market had imploded and took with it the livelihoods and ways of life for millions of Americans and much of the world. In the months leading up to my move to New York, I read the news from my rural college campus with awe and nervousness. January 2009: 600,000 jobs lost. March 2009: 700,000 jobs lost. By May 2009 nearly six million jobs had been lost in the United States and many millions more globally. I submitted dozens of applications to paying jobs with almost zero response.

At the same time, bloggers and the nascent term "social media" were increasingly hot topics of conversation, especially among journalists and other media workers. Bloggers were still considered amateurs and outsiders—interesting, for sure, but with no real expertise or credibility in the fields they claimed to inhabit. Yet editors and professors repeatedly suggested to me and my aspiring journalist peers that we work on blogs to pass the time until jobs opened up, conveniently overlooking that one typically needs to be paid to get by. My fellow department intern and I would go for walks at night, stomping around Greenwich Village in the day-old heat and wondering how it could be that the only way we were going to move forward was by selling ourselves for nothing on the internet.

Not long after, the magazine hired thirteen-year-old Tavi Gevinson to write a column. The blogger was quickly becoming a wunderkind due to her eccentric style and earnest takes on fashion that she published from her suburban Midwestern family home. That moment was existentially clarifying. I knew that the DNA of the industry I had trained and planned to work in had permanently changed—and that these changes represented a much more sweeping shift for our information and cultural environment. On one hand, as an aspiring media worker, I felt deeply the ridiculousness and unfairness in a system that essentially required preexisting economic and social capital to get ahead. I knew that I was more fortunate than most in that my family was able to help at all for those two months, but I also knew that their generosity would not be enough to float me into a paying position. I would be leaving in early August, then staying with my sister in Philadelphia and commuting to finish my internship. The commute was nearly three hours door to door on standing-room-only New Jersey Transit trains, which gave me a lot of time to worry. It was not difficult to make the connection that when the pipeline for media jobs was this inaccessible, those who make it through—and end up responsible for producing and marketing the information and entertainment that plays a significant role in constructing a society's shared reality—are probably coming from a narrow pool. On the other hand, I saw that while traditional media companies were laying off employees and demanding free labor of their entry-level and freelance workers, the public's demand for content was growing. And as our economic system crashed, it fanned the flames of deep skepticism of society's established institutions. People were hungry for content, but from providers who were "real"—who showed that they "got it" in a way that New York-based national and global media companies, from Condé Nast to the *New York Times* to the major television networks, never did.

Marching into this vacuum came bloggers. They followed different communication norms—in particular, a conversational tone and a lack of separation between their editorial content and that which was sponsored by a brand—and most of all, they portrayed themselves as driven by passion, indicating a wholesomeness and authenticity that elsewhere seemed lacking. They saw themselves as regular people searching for a like-minded community with whom to share and critique ideas, products, and more. Their independence was their power, though it would also become their meal ticket, and thus their most critical sacrifice. As bloggers and early influencers ceded independence for earning a predictable living—a perfectly rational and understandable choice, given the circumstances—they also helped create a growing digital media industrial machine interested in monetizing an authentic life, not embodying it.

I marveled over this state of affairs for another four years as I hopped around the tumultuous job market, working at a range of organizations as an assistant, then assistant editor, and later, a social media editor. I could not shake the feeling that my experience was a microscopic part of a world-shifting pattern of events, and I wanted to understand it better and help translate it for others. I went to graduate school ostensibly to study the shifting labor market for media workers and how this was impacting content. But fashion was my starting point of reference, and blogging was where these changes were going down. Turns out, as is so often the case, the fashion and retail industries were indicators of broader social and technological changes to come. Often, we get acclimated to new ways of life under the auspices of light-hearted commercialism, from viewing shopping as a route to self-actualization to handing companies our personal data (in exchange for a discount, of course).[3]

For nearly a decade, I have followed along. I conducted in-depth interviews with dozens of people, attended industry events, and analyzed thousands of press articles and corporate and individual marketing materials, as "blogger" turned into multiplatform "influencer," amateurs turned into professionals, niche content gave way to generalized lifestyle content (and started to swing back again), free product turned into multimillion-dollar deals, and an industry spun up to affirm and expand the chaotic marketplace of digital influence, repackaging and reshaping "realness" to suit its needs.

This book offers a critical history of the influencer industry's formative years in the United States. I track its development from a haphazard group of creative people scrambling for work in the face of the Great Recession to today's multifaceted, multibillion-dollar industry with expanding global impact. I contextualize the industry's origins within key cultural and intellectual histories that predate the digital era, and explore some of its consequences—which, at the time of writing, are increasingly foreboding.

The influencer industry is a complex ecosystem, comprising influencers and those who aspire to be them, marketers and technologists, brands and sponsors, social media corporations, and a host of others, including talent managers and trend forecasters. I have interviewed people from all of these groups, except for the social media companies who did not answer my queries. I examined how these stakeholders negotiated the meaning, value, and practical use of digital influence as they reimagined it as a commodity for the social media age. The systems they created for producing, evaluating, and marketing "influential" content relied on a positive association with authenticity, or "being real." Yet, as their industrial definition of authenticity shifted along with the needs of marketers, so too did the tools we use to communicate and the social norms and values that animate them. More than a decade into the influencer industry's existence, these decisions have accumulated to something more than the sum of its parts. As the later chapters show, the industry's participants created logics and tools for social media communication that have extended beyond their intentions and control, enabling propagandists (and worse) to insert their messages and misinformation into our feeds under the veil of "just being real."

Media professionals and researchers have long recognized that a sense of authenticity is critical to effective messaging. The meaning of authenticity has never been precise, but it is usually tied to some sense of genuineness or originality. As media scholar Gunn Enli wrote, authenticity is ultimately "about socially constructed notions about what is real"[4]—and thus, its exact meaning changes over time and in different contexts. In this book, I show how, in our current moment, authenticity is not just a social construction but an industrial one, continually tussled over by a sophisticated and complicated profit-making enterprise whose decisions about what expressions of reality are valuable help determine what types of content and tools for communication and self-expression are available to the world's billions of social media users.

My findings confirm that those who learn to construct and exploit the ever-shifting language and aesthetic of "realness" online hold immense commercial, political, and ideological influence, but they also show how fraught, contingent, and transactional authenticity has become. Casual observers often deride influencers for vapid self-indulgence, but influencers' messages about seemingly trivial decisions—such as how to dress, eat, travel, and work—shape our experiences of everyday life. Under the guise of superficiality, the industry has gone even further, shaping conversations about how to vote, raise children, and take care of oneself and one's community. Indeed, in the later stages of research for this book, the influencer industry seemed to be undergoing a shift—becoming less about what to buy and more about what to think.

The story of the influencer industry's development is marked by power shifts and attempts to make the intangible tangible. Democratic dreams gave way to industrial ossification. In retrospect, this story makes perfect sense. The influencer industry is both a symptom of and a response to the economic precarity and upheaval in social institutions that have characterized the early twenty-first century. Indeed, this is what enabled the influencer logic to expand and root itself so securely in our way of life. While individual participants looked for a route to autonomy, stability, and professional fulfillment that seemed impossible elsewhere, they ended up creating a value system that advanced the erosion of boundaries between individuals' inner lives and commercialism, asking us to view ourselves as products perpetually ready for market, our relationships as monetizable, and our daily activities as potential shopping experiences. As such, I argue that influencers are neither "a flash in the pan" nor "a bubble about to burst," but indicators of a paradigm shift in the way we think about each other and ourselves.

The terms by which people refer to the industry help elide its consequences. Repeatedly and across time, in interviews and in the press, people use the term "Wild West" to describe the influencer industry. They use it to describe how no one seems to know for sure what is acceptable or what the future holds, and how people are figuring things out and testing boundaries as they go. For years now, though, the industry *has* had established norms and processes. Even if they are often shifting, they do so with the participation of people working in and around it. The influencer industry's "lawlessness," at this point, is a choice—one made and recommitted to daily by social media companies, who have had too much to gain by doing nothing (and more recently, acting only after problems seemed out of control), and regulators whose attentions are directed elsewhere. Further, "Wild West" as a descriptor makes it too easy for some to shrug off the industry's lack of transparency, persistent inequalities, and role as a conduit of mis- and disinformation.

By virtue of the time period that I conducted this research, as well as my position as a researcher following shifts I first noticed in the magazine world, this book focuses heavily on blogs, Instagram, and their associated technologies of self-commercialization—that expanding repertoire of tools that allows people to monetize their digital presence and adopt the ideology of the marketplace for their own self-expression. In this way, it could also be read as a study of what particular platforms—despite their frequent attempts to characterize themselves as neutral—make possible.[5] But the patterns described here often repeat themselves: on blogs, then YouTube and Instagram, then Snapchat, then TikTok and Substack, and will likely continue in the future so long as the ideological, technological, and regulatory infrastructures that support them remain unchanged. The industrial construction of authenticity is everywhere media industries are, particularly in times when people who create media content—not just influencers, but journalists and pundits, designers and musicians, and everyday people looking for an audience—have little to lose and a whole lot to gain by cultivating the right kind of "realness" online.

Yet, at the end of the first decade of the influencer industry, I am not cynical. This is a story of rampant commercialism, questionable ethical decisions, indignities and unfairness, and frightening opportunities for negative social impact, from rabid misinformation to the commercial colonization of our very sense of selfhood—plus the environmental and psychological impacts of the never-ending onslaught of goods from consumerism's accelerating hamster wheel. But it is also a story of scrappy survival, especially for the women who have been at the forefront of this industry since its beginning, and of genuine efforts to live well and live better. In its complexity, you will see simple yet resounding calls for progress. Workers thrive with autonomy, resources, and opportunity. Our media environment best serves its consumers leading with intellectual honesty, understanding of the vast variations of human experience, and less noise. And from the technology that makes much of this possible, people demand transparency and respect rather than surveillance and exploitation. What academics, media professionals, and government and technology industry leaders need to do is listen—and act.

In the remaining chapters, I contextualize and untangle the development of the influencer industry, demonstrating how the "influencer economy" emerged as a locus of power tied to tangible economic and social rewards on the social media-driven, visual web. I critically examine how participants in this system construct and operationalize what it means to be an influencer. And I explore the consequences of this industrialization of "authentic" influence for the production of culture, technological innovation, and everyday life.

I refer to the development of the influencer industry as *industrialization* because it represents a coordinated collection, processing, and commodification of a good or service. Marketers, brands, influencers, social media companies, and others worked (and continue to work) together to make influence meaningful as a commodity—to give it social meaning as well as financial value, and to build infrastructures for its measurement and sale.[6] The book's chapters are loosely chronological, but they are not an attempt at periodization. Rather, the chronology offers a means of making sense of the industrialization of influence and authenticity *as a process* that was informed by and responsive to current events. As will become clear in the ensuing chapters, this process was not always linear or evenly paced.

In chapter 1, I explain how the logic of a digital influencer economy was born out of a long history of intellectual thinking about what influence is, as well as a "perfect storm" of events in the 2000s. In chapter 2, I show how a range of creative professionals began working together to rebuild their careers in the wake of the Great Recession and, in so doing, created the mechanisms and negotiated the terms by which the influencer industry would blossom. In chapter 3, I explore how, once the industry began functioning in a coordinated way, stakeholders aimed to maximize its efficiency by introducing various new technologies for relationship management and monetization. The industry grew precipitously, and its growing impact on various cultural products became eminently obvious. Soon, however, a sort of backlash developed. Chapter 4 highlights the changing cultural environment of the late 2010s and some specific public events that contributed to wider suspicion about—and regulation of—the influencer industry. It then explores how various participants repositioned their work so the industry could continue to thrive. Chapter 5 untangles a series of existential and practical issues brought to the fore by the social tumult at the turn of the 2020s. I explore potential futures and current concerns as the influencer industry moves beyond commercial interests and becomes a tool for propaganda and misinformation, as well as for prosocial messaging. In chapter 6, I take stock of the complex system the influencer industry has become by the start of the 2020s: one that ensnares business owners and brand executives, professional and aspiring influencers, ordinary social media users, technology companies of various sizes and scopes, and governments in a marketplace whose rules and system of value are constantly shifting and being renegotiated, yet whose successful navigation is increasingly required for understanding the flows of culture and information in the twenty-first century. I reflect on the industry's promise and peril and suggest what we as a society should consider as we reckon with it. For now, let's go back to the beginning.

Chapter 1

Groundwork

The rise of the social media influencer has propelled billions of market-ing and advertising dollars into the social media economy and instigated a chain of events that has fundamentally changed the way culture is produced and experienced, in ways both very broad and quite specific. The way goods, services, information, and experiences are imagined, produced, marketed, and consumed have all been impacted. When I speak to people about my research, I am often asked: Why does this blogger get to come on my favorite news show and opine about something? Why does this line of home goods at Target have this influencer's name and face on it? Why does my Instagram feed feel like a nonstop on-slaught of ads from people I thought I liked? What people are really asking, I believe, is: Why do influencers pop up across our main sources of information, entertainment, and consumer goods, where did they come from, and what does this phenomenon portend? We can find many of the answers by understanding the processes and pressures of the industry that supports influencers, and the way the people who comprise this industry interact with and respond to the ever-changing world around them.

The influencer phenomenon did not come out of nowhere, and it was not inevitable. It was the result of people making particular deci-sions under particular economic, cultural, industrial, and technologi-cal circumstances. It is also a product of a long history of popular and academic thinking about who can influence and how, the features of persuasion, and the promises of technology. And like people, its priorities, aesthetics, and modes of working are often in flux, but its core remains essentially the same. Indeed, what enables this industry to continue to morph and succeed despite its and the world's state of constant chaos is that it *belies* the chaos. It takes fundamental—and fundamentally slippery—ideals and processes like authenticity and influence and neatly packages them as commodities that can be measured and sold like any other product. It takes uncertainty and makes it feel manageable.

The influencer industry's core business is continually reassessing, redefining, and revaluing authenticity. Authenticity is the quality that makes one person more influential than another, even if they have similar metrics. A sense of authenticity sells products. The authentic-feeling stories shared by successful influencers sell to their followers the dream of digital entrepreneurship and the myth that technology is inherently democratic—or, at the very least, meritocratic. Carefully constructing authenticity is what has allowed some people to make real money and gain genuine satisfaction from their work making content for social media. But it is also what has enabled some to become cults of personality, spreaders of misinformation, propagators of disingenuous lifestyle ideals, or worse.

Despite the rapidly increasing significance of social media influencers in society, many pundits and commentators criticize or diminish them as silly or self-involved. This is surely wrapped up in a range of cultural scripts. First, about gender: influencers tend to be women, whose historically key position in the consumer cycle makes them both economically critical and easily dismissed. Since the beginning of American consumer culture in the nineteenth century, advertisers have targeted women as the "shoppers" of the home. Historian Kathy Peiss has pointed out how, even today, "the association of femininity and consumption remains nearly seamless. And these terms have been mutually reinforcing. Consumption is coded as a female pursuit, frivolous and even wasteful . . . in turn, consumer identity obscures women's important contributions to economic and political life."[1] Next, the influencer industry has been largely led by young people, whose use of technology tends to attract moral panics rather than nuanced understanding. And finally, the industry is driven by commercialism, which has become so pervasive in our lives as to be taken for granted.

To be sure, some influencers do silly things, and sometimes stupid or disrespectful things. For example, trampling natural wonders to get a picture, as some did during the "superbloom" in California's poppy fields, or shilling cheap clothes, diet teas, or other suspect products. In this book, however, I offer a different perspective, providing a broader view of the industry that supports and incentivizes influencers, its context, and the implications of its power.

In this chapter, I dig into the influencer industry's prehistory. Its roots are long and complex, and they far predate the digital era. A brief look into the intellectual history of influence shows how literary and scholarly contributions shaped our understandings of influence over time and, in distilled forms, came to permeate popular thought during the last century. The influencer industry's existence is, in many ways, a direct result of this intellectual history, legitimizing itself by enacting ideas advanced for decades before. In other ways, the industry is a challenge to this history, forcing us to rethink preconceived notions about what influence can be—particularly as a monetizable product.

Building upon this, I then explore how a confluence of economic, industrial, cultural, and technological factors enabled the influencer industry as we know it to develop exponentially. While the ideological and technical groundwork for the emergence of this industry had been quietly laid for decades, the 2008 financial crisis served as a critical inflection point, supercharging the industry's growth and setting a particular course for its rapid expansion. Throughout, you'll see how the notion of authenticity is consistently present, threading together conversations about meaning across time and contexts and becoming the ever-shifting construction upon which the industry relies.

Influence: From Art Form to Commodity

Intellectual attention to influence and its social consequences dates to ancient Greece, when persuasion and rhetoric were studied and practiced as arts and eventually seen as devolving into tools for social ill. Shakespeare, too, assigned influence "a darkly astrological cast," as writer Laurence Scott pointed out; a quarter of his plays plumb the various ways people exploit or fall prey to influence.[2] Philosophers over the centuries sometimes attended to influence indirectly, with some economic, political, and social theories reflecting assumptions about how people are influenced or persuaded. Max Weber's writings on charismatic authority address influence directly, illustrating how authority, authenticity, and influence are intertwined—and usually socially constructed,[3] contingent upon context and the relationships leaders cultivate with their followers. Fundamental to thinking about influence through the ages has been a concern over authority and social power: who has it, how is it deployed, and what are the consequences?

In early twentieth-century America, as waves of immigration and forces of industrialization expanded the population and rearranged the rhythms of daily life, government and media institutions began to understand that they could leverage authentic-seeming messages and new mass media technologies to influence citizens. They viewed this as a necessity in a time of immense population growth and change. In his assessment of this period, historian Stuart Ewen described how the growing advertising industry of the time worked to "habituate" people—particularly the huge population of factory workers, many of them immigrants—to its vision of life in industrial America, reorienting them away from traditional values of family, self-sufficiency, and thrift[4] and toward finding meaning and identity in the consumption of goods.[5] As Ewen wrote, "The development of an ideology of consumption responded both to the issue of social control and the need for goods distribution."[6] Advertisements typically utilized paragraphs of copy to prompt readers to consider how their lives might be improved by the product in question, or to take on the voice of a featured expert or model explaining why they approve of the product.

In his controversial 1925 book, *The Man Nobody Knows*, advertising giant and agency founder Bruce Barton cautioned that "the public has a sixth sense for detecting insincerity; they know instinctively when words ring true"[7] as he encouraged businessmen of the era to follow the example set by Jesus: "What he was and what he said were one and the same thing."[8] George Creel, head of the Committee on Public Information (the U.S. government's first organized propaganda outfit), wrote that the committee's work—"selling" participation in World War I to Americans and American ideals to the rest of the world—was successful in large part because of its authentic nature. "Our effort was educational and informative throughout," he wrote, "the simple, straightforward presentation of facts."[9] Yet, notably, it was also "a vast enterprise in salesmanship, the world's greatest adventure in advertising."[10]

Institutional propaganda efforts such as these grew in size and scope during the 1910s and 1920s, drawing both scholarly analysis[11] and popular attention. Edward Bernays's landmark 1928 work *Propaganda* summed up the ways in which large organizations had begun to understand that they could construct and enact influence at mass scale and rationalized the activities as necessary for living in an increasingly complex society. He wrote:

> The conscious and intelligent manipulation of the organized habits and opinions of the masses is an important element in democratic society. Those who manipulate this unseen mechanism of society constitute an invisible government which is the true ruling power of our country. We are governed, our minds are molded, our tastes formed, and our ideas suggested, largely by men we have never heard of. . . . It is they who pull the wires that control the public mind.[12]

As such adulation for the power of—and questionable need for—organized persuasion campaigns became mainstream, questions about how people are or are not persuaded, and the social implications of these processes, captivated researchers. Alongside the growing movement among practitioners like Bernays (known as the "Father of Public Relations") and Creel to understand the persuasive power of institutions, academics began to identify and systematically study the dynamics of social influence.

Influence Becomes Empirical

In the 1920s, social psychologists Rensis Likert and Louis Thurstone advanced the idea that attitudes—or the "evaluative judgments" that all people make about ideas, people, and things[13]—influence behavior.

They notably created the Likert Scale, a questionnaire model still in use today wherein respondents provide answers that also indicate the level of their intensity for that answer (for example, "strongly disagree"). While this type of polling is now commonplace, the ability to quantify an attitude was a significant breakthrough at the time. It helped set the stage for empirically capturing other previously intangible human phenomena, including how, when, and why people change their minds.[14]

In the 1930s and 1940s, the rise of fascism and the outbreak of World War II stirred widespread concern about propaganda and authoritarianism, and researchers turned their attention to understanding how public opinion becomes mobilized or changed. A prevailing belief had been that messages constructed in the "right" way could exert direct influence over everyone who received the message. Otherwise known as the "magic bullet" or "hypodermic needle" theories, these arguments contended that media messages could be metaphorically "shot" into the minds of audience members and elicit a uniform reaction. Nazi propaganda seemed to provide a sinister example of this possibility. Other incidents, such as the panic induced by Orson Welles's 1938 radio broadcast of *War of the Worlds*, provided more supposed evidence for this theory.[15] Yet upon further examination, social-psychological researchers realized that the message-receiver relationship was not so simple; a variety of factors, such as a person's education level, religiousness, or "suggestibility," could intercept and alter it.[16]

At the same time, sociologists explored the notion that social relations, rather than psychological phenomena, affected how people were influenced and why. The work of the Columbia School was critical in developing the sociological and popular understandings that "people were still most successfully persuaded by give-and-take with other people, and that the influence of the mass media was less automatic and less potent than had been assumed."[17] *The People's Choice*, published in 1948, was an early milestone in this way of thinking. In this study, the authors sought to understand how people made voting decisions in the election of 1940, finding that the influence of other people was "more frequent and more effective than the mass media."[18]

In 1955's *Personal Influence: The Part Played by People in the Flow of Mass Communication*, Elihu Katz and Paul Lazarsfeld explicitly outline this "two-step flow" model, wherein people who act as "opinion leaders" or "influentials" filter information from the mass media to their friends and neighbors, and ordinary people's interactions with these influential people drives some behavior and opinion formation. Drawing on a study of women's decision-making on topics from public affairs to fashion conducted in Decatur, Illinois, Katz and Lazarsfeld dispelled the common belief that people were "a mass of disconnected individuals hooked up to the media but not to each other," arguing that, instead, people comprised "networks of interconnected individuals through which mass communications are channeled."[19]

The impact of Katz and Lazarsfeld's work on academic and popular understandings of influence was tremendous. The vocabulary with which people have discussed influence for the last half century stems, in large part, from their work. And their notion of "influentials"—that is, people who have seemingly measurable effects on those who listen to them—is probably more salient in the digital age than ever before.

Within sociology, the two-step flow model became the dominant paradigm through which researchers studied influence. It inspired a decades-long proliferation of research concerned with theories of diffusion, or how influence or innovations move through a population, as well as methodological interest in social network analysis.[20] As computational capabilities advanced, researchers began to work with massive datasets to pinpoint tipping points for the diffusion of ideas or behaviors, often identifying individual "influentials" in the process—an activity that became common in influencer marketing, as will be seen in later chapters.

Some writers over the years argued that the domination of the two-step flow model caused the field to develop significant oversights. Sociologist Todd Gitlin critiqued the lack of attention to the way mass media set agendas for public discourse, as well as researchers' emphasis on finding measurable effects.[21] Feminist media scholar Susan Douglas argued that conceptualizing two-step flow as a generalizable, quantifiable process of influence obscured the role of culture and gender in that process.[22] As Douglas pointed out, the original Decatur study was composed entirely of women, a fact obscured by the use of male ("elder-statesman") or neutral ("people") pronouns in the book. "One of the central contradictions of the Decatur Study," she wrote, "is that it simultaneously disguises that only women are being studied and universalizes them as representative of the general population."[23] Still others have argued for considering three-step or one-step flows and have emphasized the increasing complexity of our media system since the radio- and newspaper-focused days in which the Decatur study was conducted.[24] All told, research on influence in the wake of *Personal Influence* perhaps overemphasized *processes* of influence while overlooking more structural questions, including what influence means in different settings and who defines it.

Influence Research Enters the Mainstream

For nearly as along as influence has been empirically studied, business leaders and entrepreneurs have looked for ways to apply research findings for their own ends. In 1957, cultural critic Vance Packard detailed in his book *The Hidden Persuaders* how public relations professionals had been leveraging "motivational research"—the term at the time for understanding how people make decisions—to sell everything from washing machines to political candidates. Their behind-the-scenes activities, he wrote, worked to "engineer consent" of citizens to receiving advertising messages. Most worrisome, they used academic theories to "train" people "like Pavlov's dog."[25] While Packard's book was a bestseller and catapulted him to the rare position of nationally renowned critic of consumer culture, the activities it detailed—persuasion professionals leveraging academic theories to sell products—have only intensified since.

Since the 1990s, research on influence by both academics and marketing professionals has gained a popular audience as entrepreneurs and businesses have found practical value in it. In his 2001 bestseller, for example, psychologist Robert Cialdini famously outlined six "weapons of influence" that he deduced from experimental and participant observation research, emphasizing how certain norms that seem to be embedded in most human cultures—such as reciprocity, compliance with authority, and looking to "social proof" (or what others are doing) when making certain decisions—can be used to get people to think or behave in certain ways.[26] This work recognized the increasing sophistication of influence tactics utilized by all kinds of individuals and groups, from salespeople to media organizations.

Another key body of work has been concerned with tracking influential people, ideas, or behaviors. This research begins at the end, analyzing things that are already understood to be influential and attempting to trace how they became that way. It looks for the human behaviors or tendencies that drive ideas or behaviors to "catch on." Malcolm Gladwell famously brought the notion of "social epidemics" (and tools for understanding them) to a wide audience with his 2000 bestseller *The Tipping Point*. And in yet another bestseller, marketing professor Jonah Berger described the six "STEPPS" that make something "contagious": it must have social currency, naturally trigger discussion and emotions, be public, have practical value, and be wrapped in a broader narrative.[27] Because a significant amount of research in this area is oriented around business management or marketing, however, an underlying question tends to be "how can we design products, ideas, and behaviors so that people will talk about them?"[28] rather than providing critical insight into existing infrastructures of social influence or their consequences.

Other social researchers have helped push the two-step flow model to a mainstream audience and emphasized its democratic potential. For example, Ed Keller and Jon Berry of the opinion research firm Roper-ASW grounded their 2003 book entirely on the notion that people are more likely to turn to friends, family, or other "personal experts" for advice than to the mass media. Arguing that "more than a handful of people control the levers of change in America,"[29] they aimed to pinpoint the sociological factors associated with being an influential person and concluded the book with suggestions for how businesses can leverage this sort of influence. Marketer Mark Schaefer, too, lauded the utility of the "influencer class" for business, highlighting in his 2012 book the economic and social benefits to be found for those who cultivate their influence online. Echoing Bernays's 1945 pronouncement that "media provide open doors to the public mind, and through them any one of us may influence the attitudes and actions of our fellow citizens,"[30] Schaefer optimistically asserts that "in this new world of social influence, even the obscure, the shy, and the overlooked can become celebrities in their slice of the online world. . . . You, too, can earn your way into the influence class."[31]

While Schaefer was correct in asserting that social media enable new meanings and uses of influence, his ideas—and that of other contemporary popular writers on influence—reflect persistent themes in the historical trajectory of scholarly and popular thought on the subject: that influence can be quantified, that certain people are and should be more influential than others, and that technology makes the whole process democratic *and* profitable. At the same time, companies and popular marketing discourse have metabolized this literature for their own ends. Their implementation of these ideas helps to set the agenda for public discourse and consumer culture.

The Role of Media and Celebrity Culture

In thinking about influence over the last century, researchers and practitioners have primarily conceptualized mass media as channels through which potentially influential messages are sent. Schaefer's mention of celebrity, however, is a reminder of the role media companies and their technologies can play in *constructing* influence. Celebrities are, fundamentally, a particular type of influential person whose social power is wholly dependent upon media industries.[32] The expansion of celebrity culture during the twentieth century—acutely accelerated by the rise of the internet and social media in the twenty-first[33]—has enabled its logic to seep into everyday life. Public visibility, personal branding, and awareness of performance metrics are all valorized in popular discourse, baked into new media technologies, and even taught in schools as a matter of professionalization.[34] Further, the heightened enrollment of "regular people" into mass-mediated visibility during the twenty-first century[35]—through vehicles like reality television, tabloid culture, and early blogs—helped centralize the notion of authenticity (or "realness") within positive industrial evaluations of content.

Critical attention to fame and celebrity culture burgeoned over this same period as scholars analyzed the relationships between the growing mass media system and the kinds of people who thrive within it. In 1944, for example, sociologist Leo Lowenthal illuminated how popular magazines had shifted their coverage from "idols of production," such as self-made businessmen and politicians, to "idols of consumption," such as stars of the budding entertainment industry. Further, Lowenthal noted, the writing he analyzed increasingly "reduces itself to the private lives of the heroes,"[36] focusing on subjects' lifestyle minutiae rather than qualifications and accomplishments.

Nearly twenty years later, historian Daniel Boorstin argued that the television- and news-saturated environment of the mid–twentieth century made it too easy to build "cults of personality," and he specifically identified the process as antidemocratic. Boorstin outlined how the growing mass media and public relations industries had introduced a culture of "pseudo-events," or events staged specifically to generate press coverage, and had given rise to a distinctly contemporary form of influential person: the "human pseudo-event," or the celebrity. Boorstin presciently described this person as one "well-known for his well-knownness," whose renown is reliant on the media reinforcing it. Later, in his expansive study of fame throughout history, cultural historian Leo Braudy provided support for Boorstin's argument that the tendency for societies to hold certain people up as important has existed for millennia, and the nature of their influence is likely tied to dominant media forms of the time. Different types of people are lauded in different eras, Braudy argued, depending, in part, on the technologies available to spread their messages.

More recently, cultural critics and researchers have noted the symbiotic relationship between celebrity culture and the commercial web, characterizing it as a function of the internet's "attention economy." Physicist Michael Goldhaber coined this term in 1997 to describe how he believed the world economic order would change in the internet age.[37] He noted that while others often characterized the internet as an *information* economy, "economies run on scarcity, and information is more abundant than ever. What is scarce is people's attention." Therefore, he predicted, "seeking attention" would become a core activity of the digital age.[38] Coincidentally, that same year, business guru Tom Peters opined in *Fast Company* that people's "most important job is to be head marketer for the brand called You. It's that simple—and that hard. And that inescapable."

The development of social media in the 2000s—an era sometimes referred to as Web 2.0—enabled new forms of seeking attention online and using that attention strategically. While the social and economic benefits of being an influential person were usually implicit in prior writing on the subject, digital media scholars elucidated these benefits for the contemporary moment more clearly. In a study of early internet users who broadcasted their private lives via webcams and gained cult followings, media researcher Theresa Senft offered a theory of "microcelebrity"[39]—the practice of cultivating a public persona and an audience for oneself online—inspiring a cavalcade of research that has detailed the many ways people use these practices for social and economic ends.[40] As the social-driven internet matured, microcelebrity practices became inextricable from simply being online. Internet users, particularly social media users, must continually be aware of their public persona or personal brand, and its hazards and potential.[41]

Of course, as media scholar Alison Hearn has written, our expanding celebrity culture "works ideologically to valorize this hope"[42] that maintaining a personal brand online will pay off in fame, money, or both. As the social media influencer industry has blossomed and so many people have followed in the professional pursuit of personal brand creation, promotion, and monetization, Goldhaber's pronouncement that the internet would become a "star system"[43] appears ever more prescient.

The Birth of the Contemporary Influencer Industry

Since the advent of the commercial web in the early 1990s, people have gone online to self-publish ideas and commentary on an endless number of topics. Some early users of email did this through newsletters. Later, blogs became popular as places where people could combine text, images, and video to express thoughts or share information. In the late

1990s, political bloggers offered perhaps the first glimpse of the agenda-setting power of self-publishing on social media, when a few were responsible for initially reporting and pushing to mainstream news the Clinton-Lewinsky and Trent Lott scandals.[44] Soon after, so-called mommy bloggers gained traction, developing fervent readerships by writing about the complicated experience of motherhood with surprising rawness. Throughout the first decade of the 2000s, the number of bloggers and blog readers grew every year; though, all told, the numbers remained fairly low relative to all internet users.[45]

As the first decade of the twenty-first century ended, however, a perfect storm of technological, economic, cultural, and industrial factors helped the work of nascent "influencers" to grow exponentially.

Technological Factors

The advent of software like Blogger (launched in 1999) and WordPress (launched in 2003) made it easy for people without significant technical knowledge to publish content online. In turn, blogs proliferated in the 2000s. Soon, social media sites such as Twitter, Facebook, and YouTube emerged, making the process of sharing information and connecting with people online easier than ever and pervading the population at a rapid clip. According to Pew Research Center, in 2005 only 5 percent of American adults used a social networking platform; ten years later, nearly 70 percent did.[46] At the same time, websites like Klout and PeerIndex emerged, offering tools that purported to measure individuals' influence based on aggregating and analyzing their social media data—and offering branded "rewards" depending on their score. Technologically-enabled entrepreneurship also became popular, as websites like eBay and Etsy grew their reputations for enabling direct commerce between people all over the globe.

Cultural Factors

These technological changes allowed individuals to have direct lines to "publics" they never had before[47] and dovetailed nicely with the cultural valorization of entrepreneurialism and self-branding and the increasingly individualized nature of work that had begun to take hold in the 1990s.[48] From enthusiastic predictions about a "free agent nation"[49] to the emergence of the so-called gig economy,[50] the 2000s saw a marked increase in visibility—much of it optimistic—for people whose "independent" work was enabled by new technology.

Further, institutional distrust festered. In the wake of historic events and scandals that shook seemingly every cornerstone of U.S. society, from government to education to banking to religion, people coming of age in the 1990s through the 2010s (colloquially referred to as the millennial generation, to which many early influencers belonged) trusted others and institutions less and less.[51]

Economic Factors

The shift toward independent work continued, albeit with a less agentic feel, as millions of people lost their jobs in the wake of the 2008 global financial crisis. For many under- or unemployed people, particularly aspiring creative professionals, the internet and its many budding social media platforms seemed to offer a chance to move forward in a time marked by inertia and uncertainty. "I realized that traditional PR was a dying breed. I was trying to figure out something else to do," remembered Reesa Lake, a senior vice president at Digital Brand Architects, in our 2017 interview.

Many people used blogs and platforms like Twitter, tumblr, and Facebook to communicate their professional expertise and personal interests with the hope of building reputations and attracting employers.[52] Doing so also provided a sense of control over an unclear and precarious professional situation. As Lucia,* a designer and influencer with several hundred thousand followers, recalled in a 2015 interview, "I started the blog when the economic downturn had affected the amount of work I.was doing at my full-time job. I had more time on my hands and, you know, I didn't really have a life that required a ton of attention—[I was] single, twenty-four—and I have a lot of creative energy. I started it as a

---

* The book contains a mix of real names and pseudonyms; pseudonyms are noted by an asterisk on first mention.

way to focus on work that interested me and hoped that I would be able to drive a few freelance projects my way. I was blogging as a way to meet people and network."

Official tracking of independent workers has not been consistent,[53] but a 2016 Pew Research Center report concluded that "the share of U.S. workers with these alternative employment arrangements has gone up significantly" in the twenty-first century. The widespread and deep-seated economic turmoil seemed to only embolden neoliberal logics of self-governance, inciting workers of all stripes to be continually mindful of their personal brands and live as if "life is a pitch."[54] Indeed, in the wake of the recession, relying on the "brand called You"[55] seemed less like a choice and more like a requirement for participating in the new economy.

Industrial Factors

The economic crisis accelerated media industry shifts that had been slowly approaching since the launch of the commercial web. Journalism was becoming a less viable career path as job opportunities dried up, pay stagnated, and revenue models became outdated and unsustainable.[56] Advertisers were looking for more effective outlets than the print establishment and found blogs—and later, the feeds of individual influencers on social media platforms—ideal. Digital influencers were becoming miniature media empires in their own right, and thanks to their personality-driven content, they offered advertisers audiences that were conveniently segmented. Their digitally native existence also made measuring ROI, or return on investment, more convenient and straightforward, a particularly attractive benefit in an era where cultural industries were becoming increasingly risk-averse and fixated on quantification.[57] Consider this: For a clothing brand looking to advertise their size-inclusive line, the loyal audience of a woman in her late twenties who creates focused blog and Instagram content on the topic offers a clearer targeted opportunity than the print pages of *Glamour* to reach that niche.

Further, bloggers did not necessarily hold themselves to journalistic standards such as maintaining a separation between advertising and editorial or disclosing personal connections to stories. This made it easy for advertisers to forge new norms of commercial messaging in the new medium of influencer marketing. Sponsored content and activities such as gifting products in exchange for coverage became typical. These technological and interpersonal capabilities of social media reinvigorated the advertising industry's decades-old love affair with word-of-mouth marketing. Driven by these forces, blogs covering topics as varied as parenting, politics, and personal style all popularized, innovating new forms, norms, and possibilities of digital self-publishing and self-expression in the process.

While it is common knowledge that advertising undergirds the U.S. media system, less frequently recognized is the fact that *retail undergirds the advertising system*, spending more than any other industry on advertising[58] and impacting the media we use, content we see, and physical environments in which we shop.[59] It makes sense, then, that in its early years blogging became a potent force in the fashion industry. For a notoriously top-down, closed-off industry, social media initially seemed to pose quite a threat: brands could not retain tight control over their brand images as social media users all over world uploaded photos of themselves styling clothing however they liked, and fashion magazines were no longer singular voices of authority on trends and critique as readers enjoyed the opinions of bloggers who seemed "just like us." Yet social media's emerging fashion stars were also irresistible to the industry itself; they were buzzy, attention-grabbing, and potentially profitable. A few popular voices in the space caused a stir by getting front row seats at fashion shows, next to top magazine editors. In mainstream coverage, the rise of fashion bloggers was an attractive anecdote to fit the increasingly common narrative that social media was going to "democratize" culture by giving voice and visibility to "anyone with an internet connection."[60]

As popular bloggers' fan bases grew, advertisers recognized an opportunity. By 2010 retail brands understood that these digital content creators offered not only opinions and style cues but direct lines to the buying public.[61] Major brands became interested in advertising on blogs large and small, and advertising networks developed to meet the need. Sometimes brands and bloggers worked together to design and market a cobranded product, such as a line of shoes or handbags. More commonly, bloggers partnered with advertisers to create sponsored posts, wherein a blogger integrated an advertiser's product into her own visual or textual content. This sort of paid-for advertising that appears to be "authentic" content permeated social media and became the lifeblood of the influencer industry.

As advertising-fueled monetization pervaded the social media landscape in the early 2010s, a cottage industry of influencer marketing agencies cropped up to serve as middlemen between content creators and advertisers. Positioning themselves as helping digital content creators earn money from their passion projects, these agencies build metrics platforms, negotiate deals between influencers and retail brands, and in some cases serve as 360-degree talent managers for influencers. Agencies' services for streamlined and predictable flows of branding deals helped to define the content that shows up on popular social media platforms. Later, affiliate marketing, when an influencer makes commission by driving traffic or sales to a retailer's site, became a widespread, multibillion-dollar business of its own.

As blogs followed in the footsteps of legacy media in being financially dependent on advertisers, advertisers improved their ability to measure how and where their messages were most effective. The notion of "digital influence" became central. Metrics that purported to measure a social media user's influence—typically drawing on numbers such as follower counts, engagement and click-through rates, unique visitors, and more—became the currency for securing the brand partnerships and advertisements that brought financial stability, public recognition, and other professional opportunities for bloggers. As visual social platforms such as Instagram, Pinterest, and Vine proliferated in the early 2010s, the term "digital influencer" replaced "blogger" as the vernacular to describe those who produce digital content and boast significant social media clout, regardless of platform.

Conveniently quantifiable, "influence" quickly became an attractive stand-in for the nebulous cultural authority on which prominent figures had long traded. Even old-media titan *Vogue* could not resist the allure of using metrics to pin down previously elusive factors. Style.com, the magazine's website from 2000 until 2015, began in 2013 to feature a continually updated graphic called "The In Cloud," which ranked fashion editors, bloggers, designers, front-row stalwarts, and models. To use its own description: "The In Cloud is Style.com's new custom ranking of the most influential people in the fashion industry . . . In fashion, no one works in a vacuum. With the In Cloud, you can see who's on top in any one category, or discover how they stack up against one another. They're all connected; they're all in the cloud . . . So happy ranking, and may the buzziest win."[62]

In the ensuing years, the influencers, marketers, brands, and technologists involved in the influencer industry created an entirely new ecosystem in which people would encounter and interact with information and cultural products. Influencers became important means of sorting information. Their easily digestible personal brands signal what type of content they provide, and in a world where people are continually overwhelmed by information, turning to seemingly like-minded people to make decisions became a utilitarian choice. Technological developments, explored more in later chapters, allowed influencers to offer seamless integration of content with the ability to shop. And in what many experts call a "post-ad world"—where consumers increasingly tune out or avoid blatant advertising[63]—influencers offer companies a crucial means of getting messages to the public.

While many influencers identify themselves as being "fueled by passion" and their work being a "creative outlet,"[64] collectively, they are marketing juggernauts and vital components of the retail system. By 2016, eMarketer estimated that influencer marketing revenues on Instagram alone totaled more than $570 million and argued that the industry as a whole was probably worth more than $1 billion.[65] By the end of the decade, *Business Insider* estimated the industry's value at $8 billion and projected that it would nearly double over the next three years. At the same time, influencers—that is, people who earn income as independent workers providing "authentically" curated content to carefully cultivated online audiences—became one of the most visible symbols of the converging worlds of social media, information, and commerce.

The Work of Being an Influencer

As bloggers, influencers, and content creators generally are a decidedly twenty-first century profession, much writing on them has considered the meaning and conditions of their work. Within academia, writers who have contributed to these "digital labor" debates consider both the labor *of* online content creation—from unpaid users moderating or posting on message boards[66] to professional bloggers who make a living from their work[67]—as well as the ways in which circumstances of the digital age, such as constant connectedness and the incitement to self-brand, could be remaking labor more generally.[68] Theories about venture labor,[69] aspirational labor,[70] hope labor,[71] visibility labor,[72] and others point to several consistent themes about work in the digital economy: risk is shouldered by the individual; self-promotional, always-on work styles are the norm; labor is oriented toward nebulous future payouts; and inequalities of gender, race, and class persist.

Underpinning this scholarship is continual consideration of whether these forms of digital labor are exploitive, enjoyable, empowering—or some combination of the three. In his 2013 study of fashion bloggers, anthropologist Brent Luvaas reached an ambivalent conclusion while describing what he called the "conscious commercialization" of bloggers.

> The question that remains, then, is whether such a position is ultimately more empowering or exploitative for those who adopt it. Are these the newly empowered subjects of a democratizing fashion industry? Or the industry's new pawns, subjected to the disciplinary dictates of self-monitoring and self-promotion, so intrinsic to the logic of neoliberalism? And is there . . . any conceivable difference between the two?[73]

The above becomes particularly fraught when one considers that the majority of the influencer industry's early participants were women.[74] On one hand, people I interviewed often framed their experience as empowering—on the other, they described how it is tied to the larger structural limits that women face in more traditional workplaces. When

I asked about the enjoyable aspects of her work, for example, Claudia,*
a design blogger, said:

> Just the flexibility of it is really nice. Very few jobs would allow me to
> be a full-time stay-at-home mom and a full-time worker. I mean,
> there's obviously a difficult side to that, you know, trying to find the
> time to fit in what I need to fit in, but, you know, for us, that works
> really well, and I really enjoy that.

The influencer industry developed against the backdrop of persistent
structural gender discrimination in many workplaces.[75] At the same
time, American mothers, even those in dual-career couples, dispropor-
tionately shoulder the burdens of caregiving and housework[76] while
having few resources for support such as guaranteed paid parental leave,
affordable childcare options, the ability to request flexible schedules
without fear of being sidelined, or other potential remedies.[77] It follows,
then, that women looking to begin or to continue doing work *that works
for them* would turn to social media at a time when it promised to deliver
professional autonomy, creative fulfillment, and potentially enviable pay
and flexibility.[78]

Indeed, one of the most talked about aspects of the influencer industry, particularly in its early years, has been the money to be made by
those who successfully cultivate and monetize their social media followings. Headlines tout the tens of thousands of dollars that top influencers charge per sponsored post, or the millions to be made in a year
through collaborating with brands. Issa,* a blogger focused on affordable fashion, shared her noteworthy experience:

> I've been so tempted to, like, publish something about myself, but it
> just sounds like bragging. But my purpose is, I want women and kids
> in college and stuff to know what's possible. Not even in blogging,
> but just as an entrepreneur, like what you can do. It's such a huge
> success story for me personally because I come from a farm in Kansas
> and my whole family, like, has never been to college. All have blue-
> collar jobs. My dad's the only one that's been to college. I feel like
> [blogging] totally changed paths for me, and making before the age

of thirty, like, way more [money] than my dad ever did . . . It's crazy.
It's so inspiring, and I want to be able to share that.

The success of influencers like Issa is important. At the same time,
exciting anecdotes like hers are often leveraged in public discussion of
the influencer industry to such an extent that they eclipse the industry's
deep-seated issues. For example, in a separate study conducted the same
year as Issa's interview, Brooke Erin Duffy and I found that top bloggers'
digital self-presentations tend to reinscribe them in the traditional role
of feminine consumer, while "the underrepresentation of women of
color, LGBT, and plus-size models reveals how the playing field for 'top-
ranked' bloggers is highly uneven—even despite the outward counte-
nance of 'real women.'"[79] Duffy further explored the tension between
representation and reality in her 2017 book, illustrating how influencers
and those who aspire to be them strive for "relatability" by aligning their
personae with an imagined "everyday girl" reader with a middle-class
background and values, a move that also allows them to reconcile the
"seemingly incongruous values of authenticity and profit making."[80]
More recently, digital media researcher Akane Kanai argued that being
seen as "relatable" online is not "universally available," but connected to
racial and economic privilege.[81]

The influencer industry was not only largely silent on issues of inequality in its earliest years, but in many ways—intentionally or not—it
seemed to rely on it. That young women were largely the ones driving
the influencer industry is symptomatic of problems with contemporary
work as well as long-standing tropes—namely, that women are primarily consumers and that using social media is just for fun and not work—
that remain entrenched despite individual and collective efforts to the
contrary.[82] Importantly, the feminized nature of the influencer industry
obscures its seriousness and widespread impact.[83] Perhaps this is how
its workers have made it all the way to the White House (which we'll
see in chapter 6)—as well as rerouting how we experience culture, information, personal connections, and ourselves—without much serious public notice. In this way, the story of the influencer industry's development adds further evidence to the message that activists have

delivered for generations: American society dismisses feminized professions at its own peril.

Industrializing Authenticity

This book focuses on the dynamics of the industry that sprung up to encourage and render valuable the forms of labor described by prior writing on the subject. The influencer industry quantifies, ranks, and commodifies those who self-identify as workers (such as professional Instagrammers) as well as casual users who do not. The industry's ideas about what influence is, how it works, and why it matters increasingly help to define what it means for a person or a cultural product to be successful (how many sales of this dress were driven by this person's Instagram Story?) and can determine whether they will be successful at all (does this person have enough Twitter followers to be a viable book author?). Indeed, in an era when influence has become a commodity—cultivated by individuals, quantified by companies, and leveraged by all for material benefit—understanding the dynamics of its production is a pressing matter.

While the remaining chapters will explore various dynamics of the influencer industry in detail, I will pause here to note that while the nuances of these dynamics are vitally important, so too is the ideological and economic project that brings them together: building and selecting "authentic" voices of authority. Authenticity in the digital realm has generated significant academic and public interest in recent years, but people have not typically described it in industrial terms. As media scholar Jessa Lingel notes, much discussion of digital authenticity emerges from an "implicit understanding . . . that the rules and norms of social life restrict people's ability to express themselves fully in person. Online interactions, in contrast, permit people to identify in new ways and to play with presentations of self in terms of their gender, ethnicity, or sexuality."[84] Lingel notes the complications inherent in this description, most notably that people's claims of digital authenticity sometimes turn out to be superficial attempts to claim certain alternative identities to enhance their egos or to persuade others for the purpose of some form of gain. She provides a memorable example of a white American man who posed online as a Syrian woman during the Arab Spring, believing "that it would be a more compelling, more authentic blog if he claimed to be a queer activist in Syria rather than a concerned political commentator from Georgia."[85]

Feminist media scholar Sarah Banet-Weiser stresses this tension around the nature and purpose of authenticity, writing that it "is a symbolic construct that, even in a cynical age, continues to have cultural value . . . We want to believe—indeed, I argue that we *need* to believe— that there are spaces in our lives driven by genuine affect and emotions, something outside of mere consumer culture, something above the reductiveness of profit margins, the crassness of capital exchange."[86] Recognizing this tension, Lingel highlights the phenomenon of self-branding and notes that "whether in the context of major celebrities or ordinary office workers, the strategic link between self-promotion and the Internet highlights the extent to which our online selves are constantly performed and constructed rather than innate or natural."[87] Indeed, in the influencer industry, the success and significance of individuals' authenticity performances hinges on shifting rules and available tools, which are created under pressure for profit.

In a 2019 essay, media and cultural historian Fred Turner reflected on the conflict between the ideal of digital authenticity and the technological infrastructure we use to express it. He argued that today's social media giants were built on a belief, entrenched in Silicon Valley and the political left, that "the key to a more egalitarian society lies in the freeing of individual voices, the expression of different lived experiences, and the forming of social groups around shared identities." Public assertions of authenticity have helped usher in social progress. For example, first-person accounts of discrimination and oppression helped fuel the twentieth century's civil rights, women's rights, and gay rights movements, illuminating and providing opportunities for personal connection to the fight for fair treatment under the law. But in the venue of privately owned, for-profit digital media technologies, the social benefits of publicly sharing our "authentic" selves become less clear. "Now user data is optimized and retailed automatically, to advertisers and other media firms, in real time. Computers track conversations and extract patterns at light speed, rendering them profitable," Turner observed. "Social media's ability to simultaneously solicit and surveil communication has not only turned the dream of individualized, expressive democracy into a fountain of wealth. It has turned it into the foundation of a new kind of authoritarianism."[88] As we will see in the later chapters, recent developments substantiate Turner's concern.

As social media have evolved, attracting billions of global users and changing the nature and content of online information,[89] digital influence—as a quantified product, made meaningful by the advertisers and marketers who co-opted academic theories—became a critical form of social and economic capital. Crises and innovations in media and technology; the cultural veneration of celebrity and entrepreneurial culture; and acute economic precarity combined to birth an industry that has come to guide the social and economic markets of the internet—and spill out to shape people's experiences of the world more broadly. The next chapter will explore the years the influencer industry established itself in earnest, when participants made ideological and business decisions that would set the industry on a particular course forward.

Chapter 2

Setting the Terms for a Transactional Industry

In February 2006, *Women's Wear Daily*, or *WWD*, ran an article covering "the blogs that took over the tents" at New York Fashion Week.[1] The piece was a one-thousand-word attempt to grapple with the new presence of bloggers in the fashion industry—both literally, at runway shows and industry parties, and existentially, as a group of "outsiders" who had somehow, through the use of the internet, become recognized as voices of authority. The article trafficked in what most scholars and industry experts now recognize as tropes about blogging: namely, that it represented a democratic process where "the population tak[es] control" of the culture. The writer made the banal observation that "the stereotype of a blogger is a lonely soul sitting in her bedroom, sending her innermost thoughts to anyone who will read them in cyberspace, but blogs are increasingly taken up by the mainstream."[2]

As the central publication of the fashion industry, *WWD* was trying to make sense for its readers of these seemingly significant shifts happening in real time. What would become of these people—mostly young women with little traditional industry experience—who were sitting front row as experts? The sense was that an imagined but entrenched industry boundary had been breached. But what did their presence signify for the industry and broader culture? It would take several years, and complete economic and industrial upheaval, before observers could begin to formulate a sophisticated answer. Tellingly, however, the writer noted, "bloggers see themselves as truth tellers in a world where the truth is hard to come by."

The Industry's Gears Begin to Turn

The influencer industry that we recognize today developed in the mid- to late 2000s amid a perfect storm of technological, cultural, economic, and industrial factors, building upon an intellectual history spanning centuries. The industry's growth accelerated precipitously in the years immediately following the global financial crisis, as aspiring and established media and marketing professionals began working together both intentionally and unintentionally, at times cooperatively and contradictorily, to refashion their own careers and create a guide for how culture could be produced in a postrecession, "post ad," socially mediated age. Indeed, it was the work of people determined to move forward professionally—or, at least, to not fall out of the workforce altogether—that built the technological infrastructure, social norms, business processes, and commodities that would comprise the influencer industry.

In every research interview, I ask participants to tell me their professional story. How did they get to where they are now? Across ages, professions, and backgrounds, nearly all interviewees traced their current position to the economic recession in the late 2000s. "[My first job] was in traditional PR, but it was of course 2008, so it lasted for five minutes," said Jessy Grossman, founder of Boldstreak Talent Management. "I wanted to work in magazines," remembered Brittany Hennessy, an author, former blogger, and senior director of influencer strategy and partnerships at Hearst Digital Media at the time of our interview. "But this was the mid- to late 2000s, and nobody would hire me."

As the above *WWD* article demonstrates, bloggers were the first to gain public visibility as potential creative change-makers of the social media age. Yet, as popular press focused on an adversarial "blogs versus magazines" narrative, the real tensions existed between bloggers/protoinfluencers and the growing cottage industry of marketing middlemen that angled to solidify, streamline, and profit from the influencer-advertiser relationship—as well as gain a "power role"[3] in charting the development of the social media marketing space.

Firms belonging to this new class of digital marketers appeared rapidly and in a range of business models. Some companies provided opportunities for influencers and brands to connect in a transactional manner by building proprietary digital marketplaces that allow influencers and brands to sign up for access, find each other, and engage in paid campaigns. Marketers search these platforms using keywords to turn up profiles that detail influencers' metrics, including their content specialties ("sustainability" and "travel," for example) and ability to drive sales. Other agencies approach influencers directly on behalf of corporate advertising clients and build up a smaller stable of influencers to whom they can reach out directly with appropriate brand partnership opportunities. Agency representation allows select influencers to have teams of marketing professionals backing their personal brands and seeking out relationships with retail brands. Much like traditional Hollywood talent agencies, these companies seek out social media personalities they would like to represent and manage their careers; this includes finding and negotiating deals, coaching influencers through brand relationships and campaigns, and providing general career guidance.

While these firms positioned themselves as helping independent content creators earn money from their passions—and to be sure, working together was financially appealing to all parties—they and early influencers often differed in their approaches to personal branding, the labor required for content production, and the meaning and value of influence and authenticity. In exploring the way these stakeholders navigated these fraught concepts as they brought the influencer industry into existence, the remainder of this chapter illustrates that their primary achievement during these years was defining and operationalizing an industry logic of cultivated-but-authentic visibility while evangelizing the values of metrics and self-monetization.

Early influencers and influence marketers had varying priorities and assumptions regarding their work, but there was a shared suspicion—and optimism—that there was money to be made, creative freedom to be had, and innovation to be done at the axis of social media, marketing, and creative self-expression. In the late 2000s and early 2010s, the industry expanded exponentially with entrants from all corners.[4] As influencers, marketers, and brands navigated their daily work of constructing, marketing, and leveraging social media personalities, an internal set of rules emerged. These early digital influence professionals arrived at four significant definitions—sometimes through tension-filled negotiations—that set the course for the influencer industry.

Brands as People; People as Brands

While marketing practitioners and scholars have long spoken of the push for commercial brands to be more like people,[5] this effort became particularly pointed as the advertising industry tried to reckon with the problem of "increasingly tuned-out consumers"[6] in the twenty-first century. As advertising scholar Michael Serazio observed, "The more obvious [advertisers'] efforts to influence, the more we screen out their messages."[7] In response to this situation, advertisers and marketers have come up with countless ways to humanize brands, from hosting parties to engaging in social activism. At the same time, cultivating a *personal* brand became increasingly critical to professional success, particularly in the digital economy.[8] As bloggers, brands, and marketers began working together in an organized way during the 2000s, they needed to come up with a common language and system of value with which to do business, and "brand" was the answer. "Brands" are neither human nor divorced from humanity.[9] As such, there occurred a simultaneous *collapsing* of self and *building up* of corporate brands so that they engaged on the same plane and were able to engage and exchange within the marketplace they were creating.

Bringing a Company to Life

A guiding principle from the very beginning of digital influencer marketing was that the days of connecting with customers in a one-to-many model were ending. As one advertising observer reflected in

Adweek, "People expect brands to talk *with* them rather than *at* them. They no longer expect brands to sell to them, but to entertain and inform them."[10]

Thomas Rankin, founder of Instagram marketing and analytics firm Dash Hudson, explained that, regardless of a company's size or the particulars of their marketing goals, the guiding question had become: "How do you really connect with your consumer through great content and deepen your engagement with people?" Social media allowed brands to transmute their "brand values"—or words they used to identify and focus the company—into "personalities" in a way that was never before possible.

Many viewed this as a powerful evolution of a classic marketing practice: word of mouth. "Word of mouth is the oldest channel of marketing in the world because it is just people talking and other people listening," reflected Ryan Berger, who was an early entrant to influencer marketing as founder of advertising and marketing firms The Berger Shop and HYPR. "But as the technology started to amplify that word of mouth, it became very clear where this was headed. [It was] so much more efficient and quicker and it reaches so many more people. [We were] moving away from interrupting people and moving into a thing where you provide value for people by coming up with ideas that become part of their world and their life."

To this end, brands undertook efforts to cultivate a "voice" online. Marketing professionals encouraged brands to ask "who would my brand be if it was a real person? What would it sound like?"[11] This was an opportunity to "inject the brand into culture in a different kind of way," Berger said. By making a brand a "personality" that could interact with people on social media, companies and friends could become social equals, with similar abilities to influence—or at least that was the hope. It helped that in their early years, most popular social media platforms did not differentiate between business and personal accounts. Everyone was just a "user," interacting away.

Indeed, as feminist media scholar Sarah Banet-Weiser observed, "building a brand is about building an affective authentic *relationship* with a consumer, one based—just like a relationship between two people—on the accumulation of memories, emotions, personal narratives, and expectations."[12] Maria,* who works in marketing for a U.S. designer, provided an example of how the designer's brand "humanizes" itself to connect with consumers and the social media strategy behind it:

> We did an event at our store on Bleecker Street and it was called the Leopard Leopard Leopard event. We had Leandra Medine of Man Repeller and our chief creative officer doing a panel. It was livestreamed. [We were] watching and following the commentary on the livestream, keeping tabs on the temperature of whether people seemed like they were interested in the conversation. We had a collaboration with the ASPCA that weekend and had a big activation at the store. So the entire facade was in leopard spots and we were highlighting our leopard print product and made leopard print cat beds; if you adopted a cat from the ASPCA you got this cat bed. So there was just this thematic leopard spot thing going on. [We could see] how many people reposted that, and said, like, "I wish we could be there, is this coming to my city." . . . [We were] seeing if it has a sort of viral effect.

Maria noted that "entertaining, being the consummate host, and throwing parties" were some of her company's brand values. By hosting events that connected their target audience to people and causes they were interested in (a popular fashion blogger of the time and a generally noncontroversial charity), the brand humanized itself in the public eye, becoming more relatable, accessible, and fun. Further, the event provided an opportunity to feature their products in a visually appealing way and share the whole experience online in an affable voice, and thus they more deeply engaged with established and potential customers.

Corporatizing the Individual

As brands worked to build themselves out into social media personalities, individuals on social media worked to simplify and distill their personalities into easily understandable personal brands, which—given the economic turmoil of the era—seemed increasingly appealing as a way to ensure one's financial and social stability.[13]

In interviews, influencers described their processes of personal branding as a practice of discipline. They must select and amplify aspects of themselves that they wish to project into a cohesive brand voice that is easily digestible to audiences. As Carissa,* a blogger, explained, "I tried to take my personality in real life and then create that, as best as I could, in this digital way . . . When you look at it online, it's very colorful. It's all about positivity and sunshine and travel and just making your life easier as a twenty-something. When you meet me in person I'm all about the same things. I think it just molded from there." At the same time, Carissa explained that "of course there's always that aspect of filtering it a little bit because I'm also a working professional."

Crucial for influencers, too, is making their personal brands legible to advertisers as a potential partner or vehicle for their own brand messages. In addition to constructing appealing social media feeds, they also use tools borrowed from traditional media industries such as media kits. Media kits distill personal brands into accessible, bullet-point language, and serve as a key means by which influencers are "assessed and subjected to valuation," as media scholar Arturo Arriagada has pointed out.[14]

As Skylar* explained, "In my media kit, when I'm explaining my brand, [I say] it is just a platform women can turn to when they need, like, a best friend." She then expands on the more complex personal history that her media kit language distilled: "I moved my sophomore year of high school to Texas and everyone had their own groups, and it was hard for me to adjust. So I was actually reading blogs and watching YouTube videos, and I kind of looked at [the content creators] as all my best friends. I felt like I knew them because they shared so much of their life. Of course, I didn't . . . [but] I loved how much it did for me. So when I started my blog, that's what I wanted."

Influencers readily acknowledge that, despite their appearances of being forthcoming, the personal brand is obfuscatory by necessity. Individual personalities are too complicated and contradictory to be captured in the clear, bullet-point legibility required by advertisers, so a distancing occurs: *this is me, and this is my personal brand.* Constructing a personal brand for social media often, ultimately, amounts to creating an avatar of the self, one that is cloaked in *discourses* of "realness."[15]

Alana,* a top-tier fashion and lifestyle influencer, was a former investment banker who transitioned into fashion writing in the 2000s, just as influencer marketing was beginning to develop. In our first interview in 2016, she described an early reluctance to call herself a "blogger" or "influencer" and to construct a personal brand online, but said she later realized that the visually oriented personal brand was becoming a necessity for success in the creative economy of the social media age.

> I live in Los Angeles and I thought, "OK, I see all these girls, they're posing on the beach literally in bikinis at sunset, rolling on the grass," and I thought, "Oh, that's what I needed to do." And I did that, but I felt weird about it because first of all, I don't do that [laughs]. I don't roll through the grass, talk about sunsets and be dreamy, I'm not that sort of person. And it made me so uncomfortable . . . When I realized why, and I realized, you know, that I need to stop trying to be whatever these girls are and I kind of stepped back. I talked to someone and she said, "You have this amazing corporate background, you're very intellectual and you have a lot of strong opinions, so why don't you just try to be yourself instead of being another LA girl, for lack of a better phrase, rolling around on the beach in a bikini?" And I said, "Yeah, that's kind of true," and I stopped doing that, kind of a 360 where I just, I became myself. An amplified version of myself, for sure. Still myself, but an amplified version. So we're talking lots of power suits, lots of photos of me working, looking like I'm out there conquering the world. And that worked, and I felt happy because I'm not pretending to be someone I'm not. Obviously, I still wear sweatpants at home . . . but back in the early days, if you look, it's lots of tailored clothing and just looking like this boss lady who's killing it. And that really worked for me.

As personal branding on social media became an answer to "a world where more people than ever are operating as freelancers and are having to invent business models to support themselves,"[16] individuals treated themselves more like media businesses and less like people who were "fun, free, and just being me."[17] While many influencers explained to me how their efforts to be "real" were genuine, they also adopted practices long associated with traditional media companies, such as scrutinizing audience demographics and adjusting their branding accordingly. Alana recalled working with a branding expert to help develop her social media presence:

> She said, "There are certain things that sound more confident and would resonate more with the kind of women you want." So we developed that. The visuals came together after a few months. And we changed the [blog] name. And honestly, once that change came, the improvement in the reach and the follow rate just sort of exploded because it resonated with what women wanted.

Ironically, Alana observed, "when you become yourself"—notably, expressed in the language of the brand—"people can see *she's not trying to fake it*."

Brand Exchanges

As corporate brands and individual people began, with the help of marketers, to understand themselves as similar types of commodities existing in the influencer marketplace, they were better able to determine who might match with whom for sponsorship deals that would be financially and reputationally beneficial for both parties. By speaking the same language of brand "voice" and scrutinizing audience demographics and engagement like a traditional media company would, they made decisions about brand "fit"—or whether a partnership would be appropriate.

In addition to being a blogger and Instagram influencer, Carissa maintains a full-time job on the influencer marketing team for an American fashion designer. When scouting brand deals for herself as an influencer, she said, "I do my research. I look at all [of the brands'] social platforms. I see what their engagement is like and how far along they are as a business. I love working with female-owned and founded businesses as well. Just little tidbits like that—that I can relate to, and I think are on brand, or I believe in paying for—are all things I take into consideration." When scouting influencers for her employer to work with, she continued, "I really take [influencers'] personalities into consideration and see how creative they are in taking on our brand voice but making it their own in a really special way that will connect with their audience."

While constructing a brand and making it profitable is quite labor- and time-intensive for individuals and advertisers, with some estimating eighty- or one-hundred-hour workweeks,[18] many interviewees emphasized that too much *effort* in these relationships could be a signal that the influencer's brand and the advertiser's brand were not a good match. Annette,* director of marketing for a digitally native women's fashion brand, said, "I don't really want to be working with girls and forcing them to create content that they don't want to create. I want to be working with girls that truly believe this is an amazing brand and they love the clothes and they love working with us and it's a relationship—and that's truly what it is behind the scenes as much as it is on social media."

As individuals and advertising brands endeavored to engage in the influencer marketplace, they adjusted their identities and means of expression to suit each other and the audiences they deemed desirable. As Erica,* another influencer marketing professional who also had begun to monetize a personal brand on social media, said, the landscape had developed to "kind of an amazing place, where people are brands and they have all the capability to fully develop businesses online through that." At the same time, she worried about the longevity of the situation, musing, "to see it grow will be kind of scary because . . . what does that look like?"

Followers as Assets

At the same time that participants in the burgeoning influencer industry redefined certain people and companies into persona-inflected brands, they came to understand other people—namely, the faceless members of the social media "audience"—as economic assets. This followed in a long historical trajectory of media companies understanding audiences as commodities.[19] The notion of "the audience" was often mentioned but rarely interrogated in the burgeoning influencer ecosystem of the 2000s. Yet various stakeholders' approaches to the audience—imagining it, cultivating it, and measuring it—were critical to influencers' transition from amateur bloggers to professional cross-platform personal brands, from unpaid to advertiser-supported workers, and from marginal to powerful cultural forces. Further, the way influencers, marketers, and brands responded to the push to view followers as economic assets also revealed their differing beliefs about the purpose of creative production and self-expression in the social media age.

Importing Ideas from Older Media Industries

Media scholar Ien Ang and others have described the "institutional point of view" that guided mass media industries' approaches to audiences throughout the twentieth century.[20] This point of view implies that media audiences are faceless groups onto which all manner of economic and cultural aspirations, expectations, and policies can be projected.[21] Audiences become economic assets that media organizations define "in particular ways, using analytical tools and perspectives that reflect their needs and interests," as media and public policy scholar Philip Napoli wrote.[22]

Continuing this tradition from the mass media industries that ruled the twentieth century, the influencer industry propels itself by measuring, analyzing, and delivering social media audiences to advertisers. Audience members' digital traces—much more easily collected than, for example, television viewers' habits—allow industrial measurement and analyses to occur at more individualized and granular levels. The notion of audience "engagement"—clicks, purchases, and other quantifiable indicators of media content's assumed *effects* on audiences—became central to the way marketers, influencers, and advertisers thought about social media audiences.[23]

Through their language and practices in the 2000s and 2010s, influence marketers encouraged budding influencers to follow their "economic and strategic imperatives,"[24] helping to guide this emergent medium into one that would support individual users as miniature media companies and establish a norm that user-generated content could be advertiser-supported. Tensions came to exist, however, between influencers' desires for more personal interactions with followers, and the marketers and advertisers who encouraged a streamlined and strategic approach.

Interacting with the Audience: Creativity and Strategy

In interviews, most influencers described themselves as primarily creative people who happen to be able to make a living from these impulses. "I've always been a little bit more of a creative versus, like, sort of the analytic type gal. So the flow [of the blog was to] kind of move with my life," explained Lucia, the designer and lifestyle influencer. "I want to create all day long now," said Issa, a fashion blogger. "I just want to concentrate on, like, making beautiful pictures and just being creative," she continued, "I have to stay true to myself."

Influencers also discussed the role of their followers in the creative process. Claudia, for example, described a more affective or emotional investment in "putting herself out there" for the audience.

> I think that my audience has become what it is because of my voice and the way that I blog, if that makes sense. Storytelling is a huge part of it. And that doesn't mean that every post really tells a story, but the majority of mine do . . . I really tried, once I started [my blog], to just be like: you know, here's me. I've really tried to just be me, and here's what I'm naturally gonna share, and I think people have responded well to that. I want myself and who I am as a person woven throughout the blog, just because that's the only way that I could enjoy doing it.

At the same time, influencers also described more business-like approaches in the way they took their followers into account creatively. "It takes time to figure out what works for you and what doesn't work for your audience, what they like, what they don't like, so they would keep coming back," Brittiny, a city-focused fashion blogger, told me in 2015. Lucia recalled the creative and strategic adjustments she made with her blog a year or two prior to our interview, as the blogging market had become more saturated: "I think I just reacted to the fact that I wanted to keep my audience," she said. Skylar, meanwhile, noted that she conducts audience surveys a few times each year to ensure that she provides content they want.

In reflecting on their creative processes and their audiences' roles in them, then, influencers ultimately described a situation of continual negotiation between creativity and strategy. The influencers maintained that honoring their own creative satisfaction and impulses ("being true" to themselves) were the ultimate drivers of their decisions. Yet they also acknowledged that they wanted (and needed, for the sake of their careers) their content to resonate with their audiences.

Marketing firms, on the other hand, sent clear messages about the nature of influencers' creative work and the role of the social media audience in it. In interviews and on their websites and other public marketing materials in the mid-2010s, these agencies described influencers in one of two ways. They might be "publishers" or "content creators," invoking an efficient, corporate approach to creative production. Or they might be "channels" who are "activated" in service of retail brands' needs—rationalizing away their personhood altogether. To marketers, influencers' audiences are often conceptualized as a receptacle for branded deliverables: "professional quality, platform-optimized content," as the HelloSociety agency described it on their website. Creativity on the part of the influencer is both encouraged and restrained; once a person becomes a bankable "influencer," her role is to be a "trusted media property" (according to theAudience) that delivers consistent and continual content across platforms. HelloSociety further explained that the influencer's goal should be making content that meets certain metrics:

A successful social media campaign means constantly monitoring your audience and making changes to the content, voice and network without compromising quality or authenticity. Through detailed ana-

lytics across our network and even through to our partners' proper-
ties, we help both brands and influencers meet their goals together.

Marketing firms described influencers as a mass of data points that
could be aggregated into categories and statistically analyzed; they became significant only when they use their creativity for an effective,
applied purpose. As agency rhetoric makes clear, a successful creative
worker in the social media age is one who "shine[s] themselves up" (as
Lucia said in our interview) to be a mouthpiece for brands.

Navigating this tension was a central theme in interviews. Many influencers preferred to hold on to a feeling of personal connection with their
audiences, complicating the idea that parasocial relationships are one-
directional. "I look at my audience like they're my friends," said Miranda.
"I've connected with so many genuine people that I've never met in person.
I talk to about fifteen girls a day that I've never met and I consider them my
best friends . . . so when I put out a post, I want to be helping other friends."

Jade Kendle-Godbolt, a content marketing CEO and longtime beauty
blogger, said that her hope for her audience is to feel that "she has a platform that's huge and she talks about the things that I care about. She talks
about the things that are good and the things that are bad that we go
through as days go on, and as women, as moms, as Black people, as all
these things . . . let's be real with our audiences."

Influencers both cultivate and care for their audiences, cherishing the
personal connections while also leveraging them in the marketplace.
Indeed, in interviews, influencers often responded to the question of
"who is your audience?" by rattling off statistics and demographics: "My
audience is primarily females who are mid-high school to mid-twenties,
but then I also do have a number of very loyal moms. I have a lot of East
Coast followers as well, but I do know that my top cities are New York,
Dallas, Philadelphia, and Chicago," Carissa reported.

Ultimately, the negotiations over how to understand the social media
audience showed that, despite influencers' desire for nuance on the
topic, the industry would ultimately expand and digitize a longstanding
marketing practice: "Friendship becomes a raw commodity to be in-
strumentalized like any other resource."[25]

Influence Is Measurable and Monetizable

Participants in the nascent influencer industry realized that for stability and longevity, they needed to offer a clearly defined product. The notion of digital influence became a convenient way to communicate the economic and cultural potential of the brands (both personal and corporate) and audiences that existed on social media. While marketers and scholars had studied and utilized quantitative measures of influence for decades before this time, the user-friendly social media technologies and metrics tools offered in this era distilled and made meaningful a particular idea of influence and made it widely accessible. Influencers used tools like Google Analytics and the individual analytics available from platforms like Twitter, Facebook, and later Instagram. Influencer marketing firms also built their own proprietary platforms, often charging a subscription fee, that measured digital influence at massive scale, tracking metrics for thousands or millions of potential influencers.

The idea that digital influence could be tracked, measured, and monetized was initially put into practice by a company called Klout. Klout launched in 2008 with the goal of tracking and ranking the influence of every person online. The company's technology combed through social media data, primarily from Twitter, and assigned every user a score based on a variety of factors including follower count, frequency of posts, the Klout scores of friends and followers, and the number of likes, retweets, and shares received. The only way to *not* be scored was to opt out of Klout on their website—meaning that even social media users who did not know the company existed were still in their database. Klout users with high enough scores were eligible for "perks," or connections to brands that were willing to give out free goods in return for "influential" online praise. Klout's executives saw the company as providing a road map for brands to find "society's hidden influencers," and envisioned a future where "people with formidable Klout scores will board planes earlier, get free access to VIP airport lounges, stay in better hotel rooms, and receive deep discounts from retail stores and flash-sale outlets."[26] "We say to brands that these are the people they should pay attention to most," a company vice president said. "How they want to do it is up to them."[27]

Klout and its competitors like PeerIndex found a fan in author and marketer Mark Schaefer, who espoused his belief that such social scoring represented the "democratization" of social influence.[28] Yet in practice these services more often amounted to discrimination. Klout received sharp criticism for its methodology, and worrisome stories circulated in the press, like that of job seekers being rejected from opportunities because their influence scores were too low.[29] In 2014, the company was sold to Lithium Technologies, which shut down the service for good in 2018.

While the marketers I interviewed maintained that they had not been inspired by Klout when starting their own influence-based ventures, Klout's initial success did help to normalize the idea that "regular people" could leverage their social media followings for commercial benefit. Further, it also lighted a path for the digitization of word-of-mouth marketing—that particularly potent form of marketing whose importance Berger, the agency founder, explained—and provided evidence that there was a market for middleman-type firms that brought individuals and brands together for advertising and publicity campaigns.

Measuring Influence

Marketers, influencers, and brands toggled with various metrics of influence in an effort to determine which most effectively captured an individual influencer's value. Early proponents of social media monetization prioritized follower counts, subscribing to the theory that bigger is better. Yet that soon fell away in favor of more specific measurements such as conversion and the crucial *engagement* metric—or the rate at which audience members click, watch, "like," or otherwise provide digital evidence that they have not just seen but have *engaged with* content. However, efforts to measure social media engagement are widely fraught, as digital media scholar Nancy Baym has noted.[30] And indeed, tensions existed among those involved in the influencer industry about the importance, accuracy, and appropriate use of various metrics.

Early influencer marketing firms built the argument for the primacy of metrics (and in turn, the value of the firms' very existence) by using the language of innovation. They touted their exclusive, cutting-edge metrics technology: Style Coalition claimed on their website that their platform was "an industry first," offering "verified stats" that measured influencers' "reach and impact by viewing their fans and followers across blogs and social platforms." Firms also hyped their own reach: theAudience announced on their website that they offered "a unique blend of creativity, proprietary technology, and influencer amplification [that] enables artists and brands to collaborate in popular culture and syndicate content to over 1 billion consumers" and boasted that their Back-Stage platform "manages every stage of the social publishing process, at massive scale."

While each influencer I interviewed described her own strategy for understanding and utilizing her influence metrics, a common arc existed in the way they characterized their relationship with metrics over time. At first, they were "obsessed" (as Claudia put it), constantly wondering how their content was doing and checking their analytics (typically via an iPhone app, readily available at all hours). Later, they experienced a period of realization as they determined they should re-center themselves around their creative voices in order to bring both personal and professional success and fulfillment. And finally, they expressed a feeling of regained control, deciding to have a less emotional attachment to the numbers, checking them occasionally to be aware of what was going on and to make rational, well-informed, creative-driven decisions from them.

Claudia was in the midst of moving into her "control" stage at the time of our 2015 interview. "I try to really let go of the numbers and love what I'm posting, and do my job well and kind of let the chips fall where they may . . . I've just found there's no way to really tell [what is going to do well]," she said. Yet, she continued, "that being said, like, I'm going through this huge Pinterest overhaul right now. I definitely do give thought to what performs well and what doesn't and why."

Issa was firmly in the stage of feeling in control when we first spoke that same year. In her nearly ten years of blogging, she had dealt with a notable amount of cyber harassment, which led her to develop a firm point of view about how much attention should be paid to people who may be reading the blog. "I want a general sense [of how things are going] but I'm also like, OK, *whatever*, you know? It is what it is," she said. Issa emphasized the affective and interactive relationship she has with her dedicated readers as paramount; she prefers to learn about what her audience likes by talking to them. "I'm a marketing ninja but a metrics hippie. I kind of have a general idea of how the audience is feeling about something because I look at comments, and there's kind of a general number of likes [I typically get], and it's, like, a general feeling," she explained. "But I am totally stubborn, and I do what I want. I'll blog about what makes me happy and that's about it . . . because I really think there's so much noise that tries to get you involved in what people are saying."

The "noise" Issa was referring to was not only the criticism of "anti-fans"[31] but also the industry rhetoric that attempted to guide influencers' attention to certain types of deals and methods for getting the deals. The influencers I interviewed who had worked with an influencer agency described these relationships as fraught ("very tumultuous," as Lucia described it in 2015). There was a clear power struggle between the influencers—who were interested in influence metrics but increasingly trying to pull away from them in favor of interaction with their audiences—and the marketing firms who were pushing influencers and brands to sign on for their metrics and management services.

Notably, the social media audience was at the center of this struggle, but the way in which the audience was implicated was a departure from prior models. For example, radio, television, and film audiences have been measured for decades through tools such as Nielsen ratings and box office sales, but with often unpredictable consequences. Low ratings are often but not always cause for cancellation of a television show. Films that bomb at the box office are typically dubbed failures, yet numerous films and television shows that were considered poor or mediocre at their time of release have later become cult favorites or had significant impact on cultural production in years following. Research on pop culture fans has shown other ways that audiences might impact production, often through individual back-and-forth relationships rather than quantification.[32] Yet neither mass media measurement tools nor fan-producer communications could ever purport to capture everyone *actually in* the audience.

While digital media scholar Nancy Baym has rightfully pointed out that "social media metrics are skewed by algorithms that foreground some messages and users over others through recommendations or automated feed editing"[33] in the influencer industry of the early 2010s, there was still an understanding that each member of the audience could be watched, their every click and "like" tracked, counted, and analyzed. The influencers I interviewed endeavored to use this data sparingly and not define themselves by it. Others, meanwhile, angled for it to directly determine content production.

Monetizing Influence

Only once influence could be measured could it be shaped into a good and assigned monetary value—and monetization was the goal, particularly given the tumultuous economic context of the late 2000s. In these early years, brands and marketers approached bloggers and other social media users to initiate a professional relationship, espousing the idea that these users could and should recognize their digital influence and monetize their followings. "I was, like, the third [Pinterest] Pinner they funded, and I was naive," Lucia, the lifestyle and design influencer, reflected on her early relationship with an influencer firm. "Honestly, it was really embarrassing. I was like, 'Oh, you can get paid?'"

While influencers and influence agencies came to share the goal of monetization, at this time they often differed in their approaches to making it happen. To agencies, optimizing monetization was central. Influencers, instead, preferred to recognize that behind every blog was a person who has her own set of goals, creative impulses, and needs. "That's the first thing when you're talking about monetization, is that every blog is so different," Issa said.

"There's so many ways you can go, and that's one thing that excites me so much," Claudia explained. "I have friends who get a third of the followers I do or less, and they make three times what I do, and they don't even have ads on their site. It's just from [things like] shoppable Instagram. And then I have a lot of friends who have just grown an awesome following, so they make the vast majority of their income from ads. That's really my goal at this point: to just continue building my brand to the point that ads and sponsorships pay my salary."

Claudia's description of monetization highlights some of the different revenue streams that influencers could pursue: banner advertising on blogs, affiliate links, and sponsored content. Each type of revenue has different implications. Banner ads, for example, require no creative effort on behalf of the blogger; they simply sell ad space on their sites. Affiliate links are particularly useful for those who frequently discuss specific products, as the blogger earns a small amount for every click-through or purchase that a reader makes. Sponsorships or partnerships require the most creative effort on behalf of the blogger, as this is when a brand or a product is fully integrated into content. Claudia's goal was to focus on ads and sponsorships; Issa, on the other hand, earned most of her income from affiliates and sponsorships. All influencers I interviewed emphasized that they had to figure out what monetization tactics worked for them, given their creative inclinations and the preferences of their audiences. As Skylar admitted, "A huge thing that goes into blogging is looking at what does well and what doesn't. Especially if you're putting that much time into it, or paying photographers, paying videographers . . . I don't want to pay for that and not reap the benefits or [have] my audience not like it."

Authenticity governs the process of monetizing influence, but it often meant different things to influencers and to marketers and brands, particularly in this early era. In the face of increased pressure to monetize, influencers aimed to maintain what they saw as the creative drive that brought them to social media in the first place. They hoped to make money in a way that felt pure to them and not as if they were "selling out."[34] Marketing firms attempted to prove that they themselves were "authentic"—or understanding of creative processes, and not necessarily looking for profit—in the way they publicly positioned themselves.[35] theAudience distanced itself from its industry, announcing, "We think like publishers, not like marketers." Reward-Style framed their work as that of empowerment: "Empowering the world's publishers & retailers to maximize market potential." Indeed, most influencer marketing firms positioned themselves as "helping"—though helping meant measuring and monetizing in ways that were not always agreeable to all involved.

Authenticity as a Perception

The process of commodifying influence through standardizing measurement and monetization revealed that authenticity was the axis on which the influencer industry would spin. The early bloggers and other social media users who monetized their influence did so by leveraging their "real" relationships with their followers—a sense of "realness" that had come to exist, in part, because they *were not* monetized.[36] Yet as individual monetization permeated the social media ecosystem, marketers, advertisers, and influencers and their followers had to figure out a way to continue moving forward. Marketers did not make it their businesses to ensure that what happened behind the scenes with an influencer's work process was "authentic" to whoever she "really" was—merely that it appeared that way. (And, as an agency executive said in an interview, "The second the influencer starts saying, 'Yeah, I do it because its authentic,' that means the authenticity has totally gone out the window.") Influencers wanted to "be true" to themselves, but faced an industrial reality that might not always support that.

In their exploration of authenticity, social media, and contemporary politics, media scholars Georgia Gaden and Delia Dumitrica point out that authenticity was historically understood "as an ethic for living a virtuous life."[37] Authenticity was linked to political engagement: by understanding oneself, one could understand others and be a better citizen. Yet, they observe, the "strategic authenticity" that has become standard for social media users of all stripes "reinforces a consumerist attitude, where the individual presents herself on social media in order to be 'consumed' by others."[38] This marriage of authenticity and strategy is not just a product of the social media age—deploying "realness" in advertising has been popular for decades, perhaps made most famous by the

2000s-era Dove Campaign for Real Beauty—but the gradual depoliticization of authenticity has also defanged the concept of any significant social meaning. In the influencer industry, authenticity is significant only inasmuch as it can be perceived and given numeric and financial value. It is instrumental, even as it remains a resonant ideal. Influencers, marketers, social media companies, and users navigated this situation as they—intentionally or not—helped bring it into being.

Being "True"

In interviews, influencers described their own drives for authenticity as a twofold desire to "be true" to themselves—meaning that they created content that resonated with them personally—and to represent themselves truthfully online. As Claudia reflected in a 2015 interview:

> You know, a lot of people out there will tell you . . . that you have to be super professional . . . You can't talk about beliefs. You can't give your opinion on anything. But for me I just—I do not function that way. I feel like I'm lying.

Claudia's comment illustrates the double bind in which many influencers find themselves, navigating the impetus to be real, but not so real that they alienate followers.[39] It also reflects the sociopolitical climate of 2015, wherein influencers were generally expected to stay away from any subject, especially political or religious ones, that could be considered controversial.

Then as now, though, being true to oneself and striving for real representation of one's life does not mean sharing everything. The process of self-branding, by necessity, entails curation. To be legible as a viable personal brand, one must have a clear message and fairly predictable posting practices, from the cadence (or how often new content is posted) to its aesthetic. Cohesiveness and consistency are key.

To this end, Skylar explained the strategic thinking and effort behind a single video she posted on Instagram and YouTube:

> I actually just hired a guy to help me work kind of behind the scenes . . . he goes through my stuff and sees what works well or what

people interact with. He said, "Every time you share something about your life or a photo that's not perfectly done, it does well. It works better than others." So he's like, "What if you started sharing just more real life?" We threw some ideas around and I was like, OK, I'm not sure I'm really comfortable with doing that video on Instagram because I feel like it's front and center to everyone. If I put it on You-Tube not as many people will click on it [laughs], but I filmed it and it did really well. I got really good feedback, emails from girls who were like, "I love this!"

Skylar further reflected on the pressures she felt to adhere to prevailing visual norms on Instagram:

Instagram is just so pretty and I put so much thought into just posing [a photo]. And my room is such a mess half the time and if I take a photo in my room, everything is thrown into a corner. And no one sees that. So [the video was] just, I don't know, to me, more relatable. I feel like that's what makes me gravitate to other girls is just, someone who isn't just all put together and fake and pretty. It's someone who actually shares their real life.

Skylar's example highlights how tenuous the line is between reality (the messy room) and constructions of it (showing herself at home, but not the mess), between "being true to yourself" (not wanting to make a video) and aligning with others' demands for a particular type of "authenticity."

Further, influencers must carefully calibrate their brand partnerships so as not to diminish their feeds' relatability. As Brittiny said, "I don't want to feel like I'm always trying to get my followers to buy something. I try not to get too many sponsored posts at any time, so that it looks like 'she's just in it for money.' I try to break everything up." Brittiny also explained how she strives for authenticity when seeking out branding deals, remembering a campaign she agreed to with a brand that did not actually resonate with her personally. She ultimately decided "this isn't me; I'm not going to do this."

The ways in which brands and marketers discuss authenticity makes clear that it exists only as a continually shifting perception. As a marketing director at a fast-growing apparel startup told me, "We value the *idea* of authenticity." The startup looks for influencers whose content "has an authentic *feel* to it" (emphasis added). They have no means—and no time—for evaluating whether an influencer's content is actually true to her life, so they rely on their "gut" reactions to influencers' content.

Further, Erica,* who had worked in marketing for American designers for a decade and was launching her own influencer career, observed, "I think if you're showing enough of your personality and *it seems like who you are* [emphasis added], then I think that's the most important thing. I think people are [following] people that they're interested in and they want to see what they're doing, or where they're going, what they're eating. You're trying to successfully capture the 'someone,' so much so that they want to be your friend or they want to be involved in your life to the point that they're subscribed, so to speak."

Influencers need to share enough "truth"—constructed textually, visually, and interpersonally through responding to followers—to be perceived as authentic. No one to whom they might be accountable—such as sponsors or the platforms on which the business is carried out—has the resources or motivation to verify whether it is accurate.

"Authentic But Not Accurate"

To reconcile the competing demands to "be true" with the needs of advertisers for predictable, reliable, and measurable media channels, participants in the influencer industry began to differentiate between authenticity and accuracy.

Brittany Hennessy, who directed the influencer division for a major media company at the time of our interview, described, for example, how influencers still needed to look conventionally attractive when selling a product. "In a way, that's where you might run into the authenticity problem," she said. "It's like, I understand you need to look pretty when you take a picture because I don't want to see a picture of you after you've run two miles. You're not gonna look super cute, and it's not gonna make me want to buy this water. So I see why you lie [laughs] . . . so maybe the content isn't 100 percent accurate, but it's probably still authentic."

Alana, the fashion influencer and agency founder, remembered:

> When I first started, I would be more relaxed in the kind of sponsors I would go for. Let's say I don't use anything but iPads but let's say Verizon comes to me with this tablet that kind of looks like an iPad but it's not. And I have to be honest. This is a decision I would not make today, but back then I would say, yeah, I can do that. It paid a lot and I needed the money, and campaigns weren't easy to come by, so you're kind of silly if you're gonna say no. It's not like these are drugs [laughs], they're tablets. So I wasn't really lying, I did talk about the benefits of the tablet and I did use it, blah blah blah, but if you want me to be honest—are you gonna use your iPad or are you gonna use this pseudo iPad/tablet, you're gonna use the iPad. But because this brand came to you, you took this campaign.

Beth,* an influencer marketing manager for an American e-commerce startup, noted that influencers are "really just about *showcasing* what's real in their lives [emphasis added]—even if it is a little bit posed or staged."

Despite the often genuine desire on the part of members of the influencer industry to "be true," their work requires them to rely on a paradoxical version of authenticity—"realness" that exists only in perception. As Brooke Erin Duffy observed, the "conceptual imprecision" of authenticity in the social media sphere "enables bloggers to deploy these terms in ways that resonate with their ever-shifting allegiances— to themselves, to their audiences, to their advertisers, and to members of the public who celebrate them for wresting power from fashion's old guard."[40]

The Way Forward

The tremendous growth and increased visibility of the influencer economy in the mid- to late 2000s helped to cement its reputation as the most accessible pathway for creative success in an age of otherwise decreased opportunities. As bloggers and other protoinfluencers began working with brands and a new class of influence-focused marketers in a formalized way, they negotiated the meaning and significance of a range of key concepts through a contradiction-filled process that included importing ideas from other industries as well as from popular trends. These concepts would come to guide the nascent business of influencer marketing to develop, within a few short years, into a multibillion-dollar industry that has rearranged logics of cultural production and social life.

Marketers aimed to encourage a new way of imagining and using social platforms that felt frictionless and inevitable, where everything is measurable and a potential channel of commerce. Influencers—those who turned posting on social media into a job—enjoyed the expanded income opportunities that marketers offered but also worked to defend their creativity and autonomy in an increasingly rationalized and competitive environment. Popular metrics platforms encouraged social media users to view their audiences as potentially monetizable or otherwise quantifiable for personal gain, such as branding deals or higher status. The ultimate consensus that people and companies should engage using the language and self-identity of brands, that these brands should view their social media audiences as economic assets, that their interactions with their followers could be quantified and leveraged as metrics of influence, and that the sense of authenticity on which this system relied was meaningful only as much as it was believable have become pervasive in our communication landscape. They contribute, in a sense, to what media scholar José van Dijck described as a social media culture of commercially focused "connectivity" rather than connection.[41]

While influencers often described themselves in interviews as satisfied with their jobs—and often, "lucky"—they acknowledged the limits. As Lucia said of this early period, "It's all about how [influence marketers] are able to best inspire or keep influencers moving on the track they want it to go."

Chapter 3

Making Influence Efficient

When I interviewed Thomas Rankin in early 2016, the company he founded, Dash Hudson, was a young and successful marketing analytics firm, offering Instagram insights and strategy to influencers and brands. As an early entrant into the growing field of influencer marketing, Rankin's company pivoted several times, from a menswear e-commerce company to an Instagram shopping app to a business that, as he said, "shines light into the darkness of Instagram." Their product and business model—providing data, analytics, and strategy on Instagram content performance to subscribing customers—gained traction and accelerated quickly. "The absence of data is always a big opportunity," he observed, recalling how little formal knowledge or processes existed in the influencer landscape just three years prior, when the company was founded. Now, he said, "we can show you a full suite of metrics on [a] person at a per post level of how they're helping you grow your audience and brand awareness."

At the turn of the 2010s, excitement continued to grow around the ability to measure and monetize individuals' social media followings to deliver targeted advertising messages. Advertising industry leaders were once again touting the "pass-around power of everyday people"[1] that Katz and Lazarsfeld had popularized in the 1950s, and industry insiders were bullish about leveraging it on social media platforms' unprecedented scale. Advertising and marketing professionals envisioned a social media environment where individuals and brands worked more harmoniously to deliver authentic-but-sponsored content to niche audiences.

During the next several years, those means of identifying, measuring, and monetizing influencers matured in particular ways aimed at maximizing efficiency. Dash Hudson was one of hundreds of third-party firms that emerged to work toward these ends. The development of various technologies and businesses norms and processes transformed the influencer space from a haphazard ecosystem of actors into a more smoothly functioning industry with clearer goals and roles for various participants.

By 2015, popular narratives about the influencer industry remained positive and sometimes grandiose: *Adweek* estimated that 75 percent of marketers utilized influencers,[2] and venture capital flowed into the space.[3] At the same time, however, a small subset of critics came forward. One of these was Tay Zonday, who had experienced the promises and perils of digital influence in a particularly heightened way since accidentally achieving viral fame in 2007 for his "Chocolate Rain" video. He reflected to *New York* magazine:

> In 2015, internet influence is an accepted fetish. No hyperbole can describe the way every person and brand is frantically inflating social-media metrics as a form of "digital plastic surgery." We all want to be influencers. Every facet of our self-actualization is enhanced by appearing to be the biggest digital Pied Piper. Digital influence is now the costume of our century and a problematic eugenics for sorting human value.[4]

Indeed, in the increasingly commercialized, social media-focused, and *sprawling* internet environment of the early 2010s, the notion of "digital influence" became an efficient means of identifying people's value: amid the immense noise of social media content, who should be singled out as worth listening to, what should they say to obtain and maintain that position of power, and how can they more consistently earn money from it? In this period, marketers and brands worked together to rationalize this process.

The influencer industry expanded rapidly as its participants operationalized the guiding definitions discussed in the previous chapter. With
this expansion came forces of rationalization, as companies and individuals sought to make influencer marketing more efficient. This chapter presents an overview of industry stakeholders' various efforts to streamline
deals, commercialize content, and optimize metrics and aesthetics.
These strategic moves enabled the industry to experience sharp growth
while at the same time undermining its democratic and authentic self-
image. By arbitrarily assigning value to certain metrics, minimizing or
exploiting the labor of countless aspiring content creators, and deincen-
tivizing creative risk taking—among other activities—the influencer
ecosystem quickly evolved into a highly lucrative and highly visible industry, critical to the marketing plans of brands of all sizes and product
specializations. Indeed, *WWD* dubbed 2015 the "year of the influencer,"
and Google noted that same year that the keyword "influencer marketing" had reached "breakout" status, meaning it was "experiencing growth
greater than 5000 percent."[5] By year's end, however, a pair of high-profile
events pushed the industry to a precipice.

Streamlining the Dealmaking Process

In the early 2010s, the rapid uptake in smartphone use[6] shifted internet
users' attention to mobile devices and, with the launch of popular apps
like Instagram, helped usher in the "decline of blogging"[7] and the rise
of the "digital influencer." As bloggers "fanned out onto other social
platforms and, importantly . . . no longer expect[ed] to make a living by
blogging alone,"[8] "influencer" became the go-to terminology for these
multiplatform personal brands that boasted impressive followings. In a
Fast Company article addressing the so-called end of the golden age of
blogging, a marketing executive noted that "influencers have a more
nuanced and complex strategy . . . they use different social platforms to
build their brand; their blogs are just one extension of this effort to
engage followers."[9]

New influencer marketing agencies continued to appear, merge, shut
down, and pivot at a rapid clip as they searched for ways to further develop and profit from digital influence. While their specific approaches

and offerings differed, influence marketers' central goal at this time was to streamline the influencer identification, selection, and pricing processes for the brands and individuals involved. As Ryan Berger, the advertising industry veteran and cofounder of influencer marketing platform HYPR, explained in a 2018 interview, "The whole idea [behind this company] is: Ryan Berger's really interesting, but he can only fit so many people in his phone and bring only so many people to the same things over and over again. So what if we had a database of everybody in the world with their contact info and their audience demographics, and brands could pay a subscription fee to connect to those people and reach out to them?"

Intensifying the urgency to streamline the influencer landscape were the early, high-profile successes of bloggers like The Glamourai (working with Digital Brand Architects) and Fashiontoast (represented by Next Management), who earned enviable incomes by starring in commercials, collaborating with brands to create product lines, and displaying ads and sponsored content on their websites and social media feeds.[10] Several early bloggers such as Bryanboy and The Man Repeller attracted the attention of traditional Hollywood talent agencies like Creative Artists Agency, which signed bloggers "left and right" to capitalize on their growing buzz and the new possibilities for visibility and monetization that the social media environment offered.[11] The seemingly overnight successes of these bloggers-turned-digital-influencers— whose "authentic" personal brands made them seem "just like us," and thus, their fame accessible—created a gold rush moment on social media. Countless users, especially women interested in fashion, beauty, parenting, and other traditionally feminine domains, began posting in strategic ways in hopes of "making it" as an influencer, engaging in what Brooke Erin Duffy called "aspirational labor."[12]

Identifying Influencers

Given the widespread enthusiasm for the influencer industry—from advertisers who looked for new channels for their messages and from social media users who yearned for the free products, glamorous lifestyles, and passionate work that early influencers depicted as accessible to all[13]—marketers and brands found it increasingly necessary to make it easier to identify who could "count" as an influencer. As a writer for Racked, the now-defunct fashion website, observed in 2014, "Originality doesn't get bloggers noticed anymore—numbers do."[14] Indeed, influence marketers continued their work to quantify and package digital influence in ways that could be easily digestible and actionable for both brands and influencers.

The first move was to set metrics benchmarks for would-be influencers. In interviews, marketing and brand executives typically characterized these as basically arbitrary. Matthew,* a cofounder of a marketing agency, explained to me in a 2015 interview that, for his agency, "the minimum number of followers across their combined social networks is fifty thousand before we consider them." Jane,* a director of brand partnerships at one of the first, and later largest, influencer marketing platforms, said in 2018 that her company's view was that ten thousand followers was the minimum point of entry. Hennessy, the author and strategic director, said, "100,000 followers—that's when you're an influencer. Unless you're . . . some weird niche where there's only ten of you. But if you're doing fashion or beauty or travel, you should be able to get to 100,000 or you're not that good."

Next, brands and marketers looked at engagement rates, or the degree to which an influencer's audience interacts with their content. "It's easy to say 'this influencer is an influencer,' but if the audience doesn't share content, doesn't engage with the content, then you just flushed your money down the toilet," said one agency founder. Similarly, Matthew said a key part of his agency's evaluation of an influencer is, "Does the audience click, does the audience care what they're doing?"

Countless influencer marketing companies offered tools to analyze engagement along with a variety of other attributes, such as audience demographics, brand affinities, and typical price point of goods advertised, and made the information readily available to brands so they could make quicker decisions about influencer campaigns. These product dashboards made searching, analyzing, and matching with influencers easier than ever. As one agency director told Digiday, "The beauty of using technology platforms to identify influencers is that it makes [influencer marketing] very turnkey. Now we can get influencer programs live in a matter of weeks."[15]

Influencer marketing and technology startups continued to introduce and refine proprietary data-driven technologies, and countless articles in the advertising and marketing industry press encouraged readers to use data and sophisticated analyses to refine their influencer strategies. As the trend toward data-driven influencer marketing gathered steam, marketers identified potential influencers within smaller and more specific niches. A MediaPost article cheered on these efforts, arguing, "It's essential to identify if certain personalities have microaudiences centered around specific interests and passions. By taking a closer look, you'll have a diverse arsenal of influencers available."[16] A focus on "microinfluencers" and, later, "nano-influencers"—individuals who boasted high engagement rates, even while their total number of followers may have numbered in the low thousands—followed.[17]

Selecting Influencers

Data-driven, user-friendly influencer marketing technologies evolved. Yet as they aimed to simplify the influencer marketing process, it was not always clear how influencers were being judged. One agency's head of influencer marketing explained his company's approach to me as such:

> We look at demographic data, and then we run them through a proprietary qualitative scoring methodology that allows us to rate and rank influencers so we can help our clients make smarter decisions . . . We rate them qualitatively based on a few different factors and those factors, in general, are their reach, that's one piece of it, potential and actual reach or a selection of both. We look at their authenticity or credibility. Then we look at their—what we call potential impact or resonance, and there are a number of factors that we use to qualitatively determine that. But we pull those three things together to give a recommendation to our clients.

These sorts of rambling, specific yet vague descriptions were common as agencies situated themselves as always being on the cutting edge of an industry that was constantly changing.

Sabina*, an executive at a Los Angeles-based influence marketing agency, explained, "Almost every first influencer project is a test-and-learn project because we're seeing what audiences respond the best to. Are the audiences that the client thinks are the right audiences really the right audience? Or is it some random group that's actually responding better? What content really drove people to particularly engage with this product?" Further, she explained, "we'll be able to see what to do if someone's really difficult to work with, or their content performed really poorly. We'll probably just make a note on that for ourselves because we wouldn't want to leverage them again."

While followers and engagement metrics were the gatekeepers that opened aspiring influencers up to the possibility of securing branding deals, once they were in the door, agencies reserved a level of human touch to verify whether an influencer could become viable—and in what ways. Many agency employees combed social media profiles to look for an appealing aesthetic and consistency of content, and some read comments for a "gut check" on the "health and quality" of the audience, as one agency founder said in an interview. As media scholar Sophie Bishop has pointed out, "Like Bookscan and Soundscan in publishing and music industries, intermediaries such as brand representatives and talent managers use automated tools to sharpen and justify decisions, which in practice are based on a number of subjective feelings."[18]

Jessy Grossman, founder of influencer talent agency Boldstreak, explained that, for her, "comments are weighted a lot more heavily because you can easily tap on the photo and like it, but to actually sit down and write a comment because that content resonated with you so much that you felt compelled to comment on it, that has so much more weight than just tapping a photo. So if I see someone with hundreds of comments on a piece of content they're creating, that's someone I'm really interested in."

Further, Hennessy emphasized the importance of paying attention to the personal details influencers post in the event they offer new branding opportunities. "I have a list of influencers who are pregnant and when they're giving birth based on the fact that they hashtagged something like, #36weeks! So I'm like, OK, that means you're due in four weeks, so right around this time we should start pitching you for new mom stuff."

Renee,* a director of influencer marketing for a legacy public relations agency, characterized the influencer identification and selection process as a "mix of art and science."

> The science part being those data-driven points, from audience demographics to engagement rate and total following but also looking at their momentum—seeing whether their audience is growing over time or whether they're static. We obviously want to be working with someone who is growing, we want to work with someone who is on the rise, who might not be at their peak at this point because the more that they grow the more we can grow with them. And then from an art perspective, we look at their overall content aesthetic of course, whether they've worked with competing brands previously, other branded content that they've done and whether that measures up to their organic content.

Indeed, marketers and brands expected influencers' sponsored content to be just as engaging to audiences as their "organic," or not sponsored, content. A sponsored post advertising a handbag line must be legible within, and resonate similarly with audiences as, the same feed that showcases organic photos of an influencer on vacation or playing with her children.

While it can be understandably difficult for influencers to muster the same enthusiasm, personal touch, and audience outreach with sponsored and organic content, the degree to which influencers were successful at it correlated directly with their value in the marketplace. By further collapsing the "self" and "brand" into the same aesthetic and rhetorical plane, influencers' level of authenticity supposedly became clearer to others, particularly the marketers whose work was to assess and sell it. Authenticity had come to moderate the value of digital influence. In a 2018 interview, Corey Martin, director at the 360i agency, reflected on the role of authenticity in the influencer selection process:

> Authenticity is really subjective and really hard—so we need to make it less subjective. The assumptions that we make are: The more that an influencer is engaged in promoting products from a paid standpoint, the less authentic their overall content is. So we evaluate how often they do that. But other factors play into that, [such as] their expertise, their credibility, the kinds of content they produce, quality of content. And the last piece of it is the engagement—and not just the number of people that engage with an influencer but reciprocal engagement, the depth to which an influencer is engaging back with their audience.

Indeed, as other scholars have noted,[19] influencers need to carefully navigate the imagined boundary between being "authentic" and "selling out," which means calibrating the frequency with which they post sponsored content as well as partnering with the "right" brands. As one industry watcher wrote:

> [A]n influencer accepting payment to endorse a product should be seen as more of an "access fee" to their audience. They are the gatekeepers of their audience and their credibility depends on who they let through that gate. The less scrupulous their "door policy," the less their audience will respect their judgment. *Entry* must come down to more than paying the right price or influencers will lose their audience's trust. Influence is built on a foundation of trust. Without trust, you cannot influence.[20]

Yet, while industry insiders urged each other to centralize authenticity and trust in the influencer selection process, they also turned to older entertainment industry shorthand to help carry it out. One executive urged brands to "have a 'casting' hat on when selecting people," even though influencers should not be "treat[ed] like a cast for an ad."[21] As research from this period has pointed out, often the influencers who were "selected" most frequently—who were ranked as most influential—

represented stereotypes and homogenous beauty ideals (young, thin, feminine, blonde, and overwhelmingly white) long relied upon in traditional advertisements.[22]

Constructing these visuals also often required preexisting social and economic capital, such as savvy in dealing with advertisers and money to buy clothes and accessories, as well as a "brand-safe" digital presence. Worryingly, recent research by Sophie Bishop has shown that some tools brands and marketers use for identifying influencers' "brand safety" systematically devalue queer people and people of color by red-flagging their use of emic words—"queer," for example—thus making those influencers less likely to be selected for brand deals.[23]

To deal with the influx of influencers in the mid-2010s, marketers and brands created loose, internal methods for sorting influencers for selection. Annette, the director of marketing for an American fast fashion brand, explained her department's tier system:

> The fourth tier, which is the lowest, is more organic. So we've got tools that look at our Instagram and look at people that are talking about us in the social sphere, and they're not really influencers, they're just everyday girls who have an affinity for the brand. So you know, we're connecting with them on a regular basis and there's no dollars exchanged, it's just really, "Hey, we noticed you like the brand and we'd like to sort of bring you into the fold." We've got a showroom in our office where we've got a pretty steady stream of girls who come through and are gifted pieces from our collections and so forth. So that's really relationship building, we're not expecting any sort of KPI [key performance indicator], it's just about celebrating these girls who are just fans of the brand. I'd say the next level is really digital influencers, so kind of your true kind of fashion blogger girls, where this is what they do for a living, and in that regard it really is all about the content that they are creating and ensuring that is content that we can then use on our own channels to drive sales. So they're kind of like the workhorses . . . Then I would say the next tier up is what we would refer to as brand ambassadors. So these are girls

that have a following, they have great engagement, they're producing great content, it's all in line with who we are as a brand and we really want to kind of champion them to be an ambassador for us . . . But they may be models, they might be singers, they might be something other than a digital influencer and a blogger, you know, these girls sort of live and work across a number of different mediums but they have an amazing presence on social. And then the top tier is this celebrity grouping. So we work with an agency who gifts out pieces to celebrities on a regular basis and we can choose to engage with them, kind of a pay-to-play model. And again, these are women that are identifiable throughout the world, who people are looking to for style inspiration, who are getting picked up in editorials and PR and their goal is not so much revenue but more so the brand awareness, engagement play.

Most brands and marketers described some form of a "tier" or "bucket" system when explaining how they think about the influencers they work with, especially when discussing pricing. Buckets—often, though not always, corresponding to arbitrary metrics benchmarks— help determine how much an influencer can charge for campaign work. However, the lack of a shared or transparent industry understanding of how metrics correlate to pay leaves ample opportunity for exploitation and discrimination, even if unwittingly. Most commonly, this happens when brands pay in product rather than money, or pay different influencers different rates for the same work. "There's not a lot of structure to it, to be honest," an influencer manager for a trendy clothing and home goods retailer told me. "I wish that there was."

Pricing Influencers

Buckets were a way of streamlining pricing schemes in an industry that was still determining the value of digital influence in various contexts. For example, while some firms indicated that pricing was directly correlated to follower counts or engagement rates, others described a system of valuation that shifted depending on various stakeholder perceptions. Martin pointed out in 2018 that "somebody who has 150,000 followers may be more valuable to a particular client than someone who has two million followers." Matthew explained in 2015:

> Instagram can range from, say, $100 to $15,000 depending on the influencer and the amount of "asks" that are required with the Instagram—like if they have to travel somewhere. So someone with 100,000 to 500,000 followers might make $2,500 to $5,000 for an Instagram. Somebody with 500,000 to a million followers might make $4,000 to $10,000. Someone with a million-plus normally is looking for a minimum of $4,000 but up to $15,000. We've offered some celebrities up to $30,000 for an Instagram. It depends on a lot of factors but those are the ranges. The way we break down influencers is by four categories . . . that is by social following, and we have prices associated with each of those so the brand knows how much they can expect to spend.

As brands and marketers streamlined the influencer marketing process, they hoped to make things easier for "everyone"—though in practice, these changes did not always benefit influencers, as they were often left having to guess how much their own influence could be worth. Hennessy, in her position at a major media company, worked with countless agents, marketers, brands, influencers, and other participants in the influencer industry. She described how the industry's approach to pricing put the burden on individual influencers to guess and advocate for their own fees. "The discrepancy in fees is mind-blowing . . . I once did a campaign where I had $10,000 allocated for this girl and she asked for $2,500. It just blew my mind. She has no idea how much she's worth," she said.

Further, the process of streamlining dealmaking also changed the rules for influencers' creativity with campaigns. As the influencer industry grew and brands increased budgets for influencers, the stakes became higher. Contracts, my interviewees noted, dictated the language to be used in captions, specific times posts should go up, and other details that previously had been left to influencers' discretion. They also increasingly required influencers submit their exact content for brands' approval before they post it.

"Some of the old guard are like, 'Wait. I never used to have to send my content for approval. Doesn't the brand trust me? Don't they just want to work with me because of who I am?' And yes, that is true, but now maybe they're paying you six figures instead of $2,500, and they want to make sure that the brand messaging is correct," Reesa Lake, of Digital Brand Architects, explained in 2017.

Influencers and brands often take cues from each other when crafting a presence on social media, trying out different looks, captions, and ways of engaging with followers in service of bolstering their reach. Sabina, the LA-based marketing director, explained, "We are very discerning in terms of what we put on our own social channels. So . . . the expectation is that all of these girls are on-brand for us and are creating content that makes sense for our own feed."

To get by in the influencer industry's new processes for identification, selection, and pricing, influencers needed to present themselves in more consistent, polished, and predictable ways—to more fully transmute the *personal* of their brands into language and aesthetics that were kin to those used by sponsors and marketers. After Instagram introduced ads in 2015, it made further aesthetic and ideological sense within the platform for influencers and advertisers to model their content after each other, as they all became mixed together in an endless scroll of square-shaped imagery. The seemingly impossible feat, of course, was to do it in a way that still, as Sabina said, "feels organic."

Influencers were expected to toe a growing line of contradictions: be yourself, but be predictable and polished. Be "organic" but strategic. And, as I have written elsewhere with Brooke Erin Duffy, be "real" but not "too real"—a particularly gendered imperative that's indicative of the double binds in which women find themselves across many professional sectors, especially ones that entail public visibility, as they navigate a heightened risk of harassment or other negative repercussions.[24] In other words, the tools and practices intended to stabilize the influencer industry shifted power away from those who had spearheaded the industry: away from those who created social media content and toward those who constructed the new means of amplifying it. Unsurprisingly, these shifting expectations impacted how and what content was produced.

Niche Content Dissolves into "Lifestyle"

By the mid- to late 2010s, influencers, brands, and marketers realized that income and visibility might come more efficiently if influencers presented themselves as "lifestyle" brands rather than experts in fashion, beauty, or otherwise. The prevailing idea was that in sharing more about their homes, families, travels, and more, influencers could prove their "realness." As Grossman, the talent manager, said, "We like people to discuss all parts of their life. We're human. That's why I'm like, we don't really represent people who—I keep going back to beauty influencers. Like, I love that you love makeup, but I also know you're a human being and you like other things. In remaining authentic to yourself as a human, what else are you interested in?"

This reorientation to lifestyle content followed trends in popular media more generally. In 2008, media researcher Tania Lewis chronicled the rise of "lifestyle media," noting how television and print media were "increasingly concerned with teaching audiences, both men and women, how to manage their everyday lives through a seamless focus on food, home decoration, health, style, and grooming."[25] The proliferation of experts concerned with the tasks of day-to-day life had, even before the dawn of social media, contributed to a "commoditization of information and advice," positioning experts as a "friendly guides rather than authorities."[26] Through Lewis's work, we can see how the immense popularity of such guides, from newspaper columnists devoted to homemaking to the original casts of *Queer Eye for the Straight Guy* and *What Not to Wear*, helped set the stage for the normalization of lifestyle influencers.

Grossman, the talent manager, reflected on the importance of influencers' more accessible but still aspirational sociocultural roles:

Celebrities are this like aspirational sort of figure, where influencers are exactly the opposite—they're relatable, they're just like us, but they're still—it's this desire to, like, *learn* from them. They're not *just* like you and me, there's still some sort of distinction between the two, but they're so much closer to who [we] are, and that I think is why people relate to them so much.

Shifting to lifestyle content also provided more material and immediate benefits. In sharing a wider range of content, influencers could also diversify what aspects of their personal brands could be monetized. They were no longer limited to earning income from "just" fashion or beauty partnerships, for example, but could partner with car companies or hotels. Further, in building out their personal brands to encompass more areas of daily life, they could potentially appeal to greater numbers of followers and thus hopefully burnish their influence metrics. As such, dissolving content specialties in favor of a more general lifestyle-oriented strategy became a practical choice for many influencers, one encouraged by marketers, advertisers, and other stakeholders.

Together, the streamlining activities of influence marketers enabled influencers and brands to "buy and sell 'influence' as easily as they can buy and sell used books on eBay"[27]—and enabled the commercialization of social media self-presentations to become widespread.

Commercializing Content

While monetization had nearly always been a priority of the influencer industry, by the mid-2010s, brands, marketers, and influencers looked beyond the sponsorship models they had been working with to a future where an influencer's social media presence could be more wholly and efficiently commercialized, from each item in her photos to the very social media platforms on which influencer marketing was carried out. In other words, rather than advertising a specific clothing brand in a photo, why not earn a commission from the shoes, the sunglasses, the handbag, and the hotel in which the photo was taken? And rather than directing followers to outside e-commerce websites where they could find items displayed in the photos, could it be possible to shop within an app like Instagram? As a variety of stakeholders explored these possibilities, they changed the technological infrastructure supporting the influencer industry in important ways. Social media companies that had previously not paid much attention to influencers now recognized the industry's economic and cultural power and began to assert a dominant role. These shifts enabled blatant commercial messages as well as a commercial *logic*—wherein anything could potentially be sponsored or for sale—to fully engulf our primary digital spaces of social and self-expression.

Technologies of Self-Commercialization: The Case of RewardStyle

The most commercially and socially impactful force in this arena was the company RewardStyle, whose tools allowed influencers to earn money off of their blogs or Instagram content without needing access to an agent or even to interface with a brand directly. RewardStyle was launched in Dallas in 2011 by Amber Venz, who at the time was a fashion blogger looking for more efficient ways to monetize, and her partner Baxter Box, who helped build the technology that would make this possible for her and thousands of others. Their first, eponymous product was simple: by embedding RewardStyle links into blog content, bloggers could earn commission for the traffic and sales they drove to retailers' websites. The technology works by saving a cookie in the user's browser. If a person clicks a RewardStyle link that brings her to a retailer's website where she makes a purchase, the retailer can see the cookie and then pays out a commission to RewardStyle. This model, known as affiliate marketing, had existed for nearly as long as the commercial web—but had yet to be utilized in the fashion blogger space.[28] Success was nearly immediate. By 2013, the company had eighty-seven employees and had signed on four thousand retailers and more than fourteen thousand "publishers"—mostly individual bloggers and influencers, but also some legacy media outlets like *Vogue* and *Glamour*. That year, RewardStyle's publishers drove $155 million in retail sales.[29] By 2022, they were driving more than $3 billion annually.[30] RewardStyle was not the only affiliate marketer in the influencer space, but they were the largest and most pervasive.

A key reason for RewardStyle's continued growth and market dominance was their second product, LikeToKnowIt, which launched in 2014 with the aim of making Instagram posts shoppable at a time when the platform was still resisting any kind of commercialization. The product worked like this: An Instagram influencer who had been approved for the service (publishers must apply to be a part of RewardStyle) posts an Instagram image through LikeToKnowIt, providing information about where to buy the items in the photo. Followers, meanwhile, sign up for their own LikeToKnowIt accounts. When they encounter an image on Instagram from which they would like to buy something, they could "like" the photo by double tapping it. They then automatically receive an email with affiliate links through which they can purchase the items from the Instagram post. In 2017, RewardStyle updated Like-ToKnowIt into a standalone app whose technology can be used across the web rather than only in Instagram, now by utilizing screenshots rather than Instagram's "like" function.

By the time of LikeToKnowIt's 2014 launch, Instagram had been acquired by Facebook and was well on its way to transforming from a nostalgia-tinged photo editing and sharing tool to a central vector of sociality, commerce, and culture. Its sleek user interface that enabled infinite scrolling through image after image, uninterrupted by the advertising or excessive linking or commenting that plagued other platforms, proved appealing. Its user base mushroomed to more than one billion, and even as the company added new features such as video, replaced the chronological feed with an algorithmic one, and allowed advertising, the app maintained its reputation as the nicest and most "authentic" place on the internet.[31] Indeed, Instagram quickly became the top destination for brands and marketers looking to engage in influencer marketing.[32]

The commercialization of Instagram—including efforts by third-party companies like RewardStyle to make the platform shoppable in the face of corporate resistance, and later the corporate-sanctioned commercialization that began with its 2015 decision to allow ads—was a defining shift for the influencer industry and for the experience of mediated social life more generally. A MediaPost writer reflecting on the Instagram influencer landscape noted that "the human attention span has decreased from twelve seconds in 2000 to eight seconds in 2013" and concluded "there's something beautifully disposable and playful about this world that brands and agencies should embrace."[33] And indeed, the shift to Instagram as the central marketplace for influence opened the doors to more immediate and more socially embedded forms of commerce and gave the platform's users access to the dominant technologies and visual codes for commercializing themselves.

Aside from capitalizing on the enormous and engaged user bases of fashion blogs and Instagram, RewardStyle's services appealed to brands and influencers for other reasons. For brands who are continually on the lookout for more data that can make their operation more efficient and less risky, in 2013 RewardStyle launched a service called Campaigns, which uses historical performance data to cast influencers for brand campaigns. As Amber Venz Box told *WWD*, "As a brand, when you're giving us your exact goals and targets, like 'I need to hit this many sales and this much traffic and this is my target demographic,' we're using all of that data to cast. Brands are always very surprised at who we cast for those campaigns because it might not be celebrity influencer A, B, or C, who they thought, but we already know who that person's audience is and what type of products they convert at. We're able to rationalize their rate because we know what kind of sales they drive."[34]

Increasingly, brands were indeed looking for proof that influencer recommendations resulted in sales, or conversions. As Lake, the senior vice president of influencer marketing firm DBA, told me in 2017, "Something that we are really paying attention to . . . is conversion. So looking at RewardStyle, who are the top converters through those platforms? We manage most of the top converters, because we know that's what brands really want right now." Nadia,* a trend forecaster for a global firm, confirmed: "I think that it all becomes about point of sale . . . an influencer is someone who influences someone to make a purchase."

For influencers, RewardStyle offered an attractive way to earn income that seemed nearly effortless. Affiliate links allow money to be continually deposited in publishers' accounts according to the clicks and sales made off their posts. "Every time someone clicks [an affiliate link], I get [some] change, which is fine for me because it adds up—and it's still money coming in somewhere," explained Brittiny, the city-focused fashion blogger. Being a RewardStyle member was also a status symbol; because the service was invitation-only (and most influencers needed to apply in order to be invited), getting in symbolized a rite of

blaireadiebee ✓
West Village

blaireadiebee ✓ <*sees my fair lady
once* // never enough lady like skirts in
my closet. This full look on Atlantic-
Pacific now!> http://liketk.it/2vBBC
#florals #westvillage #springishere

strathberry

zimmermann

vivetta

MAY 2, 2018

Add a comment...   Post

FIGURE 1. A 2018 Instagram image by Blair Eadie featuring LikeToKnowIt links. Eadie launched her fashion blog Atlantic-Pacific in 2010 and over the following decade evolved to become a global influencer with nearly two million Instagram followers and brand partners including J. Crew, L'Oreal, and Veuve Clicquot. Reproduced with permission from Blair Eadie.

passage—that they had "made it" as an influencer. "It was so—almost secretive, and not everyone was getting in," Skylar, the fashion and lifestyle blogger, remembered. "So [getting in] was super exciting for me." Danielle, a fashion microinfluencer, told me, "The LikeToKnowIt thing, it definitely gave me that confidence. I was like, 'Yes. I'm actually a real blogger since I'm doing LikeToKnowIt.'"

The massive success of RewardStyle's products hinged on their ability to be implemented seamlessly, providing minimal disruption to influencers' carefully constructed authenticity. RewardStyle affiliate links embedded in blogs were virtually invisible; only by hovering a mouse over a link and looking to the URL preview at the bottom of the browser could one notice the rstyle.me extension—and even then, only the savviest readers would know what that meant, since RewardStyle was primarily a business-to-business company. LikeToKnowIt's existence was more obvious, as influencers' followers had to join the service to use it, and posts using the technology usually featured a "liketkit" link and hashtag, but it capitalized on a social action central to Instagram—liking photos—and thus barely disturbed the established influencer-audience dynamic. Pulling off this technological and social feat meant that RewardStyle accomplished what others who had tried to enter this space could not: finding a way to commercialize social media users' self-presentations without making it seem, to audiences, overtly commercialized. As a writer for marketing firm Econsultancy observed:

> One of social's most powerful attributes is that it's widely seen as a more authentic medium. If consumers start to believe that it's just an extension of the Madison Avenue marketing machine, brands could find that it becomes a much more difficult medium to take advantage of. Obviously, many consumers know that much of the content posted on services like Instagram . . . isn't exactly *au naturel*, and a growing number are aware that brands are paying their favorite internet celebrities to incorporate their products into content. But if large numbers of consumers come to see influencers as fakes and sell-outs, and *distrust* the content they post, brands could find that they've contributed to killing the goose that laid a golden egg.[35]

Indeed, as an influencer marketing agency founder told *Philadelphia Business Journal*, "We live in a world with a trust deficit. We tend not to trust governments, we don't trust corporations, and we don't trust advertisers. But what we do trust is people."[36] By building technology that allowed that person-to-person sense of trust to be mostly uninterrupted yet financially profitable, RewardStyle effectively ushered in a new era of socially embedded, technologically driven consumer culture.

Perhaps the most significant externality of RewardStyle and other similar technologies of self-commercialization was the widespread normalization of monetizing one's *lifestyle*—not just people becoming salespeople for their digital personae, but looking at the entirety of one's material surroundings as a potential source of profit. Against the backdrop of heightened economic and career-related precarity, these technologies emerged as means of gaining both income and a sense of autonomy. They were part of a rising tide of marketplace logic seeping into public spaces and cultures, where almost anything could be "shoppable"—and where there could be "commercial opportunity in every image, intimacy, and interaction."[37]

"Our everyday lives are becoming increasingly commercialized, our attention and private data sold for ad dollars," observed a writer for Refinery29 in 2018, arguing that this situation had desensitized people to the idea of allowing brands intimate access to their lives, or what used to be derided as "selling out."[38] Increased income inequality and lack of opportunities for middle class jobs and lifestyles "creates a strange kind of pressure: if only you can figure out what it is you've got to sell so you don't end up at the bottom, and once you do—cash in. That divide has brought with it the birth of a new ethos: Get that money . . . Get those #lifestylegoals. Monetize everything."[39]

RewardStyle's Discontents

This logic of self-commercialization has practical ramifications on personal, professional, and industrial levels. For RewardStyle specifically, many influencers were confused by what they experienced as a lack of transparency in the application process. Jennifer, a fashion blogger, recalled her experience in a 2018 interview: "I applied four times. The first time I applied I had just started blogging, like a month in. The second time was probably six months later. The third time I was actually—I had a referral. I don't know why I got denied, I'm not quite sure and I don't think the girl [who referred me] was either. But then I applied again a week later with a different email and I got it. So, I'm not quite sure. Because I really didn't change anything, it was just—I used a different email." Other influencers were surprised to learn, after joining, that they could not receive payouts for commissions until they had earned at least $100. "For me, that took a really long time to get to that $100 because each thing would be $2, $3, $5," said Danielle, the fashion blogger.

Carissa, who runs a fashion blog and works full-time on a designer's influencer marketing team, illustrated how using RewardStyle—particularly when it has the potential to become a significant income stream, with top influencers earning millions annually and thousands more making six figures[40]—can disrupt the "realness" of an influencer's social media self-presentation. "It's definitely lucrative, but you have to be consistently linking up products and be strategic about which brands you link to because certain brands have higher commission rates than others," she said.

Cara,* who closed her successful decade-old fashion blog in 2018, agreed: "People now say that, like, 'Oh, I only post authentic things.' But a lot of it's, like, you're not. You're just posting your LikeToKnowIt so you can get more sales." She remembered a blogger who "always had really cool, vintage pieces and always had just a pretty style. And once she got big on Instagram she was just posting like, 'It's available at Old Navy.' Then I noticed other people doing that, and it's because that's what generates the sales. And I just felt like her style changed to conform to that. I get we want to make the sales and stuff, but I never really *got* it."

Inside the closed doors of retail brands, RewardStyle also offered an efficient way to profit from influencer-driven product demand without publicly working with certain types of influencers. The influencer manager for a trendy retailer told me that, through RewardStyle's affiliate program, her company would work with people who were not exactly the right "feel" for the brand, but who drove sales. "We like to call them mommy bloggers, because they are demand drivers," she said. "It's like, they're at this age where the people who are following them also have money to buy furniture, buy a bunch of tops. But they don't necessarily feel technically on-brand."

Further, content creators have raised questions about RewardStyle's lack of ethnic and economic diversity on the company's own social media feeds, which they use to promote some of their users, and at RStheCon, their invitation-only conference where influencers get specialized training, networking opportunities, and the cachet of being included in a closed-door event.[41] The same influencer manager confirmed this when she described her experience at RStheCon.

Every influencer comes with their photographer. They usually have an assistant. Everyone has long, blonde barrel curls, a spray tan, and a big-brimmed hat, usually. It's just like a totally different world, and they go over the top. It's so wild . . . then you're talking to everyone, and it's just like, everyone is redoing their house, everyone has a vacation home.

Brands also felt pressure to adjust creative decision-making based on the data they got from RewardStyle and other social platforms. When asked whether a product was "doing well" on RewardStyle or other social media platforms impacted future product decisions, Annette, the director of marketing for an American fast fashion brand, responded, "Oh yeah, absolutely." She continued:

> A lot of what we do is test and repeat. So if a product is working, we order more of it, we order in different colors. So really it's a conversation with our influencer team and our merchants and buyers on a regular basis in terms of what product are we even gifting to these influencers, what products should they be choosing from . . . we have a pretty much weekly conversation, take a look at the last week or so on social and just say, like, we posted six things that featured product, how did each of those do?

In interviews, influencers and brand executives voiced some questions and concerns about the way in which the influencer industry's commercialization was proceeding, primarily around the growing incentive, which Carissa and Cara pointed out, to sacrifice personal creativity in service of sales. At the same time, writers in the industry press rationalized these efforts as a form of giving the people what they want. "The truth of the matter is that consumers are largely an aspirational bunch," proclaimed the Econsultancy firm.[42]

Optimizing the Influential Look

As agencies, brands, and other intermediaries like RewardStyle began to understand digital influence through technological and organizational systems intended to translate metrics and aesthetic coherency, pressure intensified to optimize posts around what was believed to work in those structures. As a result, a variety of aesthetic- and metrics-related trends—and services to help users participate in them—emerged throughout the 2010s. Participating in the influencer industry continued to be considered a reasonable route to professional success in an entrepreneurial- and fame-obsessed culture, particularly as people continued, even a decade on, to reckon with the recession's damage to career prospects.[43] Thus, the stakes for successfully utilizing these numeric and aesthetic codes remained high. A writer for Slate keenly observed the landscape in 2014:

> If people believe those [influence] scores are being judged, especially in life- or career-affecting ways, they have every incentive to game the scores. They are goaded into behaving artificially on social networks: sharing safe like-bait, and holding back anything they deem quirky, eccentric, or controversial. Anyone who doesn't want to be an "influencer" comes under intense pressure to be, especially as "influence" becomes a measure of self-worth. The result: a lot more people trying to pass around the same articles, memes, and themes. A lot more homogeneity. A lot more noise, masquerading as signal. A self-defeating search for quality in an ocean of quantity.[44]

The "Right" Kind of Metrics

Because follower count and engagement rates were the primary means through which influencers were identified and selected by brands, a number of services appeared that purported to sell followers and even commenters to boost these metrics. While these services attempted to operate under the radar—and the practice of buying followers had existed on Twitter for some time[45]—their existence became obvious through sudden boosts in high-profile users' follower counts, sometimes gaining thousands or even millions of followers in a matter of hours. The notion of "fake followers"—a topic that would, a few years later, become a hot button public issue (discussed more in chapter 4)—was by the mid-2010s a source of discussion and controversy within the influencer industry.

In 2014, the website Racked published an exposé on the growing trend, particularly as it related to blogs and Instagram. Primarily, they detailed a service called Buy Instagram Followers that claimed to operate real accounts that people could purchase to be their followers and comment on posts. Racked noted that its offering ranged from $90 for a thousand followers to $1,350 for fifteen thousand followers.[46] The reporter described a turning point in the way the industry understood influence metrics: follower count could no longer be relied upon as a meaningful measure of users' influence, and metrics could not be taken at face value. The notion of authenticity as an evaluative measure of influencers' worth took on new form, as aspects beyond the personal brand—particularly the audience—became potential grounds for contention. "You begin to realize after a while that it's all fake," a blogger bemoaned to Racked. "The focus is not on fashion, it's about how they can get bigger and richer and more famous. To the blogger, it doesn't matter if it's real. The sad thing about the last few years is that it's become all about appearance."[47]

Brands, marketers, and influencers all began devising strategies—some crude, some sophisticated—for ferreting out "fakes." Many of these centered on paying more attention to audience engagement and devising norms and expectations for what sorts of engagement could be considered *authentic*. Often it relied upon setting up imagined boundaries for *believably* authentic metrics. "If someone only has a 1 percent engagement rate, that's gonna give me some pause," explained Sabina, the executive at an LA marketing firm, in 2018. "[But] honestly, an incredibly high engagement rate is also suspicious at this point. So if I see a really high engagement rate I'm gonna dig in, what does that engagement look like? What are those comments? Is it a lot of comments that look like they maybe automated or spam or just disingenuous in some way?"

Jane, a director at a large influencer marketing agency, detailed her firm's process, which included multiple steps of vetting the influencers and their audiences through in-person discussions paired with behind-the scenes qualitative and quantitative assessments.

The way we vet authentic or real followers is—a lot of it is relationship-based. So we meet with these people. We'll have one-on-one interviews with [influencers] in LA and New York. We have an in-house data science team . . . all of our influencers are plugged into a computer system and we're able to [see] where the majority of followers are in terms of demographics or whatnot. Also we chart their following and . . . if there's a huge spike in the follower count we're like, "OK, what happened here?" And then . . . we'll have a human being actually look into, OK, what happened around this day? Like, did they get an interview on a dot-com or something like that? Or is it a time where followers were purchased?

There's actually a lot of tactics to recognizing that someone has fake followers. For instance, if someone has twenty thousand followers but they are only getting two hundred or something likes on a photo, that's not the regular . . . [there's] a ratio of, if you have a certain amount of followers then you should get X amount of likes on average for every post. There's an equation that is in place that they can see if it's normal or not normal. So if you have below-normal average of likes based on your following, there's something fishy there.

Other countries are in the black market of faking accounts. So if you look into . . . just check the first fifteen followers of influencers and just check if they're authentic. Are [followers] posting themselves? If the influencer is international, like they're from Germany, are there a lot of German followers? Because in theory, if you are an LA-based influencer, your following should have come from LA, New York, maybe Chicago, Miami. There's a common sense to it once you start looking through the followers.

As influencers gradually discovered the strategies that brands and marketers were implementing to evaluate audience authenticity, they began devising and implementing new numbers-boosting strategies in response. These ranged from interacting with their audiences more often or in a different manner (public comments instead of direct messages, for example) to collective behavior such as joining "pods," groups of a few dozen influencers bound together by a mutual agreement to like and comment on each other's every post to boost "authentic" engagement metrics.

Cultivating an Aesthetic

Along with metrics-related maneuvering, influencers adjusted their content to fit with visual trends and themes that tended to gain more "authentic" positive feedback. When blogs were the primary home of digital influencers, the notion of cultivating an "aesthetic" was less important. The increased competition and the shift to image-centric mobile platforms like Instagram in the early 2010s helped particular visual trends gain traction and ultimately precedence in the influencer industry. Instagram, in particular—and its users' perceptions about what sorts of content did well there—became the arbiter of influential looks, and influencers and advertisers turned their attention to optimizing content for the platform.[48]

Within a few years of Instagram's launch, a particular "platform vernacular"—or shared understandings about how to communicate[49]—emerged on the app. Instagram's filters that bestowed a nostalgic feel to photos, the clean square crop applied to every image, and its visual-first layout provided an ideal environment for particular aesthetic trends to flourish. As the influencer industry became increasingly Instagram-centric and focused on lifestyle content in the mid-2010s, images that purported to document a user's authentic but highly edited and curated lifestyle popularized.

These were perhaps best summarized by a satirical account called Socality Barbie that launched in 2015. The account's feed featured images of a Barbie doll wearing clothes and accessories and doing activities in locations that had become particularly trendy for many influencers, all punctuated by aspirational but vague captions. As one observer described it, Socality Barbie "takes jabs at all the things that make Instagram ridiculous yet addictive: still-life outfit photos, artsy candid shots, and, most recently, pumpkins and fall foliage. The captions contain dozens of hashtags and cheesy lines such as, "I believe in the person I want to become."[50] The account resonated with Instagram users quickly, gaining more than one million followers within a few months and receiving attention from a number of press outlets. After five months, the person

FIGURE 2. An Instagram image by Socality Barbie. Reproduced with permission from Darby Cisneros.

behind the account suspended her activity, posting on Socality Barbie's last image caption:

> I started SB as a way to poke fun at all the Instagram trends that I thought were ridiculous. Never in 1 million years did I think it would receive the amount of attention that it did but because of that it has open [*sic*] the door to a lot of great discussions like: how we choose to present ourselves online, the insane lengths many of us go to to create the perfect Instagram life, and calling into question our authenticity and motives.[51]

While Socality Barbie neatly summarized and skewered the ways that influencers (and those who aspired to be them) relied on visual and textual tropes and themes to gain attention, build audiences, and monetize their followings, it did not alter influencers' industrial reality: metrics reigned, influencers needed to dedicate significant time and energy to figuring out how to boost them, and authenticity was a shifting construction that was nevertheless crucial to master. If they hit on a strategy that worked—a particular way of posing or editing photos, or a frequency or tone of interacting with followers—they continued to do it because their livelihood directly relied upon it.

Alana, the fashion blogger and agency founder, reflected on her experience, "For some reason, people love the quotes. I didn't even know when I posted that it was going to be such a hit, but . . . the number one thing people love on my feeds are the OOTDs [outfits of the day], number two is selfies, and number three is the quotes. Anything like, you know, 'Maybe she's born with it, maybe it's caffeine.' That got, like, literally seven hundred saves. That's a record for me. People just love it, I don't know why, I wish I could tell you. When the numbers show that, we do more of that."

Marketers, too, relied on influencers' increasingly disciplined aesthetics as shorthand when matching them with advertising clients. "I'm looking for specific aesthetics depending on the client that I'm working with," explained Sabina. "I'm doing a project with Nickelodeon right now, and first of all, one of their goals is to have content that they can share on their page. So immediately I'm looking at their page, seeing what they're doing there. OK, a lot of bright colors, a lot of pretty colors, a lot of bubbly personality space. So then that is really going to kind of filter [what influencer] I'm looking for." "It's a visual language," Lucia, the design influencer, said of Instagram, noting that she used the language metaphor to determine how to present herself and her work on the platform.

Indeed, from colors such as "millennial pink" and "matcha green"[52] to poses such as the "lay flat," when influencers artfully arrange items on a floor or other flat space for a photo, particular aesthetic trends emerged, inspiring widespread adoption in hopes of gaining the likes and comments—and boost in influence—that these trends seemed to induce. Many influencers described the effort they put into planning their Instagram feeds to ensure brand cohesion and visual appeal.

"I'll look at the greater color story of what's happening [on my feed], or the mood of the previous post. And if it all kind of fits, like, it goes together," said Erica, the influencer marketing professional and aspiring influencer. Because influencers' aesthetic cohesion was so important to advertisers, services like Planoly launched to help influencers plan their Instagram feeds *before* posting—and potentially making a major content mistake.

Participants from across the influencer industry explained how the pressure of market saturation in the mid-2010s intensified competition, setting higher bars for what metrics made influencers "count" and incentivizing influencers to mimic the "looks" of other successful people. Nadia, the trend forecaster whom I interviewed, described it in this way:

> [Social media] just distilled everything down to its lowest common denominator, and it's made these very specific visual trends. There is an aesthetically pleasing style that is very digestible, and if you are an influencer or brand that is wanting high engagement . . . You're looking at your numbers, and certain posts are going to gain higher engagement than other posts. I think it's pretty obvious that you're going to do more posts like that . . . and a lot of times that is this very simplistic visual narrative that comes through that makes everybody the same.

As Jennifer, a fashion blogger, explained, "Comparison is very big in the blogger world, especially with Instagram. And I know I do it sometimes. I'll see an account and think, I want to be just like them." Sometimes the mimicry went beyond particular color schemes, poses, or editing techniques. Fashionista, for example, described how people were imitating, through use of makeup and even plastic surgery, the physical features of top influencers in hopes of gaining likes and other forms of social media acceptance.[53]

These popular features coalesced into a singular look that came to be colloquially known as "Instagram face." "It's a young face, of course, with poreless skin and plump, high cheekbones. It has catlike eyes and long, cartoonish lashes; it has a small, neat nose and full, lush lips," writer Jia Tolentino described it. "It looks at you coyly but blankly, as if its owner has taken half a Klonopin and is considering asking you for a private-jet ride to Coachella. The face is distinctly white but ambiguously ethnic— it suggests a National Geographic composite illustrating what Americans will look like in 2050, if every American of the future were to be a direct descendant of Kim Kardashian West, Bella Hadid, Emily Ratajkowski, and Kendall Jenner (who looks exactly like Emily Ratajkowski)."[54]

While influencers worked to present the appropriate lifestyle aesthetics to court audiences and help ensure security for their personal brands, retail brands also began actively rejiggering their own aesthetic strategies for success in the Instagram-centric influencer industry—often taking cues from each other. Lauren Jung, cofounder of data-driven marketing agency theShelf, shared a memorable example in a 2015 interview:

> We've been looking into the J.Crew pavé bracelet. They came out with this [a few] years ago and we've seen it pop up on so many blogs. The volume of mentions they've been getting on this bracelet is just ridiculous. Usually with J.Crew you see things in one season and out the next, but it's still being sold and it's still being talked about like crazy. We looked to see—I'm not sure if J.Crew started this trend—but after they started, we saw a number of other brands come up with almost an identical bracelet. They really hit it hard on the influencer scene with that, and I don't know if it was done on purpose or if just a couple of influencers liked it and started this trend, but it's really gotten big.

Indeed, in interviews, several industry professionals shared anecdotes about the increase in the production of goods seemingly made for the visual culture and instant commerce of Instagram, describing a sort of endless creative feedback loop. As Refinery29 observed, "Because of this 'gram-it-or-it-didn't-happen mentality, certain It items blow up once one celebrity or influencer posts about it . . . before you know it, your feed is clogged with the same scalloped bikini or designer-collab sneaker."[55]

Doin' It for the 'Gram

For brands and influencers, the "made for Instagram" mentality eventually moved beyond products and the way they were photographed and presented on the app, and into the realm of experiences. As the Business of Fashion urged its readers, "Stop thinking *product* and start thinking *productions* [emphasis added]."[56] Brands of all types heeded this call. For example, Chanel explored new heights of fashion-show spectacle, staging an entire supermarket scene for one runway show and a controversial feminist-themed protest march for another. "These photogenic, shareable, 'Instagrammable' moments are now essential for designers seeking global publicity," a writer observed in Quartz. "Our first impressions of a fashion collection no longer come through the pages of a newspaper or magazine or the windows of a store, but through our phones."[57]

Maria, a marketing director for an American designer, explained her approach for optimizing the brand's social media presence:

> What I do is pick interesting venues and create experiences that engage all of the senses as much as possible. Something that we found that's really popular is repetition. So doing something that's incredible like, you can't even believe your eyes that there are so many of something that have been stacked up so high or arranged in such an incredible way that it creates this super lush texture. Something else that we've noticed and that we've been talking about a lot on our team is where, a few years ago, it felt like people really wanted there to be a designated photo moment, like a photo area that was prescriptive in a way, like, "This is where you take your photo of yourself." And now, everybody is so kind of—everybody is so used to being a content creator and like, a creator of content of themselves, that people respond more, I think, to just having an environment that feels, like, very photogenic so that they can decide how to position themselves in that environment and create content that feels more original and authentic to them. So it's less about having, like, a beautiful step-and-repeat—although if you have a beautiful step-and-repeat, people will use it—they'd rather have, like, an art installation that they can decide whether they want to pose in a formalized way, or take a selfie, or have somebody take something that's a little more tongue in cheek. People want to be able to do more of their own thing in a space where that reflects their personality more than a step-and-repeat moment did.

And then lots of details. Like an obnoxious attention to detail. We've done things like putting a fill in the blank mad-libs letter pressed on paper cocktail napkins. So it's like down to the tiniest detail where, when somebody gets their drink and they're handed whatever the napkin is, they realize it's actually really clever copy that speaks back to the brand voice. And that's an easy instant photo for them that we're just kind of serving up, like a million tiny details that they can take photos of and those often seem to be hits.

Experiences designed for social media success extended beyond the world of retail brands. In 2014, the digital media outlet Refinery29 launched "instameets," wherein they brought prominent Instagram influencers to their studio, "surrounding them with models and props like edible Pantone chips, brightly colored candy and disco balls."[58] "It was a playground," Refinery29's executive creative director told the *New York Times*. "The event generated 128 posts tagged '#r29instameet' that drew more than 78,000 likes. That day, 590 followers joined the Refinery29 Instagram feed, more than 50 percent above the usual daily rate."[59]

While the goal of the companies that created these experiences was to access and leverage influencers' audiences for their own ends, participants often viewed it as a quid pro quo. "I don't have a problem with it," an influencer told the *New York Times* in the same article. "I have my own brand and they match with it a hundred percent."[60] Further, the likes and subsequent visibility that images like these garner is valuable for the influencers, as well. Refinery29's instameets later evolved into their 29 Rooms exhibit, a traveling "funhouse of style, culture, and creativity"[61] that charges roughly $40 for entrants to "create, play, and explore our multisensory playground."[62]

Other Instagrammable experiences cropped up in the wake of 29 Rooms, tweaking and amplifying the impetus for influencers and other users to "do it for the 'gram" and take advantage of the opportunity to build their digital influence. In 2016, for example, the Museum of Ice Cream opened in New York City, selling out tickets for its forty-five-day run in less than a week. The waitlist included more than two-hundred thousand people, some of whom slept outside the museum's pop-up

FIGURE 3. The Museum of Ice Cream. Reproduced with permission from Museum of Ice Cream.

location in Manhattan's Meatpacking District to wait for an opportunity to enter the "sprawling warren of interactive, vaguely hallucinatory confection-themed exhibits . . . with seemingly infinite backdrops against which to take a cute selfie."[63] By 2018, influencer marketing agency Village Marketing bought and began renting out a New York City apartment designed for the express purpose of Instagram photoshoots. A writer for the *New York Times* described the apartment as:

> awash in natural light, with high ceilings, gleaming hardwood floors and a rooftop deck. The living room area includes a sofa in the rosy hue known as millennial pink, the kitchen comes equipped with a floor-to-ceiling wine fridge, and the library nook is filled with books chosen for their appearance, not their contents. The white walls are spotless, and there is never any clutter. Nobody lives here. The 2,400-square-foot space—which rents for $15,000 a month—was designed as a backdrop for Instagram stars, who have booked it through October.[64]

Some companies and researchers at the time attempted to answer the question of *why* these particular visual trends become significant. Curalate, a Philadelphia startup that worked with brands to optimize their social media posts, released a series of reports on analyses they had conducted of Instagram and Pinterest images, listing findings such as:

- Single-colored images were more popular than images with multiple colors, with 17 percent more likes.
- Images with a high amount of lightness receive 24 percent more likes than dark images, and low saturation images received 18 percent more likes than photos with "vibrant colors."
- Images that had a high amount of background receive 29 percent more likes than those without backgrounds. Images with texture get 79 percent more likes.[65]

Curalate's founder Apu Gupta told *Wired* that eventually, Curalate and companies like it "will be able to predict image performance as soon as a photo is uploaded, based on past results. The prediction engine will even adjust itself to the peculiarities of a particular group of Pinterest or Instagram followers."[66]

Brands, influencers, and other social media users embraced the release of such data, which seemed to confirm the anecdotal evidence that there really were particular things they could do to optimize their aesthetics for maximum metrics benefit. But as industry participants became better at predicting what types of content, brand partnerships, and audience interactions would best help them gain visibility, profit, and influence, their behaviors brought into question the very nature of the system's alleged authenticity.

In 2015, a pair of high-profile events publicly illustrated the promises and pressures of working in the influencer space. The industry received a noteworthy level of validation when Harvard Business School created a case study on fashion blog The Blonde Salad and its related entities. Founder Chiara Ferragni had started The Blonde Salad in 2009 while studying law in her home country of Italy, and by 2014 had grown the business to include a shoe line, a talent management division, and a range of other projects carried out under the parent company she created and ran, The TBS Crew. Boasting millions of Instagram followers, high-profile advertisers, and brand collaborators such as Gucci and Louis Vuitton, and several international magazine covers, Ferragni was widely regarded as one of the top social media influencers in the world. That Harvard Business School deemed her and her company a worthy subject of one of the school's notorious case studies provided industrial validation and represented wider normalization for the personal brand-as-business model. Bustle raved about Harvard's decision: "Can we get a hell yeah?" adding, "Maybe the coolest part about this particular study is that it's the first of Harvard's case studies to focus around a blogger—a testament to the unstoppable growth of bloggers and their future in business."[67]

Yet in the midst of 2015's influencer fervor, cracks in the newly hyperefficient system—built on converting arbitrary metrics of influence and perceptions of authenticity into saleable commodities—began to show. In November of that year, Australian teenager Essena O'Neill, who had more than half a million Instagram followers and had been earning roughly $2,000 Australian dollars per sponsored post, deleted thousands of images from her feed, updated the captions of those that remained to detail the sponsors and emotional turmoil she had obscured in each one, and uploaded a tearful video to YouTube in which she proclaimed "social media is not real life."[68] Her seventeen-minute testimony focused on the hidden industrial dynamics of being a social media influencer and her belief that they did not serve prosocial ends. She said:

> There is so much I want to say . . . I have an insight into a world of social media that I believe not many people are aware of, in terms of how it works with advertisements . . . and just how fake it all is. And I say fake because I don't think anybody has bad intentions, I just think they're caught up in it like I was.
>
> I was surrounded by all this wealth and all this fame and all this power, and yet they were all miserable. And I had never been more miserable . . . I was the girl who had it all, and I want to tell you that "having it all" on social media means absolutely nothing to your real life.

Everything I was doing was edited and contrived and to get more value . . . everything I did was for views, for likes, for followers. Social media is now a business . . . if you don't think it's a business, you're deluding yourself.[69]

O'Neill's video garnered worldwide media attention and became a flashpoint for discussion about the alleged authenticity of social media and its attendant, unseen pressures. O'Neill also received sharp criticism by people who suspected that it was all a hoax.[70] While her critics appeared to be incorrect in their assumption that O'Neill staged the event to leverage attention for greater visibility and branding deals—O'Neill soon stopped posting to social media altogether and press coverage faded—the nature of the backlash was telling. It revealed a growing cynicism among social media users and industry watchers who had come to expect that influencers were simply using the norms and tools related to the influencer industry to construct a Russian doll of publicity stunts, wherein one seemingly authentic "reveal" just obscured the next round of payments and machinations behind the on-screen persona.

In the first half of the 2010s, the influencer industry made its business efficient through streamlining its central activity of evaluating, selecting, and pricing influencers for advertising campaigns; exploring more pervasive and efficient means of commercializing content; and figuring out how to optimize both the metrics and aesthetics that powered the industry. The externalities of these new tools and practices—such as stricter rules for influencers creating sponsored content, particular visual trends pervading both online and offline experiences, and rampant self-commercialization—undermined the industry's democratic and authentic self-image. At the same time, these activities enabled the industry to grow at a startling rate. Its estimated value was more than $1 billion by the middle of the 2010s,[71] and its peculiar logic of self-branding and self-monetization infiltrated day-to-day social and cultural experiences as platforms like Instagram became increasingly central for socializing, shopping, and self-expression. This is not necessarily surprising; as media researcher Alice Marwick pointed out, "The technical

mechanisms of social media reflect the values of where they were produced: a culture dominated by commercial interest."[72]

These rationalization efforts, however, did not introduce a flawless
business model, even as the industry strove for assembly-line efficiency.
(As Hennessy explained, "My job is a very teeny tiny part of a giant
machine that's happening when somebody makes a buy . . . There's an
entire team that's in charge of hitting the KPIs and conversion and—
that has nothing to do with me. I don't even have to touch that stuff
because that's how nuanced we are . . . it's a long assembly line. I step in
for my part, do my part, and step back out.")

The attention received by Chiara Ferragni and Essena O'Neill, while
very different, reminded the industry and the public that influencers are
workers first and foremost, creating value for a multitude of businesses.
Importantly, it also revealed that even these aspirational lifestyle exemplars were subject to various industrial pressures that could determine,
to an extent, how they present themselves—and that behind even their
most "authentic" content was a complex system of stakeholders. In the
next chapter, I examine how the influencer industry evolved in the late
2010s as it continued to grow—and as the public became more aware
and suspicious of its inner workings.

Chapter 4

Revealing and Repositioning the Machinations of Influence

April 2018, the tenth annual Shorty Awards—which honor "the best creators on social media"[1]—made headlines for having been a particularly raucous event. Adam Pally, an actor who presented an award, went off script and delivered a meandering ten-minute speech that roasted the social media influencer landscape. In particular, Pally criticized the fact that no creative professional seemed to be able to escape the influencer industry's logic. He noted that he was "really worried" about the young influencers who were being celebrated that evening purely for their social media presence. "I struggled as an actor for, like, a really long time," he huffed, alluding to the absurdity that he was now presenting an award for social media marketing. When an audience member called out, "Delete your account!" (a phrase typically levied as an insult in online communities), Pally responded, "God, I wish I could." Presumably returning to script, he said, "This award honors brands who have the best year-round presence on Instagram . . . considering how many brands are putting resources into Instagram, it's very impressive." He then added, ". . . *Is it?*" Eventually telling the crowd, "This is hell," Pally was later escorted off the stage.

Video of Pally's performance circulated widely, gaining nearly unanimous support from the many media outlets that covered it. Characterizing Pally's diatribe as "hilarious"[2] and the Shorty Awards as "terrible,"[3] press outlets piled on to construct a portrait of the influencer industry as unilaterally toxic and Pally as the respected outsider who dared say it to their faces. "Pally's exasperated and wildly out of place monologue still seemed genuine—and for those of us dealing with social media overload, relatable," observed Quartz.[4] "We can't say we blame him," wrote the A.V. Club.[5]

Indeed, Pally's outburst seemed apropos amid a wider sense of social media saturation and mounting distrust of technology companies and the governments tasked with regulating them. In 2018, more than three-quarters of American adults aged eighteen to forty-nine used social media, and most used multiple platforms. More than one-third of all American adults used Instagram in particular.[6] Three-quarters of American adults owned smartphones, which facilitated near constant connectivity to social media—a situation upon which brands and marketers eagerly looked to capitalize.[7]

More pressingly, in the eighteen months immediately preceding the Shorty Awards debacle, a rash of gravely serious and far-reaching scandals—including near continuous reports of Facebook's wrongdoings, from their leak of user data to political consulting firm Cambridge Analytica, to the user manipulation and misinformation campaigns that went unchecked by the company for years—meant that anxiety about the social-mediated world was nearly inescapable, and imaginings of its potential ill effects overwhelming. In particular, a sense of anxiety about fakery—from "inauthentic" social media personae to corporate and governmental misrepresentation of facts—marked the late 2010s. Influencers, of course, were an easy target for collective disdain. Weren't these aspirational exemplars just insincere egotists, using their "authentic" self-brands to, at best, sell products and, at worst, participate in a system that is rife with fraud and perhaps even contributing to civic crises?

The one Pally detractor published in the popular press, Taylor Lorenz, writing for the Daily Beast, characterized his rant as "rude, entitled, insensitive" and urged others not to "call him a hero."[8] As Lorenz pointed out, hundreds of creative professionals—social media content creators as well as various marketing and advertising teams—were in attendance, and these were people who were just trying to do their jobs well. Indeed, while the late 2010s brought a nearly palpable cultural shift toward questioning the ethics and motives of those involved in the influencer industry, none of the structural conditions that had rendered their existence not only possible but thriving had substantially changed. Personal branding and entrepreneurship continued to be valorized while, for many, the professional "scars" inflicted by the recession persisted.[9] As people came to view advertising as inescapable (and even traditional journalistic outlets such as the *New York Times*, *Forbes*, and others set up in-house sponsored content studios), ad-blocking and other forms of "tuning out" had only become more prevalent—meaning that advertisers continued to seek ways of sharing their messages through unassuming channels. Social media use increased substantially, and each year advertisers directed more and more resources toward influencer marketing on the belief that the "real people" of social media fame were more impactful than traditional celebrities. In 2016, the Collective Bias agency reported that people spent seven times more time looking at influencer content than looking at digital display ads.[10] In 2017, *Entrepreneur* reported that 92 percent of consumers trusted influencers more than traditional advertisements or celebrity endorsements.[11] The total number of influencer campaigns doubled in 2018, and Instagram was part of 93 percent of them.[12]

In other words, at an estimated value of more than $2 billion in 2018 and projections to reach $10 billion to $20 billion by the 2020s,[13] influencer marketing was bigger and more powerful than ever, even as public trust in the technological and regulatory establishment had experienced a potent and fundamental rattle. As a general skepticism about the hidden mechanisms of social media grew, grassroots social media campaigns like #DeleteFacebook encouraged users to disengage from social media. The influencer industry's stakeholders had to reckon with the damage done and determine how best to move forward.

The Chiara Ferragni and Essena O'Neill events described at the end of the last chapter differed substantially in their nature, but they shared a role in revealing to the public just how thoroughly commercialized the social media landscape had become. They also exposed some of the influencer industry's underlying—and sometimes unpleasant—issues that had heretofore been hidden from public view. In the ensuing years, a series of significant events continued to expose cracks in the industry's foundation, which—against the backdrop of larger social media scandals such as those plaguing Instagram's owner, Facebook—contributed to a so-called influencer backlash.[14] In this chapter, I outline three events that issued significant public challenges to the influencer industry. I then explore how various industry stakeholders made strategic decisions in an effort to succeed in an environment where influencers' authenticity was no longer easily believable—and their work was increasingly met with suspicion and, as evidenced by the Pally event and resulting coverage, cynicism. Finding new forms of defining and expressing authenticity became critical to maintaining their influence.

Public Controversies

Federal Crackdowns

In June 2015, the Federal Trade Commission (FTC) updated its endorsement guidelines for the first time since 2010. Maintaining their long-held position that "material relationships between brand and endorser on social media must be 'clearly and conspicuously' disclosed,"[15] the FTC added detailed guidelines about various social media advertising issues that the agency had not previously addressed, from specifying where in a caption disclosure must appear (before any links) to which hashtags are appropriate (#ad and #sponsored are acceptable; #spon and #thanks are not). Many marketers interpreted these updates as a signal of an impending crackdown—and they were correct.

In perhaps the most noteworthy case, the FTC filed a complaint against department store chain Lord & Taylor for coordinating a deceptive influencer marketing campaign. In March 2015, Lord & Taylor partnered with fifty Instagram influencers and *Nylon* magazine to promote a particular dress from its new Design Lab line. The influencers and *Nylon* posted images of the dress during the same weekend (using Lord

& Taylor–approved language), and *Nylon* ran an article (edited and sponsored by Lord & Taylor) about Design Lab. Influencers were given the dress for free and were paid between $1,000 and $4,000 for the posts.[16] The dress sold out in a matter of days.

"The program was designed to introduce Design Lab to this customer where she is engaging and consuming content every day," Lord & Taylor chief marketing officer Michael Crotty told *Adweek*.[17] "The goal was to make her stop in her feed and ask why all her favorite bloggers are wearing this dress and what is Design Lab? Using Instagram as that vehicle is a logical choice, especially when it comes to fashion." However, none of these partnerships—from the exchange of goods and payment, to Lord & Taylor's role in creating copy—were properly disclosed.

In settling the complaint, the FTC explicitly prohibited Lord & Taylor from "misrepresenting that any endorser is an independent or ordinary consumer," established "a monitoring and review program for the company's endorsement campaigns," and noted that future infractions would carry "the force of law" and result in major fines.[18] Industry watchers viewed the case as a potential harbinger of what was to come if brands, marketers, and influencers did not change their approach to sponsored content. An advertising attorney interviewed by the *Wall Street Journal* emphasized that the Lord & Taylor event was a "good example of the rise and extensive use of integrated campaigns" and that advertisers "need to ensure their processes and systems are in place and that what needs to get done gets done."[19]

Government bodies aside from the FTC also became ensnared in influencer marketing issues. In 2015, the U.S. Food and Drug Administration (FDA) issued a public reprimand to Kim Kardashian West, the "reality star turned mega influencer,"[20] and the drug company Duchesney after the two parties collaborated on a post for Kardashian West's Instagram account, which had more than 130 million followers at the time. The post featured an image of Kardashian West holding a bottle of Diclegis, a medication for morning sickness, along with a caption praising the drug for helping her feel well during pregnancy. The post failed to include information about potential side effects or risks, as well as the fact that it had not been studied in women officially diagnosed with the condition (severe morning sickness, or hyperemesis gravidarum) it was intended to treat. The FDA issued public warning letters to Duchesney and Kardashian West, requiring that the post be taken down and replaced with a new one that noted their mistake and contained the extensive details omitted in the original.

Federal agencies and departments continued to closely monitor influencers. Even the Department of Homeland Security compiled a list of "media influencers" to monitor to "identify any and all media coverage related to the Department of Homeland Security or a particular event," causing waves of worry about the government's interest in protecting or monitoring a free press.[21] But the FTC remained the most prominent and active agency in monitoring social media influencers and enforcing regulations about sponsorship. Between 2016 and 2017 the agency issued more than a hundred warning letters to top influencers regarding lack of adequate sponsorship disclosure. It also updated its guidelines several times to stay abreast of the industry's rapid changes to technological capabilities and social norms around disclosure. Instagram, for example, introduced the option to tag a brand as a location on a photo to denote a relationship. Doing so would note the brand's name in small type at the top of the post, but the FTC ruled that doing this alone was inadequate disclosure.[22] "We don't say you have to use a specific word or term, but disclosure has to clearly convey a financial relationship or exchange between brand and poster. The disclosure also has to be placed in such a way the consumer isn't going to miss seeing it," Mary Engle, the FTC's associate director for advertising practices, told PRWeek.[23]

Fyre Festival

In December 2016, dozens of so-called mega-influencers—including Bella Hadid (twenty-three million Instagram followers), Emily Ratajkowski (twenty-two million), and Hailey Baldwin (twenty million)— posted a solid orange square to their Instagram feeds. The accompanying captions expressed excitement for something called Fyre Festival (#fyrefestival) but provided few details other than links to the festival's website. A promotional video was released the same day on Fyre Festival's website and on YouTube, showing the influencers and others (including rapper Ja Rule, who was involved in the festival's planning) frolicking on a Caribbean beach, jumping off yachts, racing jet skis, and enjoying frozen drinks. The video promised "two transformative weekends" of "an immersive music festival" to be held on "a remote and private island . . . once owned by Pablo Escobar."[24] *New Yorker* writer Jia Tolentino characterized the video as a "perfectly generic fantasia of what an Instagram come to life would be . . . nothing but backdrop with montage-friendly bliss."[25] The video did little to provide real details about the event (information about performance lineup or travel and lodging logistics was absent), but the coordinated influencer marketing effort proved immediately fruitful. Tickets—which cost thousands of dollars and claimed to include entrance to the festival, luxury accommodations, and, in many cases, private airfare from Miami to the island—sold quickly.

The festival was scheduled for the last weekend in April and first weekend in May 2017. In the months leading up to the festival, a number of people raised questions about the seemingly over-the-top promises in the festival's marketing. The advertised location for the festival, Fyre Cay, was not a real place but rather the name festival promoters gave to a small Bahamian island where they hoped to hold the festival. The island's lack of infrastructure, however, proved to be too big a hurdle for festival planners to mount, and they moved the event to a larger island called Great Exuma. New marketing materials indicated that the festival's location was still remote and exclusive, but maps of the site provided by Fyre Festival seemed to be heavily cropped aerial views of a stretch of concrete behind a Sandals resort, as pointed out by an anonymous Twitter account called @FyreFraud that appeared in March 2017 and regularly tried to draw attention to Fyre Festival's inconsistencies and behind-the-scenes maneuvering.

As the event drew closer, organizers contacted ticketholders with odd requests. One message announced that the event was going to be cashless and requested ticketholders immediately upload cash to accounts that would be associated with wristbands they would receive on the island; the organizers recommended uploading several hundred dollars for each day the ticketholder would be there. In April 2017, the *Wall Street Journal* reported that none of the supposed headlining acts had been paid and argued that the festival "woos wealthy to stay afloat."[26] In the days leading up to the event, ticketholders had still not received information about their flights or lodging, and their attempts to gain answers from the organizers were ignored. Fyre Festival began deleting Instagram comments that questioned or expressed negativity about the festival. Finally, the day before the first weekend of the festival, one of the headliners announced they were pulling out of the event.

Despite the red flags, hundreds of hopeful attendees boarded planes to Great Exuma with the conviction that the influencers had been honest and the luxurious event they promoted would come to fruition. Yet what happened upon attendees' arrival, journalists observed, was a "fiasco," "disaster," and the "world's biggest flop."[27] Rather than the luxury transportation and lodging attendees were been promised, school buses brought them to the festival grounds, which were still under construction aside from disaster relief tents and wet mattresses that had been set up to serve as accommodations. Electricity, food and water, and bathroom facilities were all extremely limited. Panic ensued as attendees rushed to claim resources—or to get back to the airport to await a return flight. Social media posts documented the festival's unraveling in real time, with angry attendees sharing images, videos, and descriptions of their experience with hashtags such as #fyrefraud and #dumpsterfyre, and journalists amplifying these reports to a wide audience. A *Vice* reporter characterized the situation as "a *Lord of the Flies* situation with Instagram's top influencers."[28] After twenty-four hours, festival organizers officially canceled the events and all incoming concertgoers' flights. Instead, empty planes arrived from Miami to "rescue" those on the island.[29] As *Vanity Fair* observed, "The Fyre Festival, built on Instagram, dies by Instagram."[30]

Within days, several lawsuits were filed against Fyre Festival's organizers, specifically its founders Billy McFarland and Ja Rule. The lawsuits alleged fraud, negligence, and violation of consumer protection law; one noted that McFarland and Rule "tricked people into attending the event by paying more than 400 social media influencers and celebrities" to promote it.[31] McFarland was arrested in July 2017 and sentenced to six years in prison for fraud in 2018.[32] While the influencers who were central to the festival's marketing strategy were paid,[33] almost none of the other people involved—local Bahamian laborers who set up the site and the ticket buyers—had received payment or restitution at time of writing.[34]

Fyre Festival gained instant notoriety for its total collapse that was live-updated on social media. Watchers seized upon the juxtaposition of wealthy and aspirational attendees with the circumstances—stuck, after following the call of glamorous social media stars, in a situation wherein they lacked basic necessities—as well as the nearly unbelievable level of hubris required of Fyre's founders to scam thousands of people out of millions of dollars. These narratives were so salient that they became the focus of two documentaries released in early 2019. (In another testament to how financially and culturally powerful the influencer industry had become, the Netflix documentary *Fyre: The Greatest Party That Never Happened* was produced by Jerry Media, a company started by an Instagram influencer who was involved in the promotion of Fyre Festival.)

Fyre revealed just how much trust influencers had cultivated with their followers. Despite all indications that the festival was never going to live up to its claims, festivalgoers hoped for the best, boarding planes to the island even while reports were already surfacing about what awaited them. Influencer marketing was so effective—followers trusted that what the influencers represented was real and that they could be relied upon, even in the face of contradictory information, because of their authentic and friendly personae—that it overruled logic.

"The cacophony of sound that they were able to create using the influencers and their social media strategy was so overwhelming that not only did various financial guys give them money, but facts were basically ignored," said one participant in Hulu's documentary *Fyre Fraud*. Further, the Fyre calamity offered a meta-comment on the precarity that undergirds the influencer landscape; the pressure to continually seek money and status is so high that those at the top still take deals that promise to deliver these things, even if the details are foggy. Followers' willingness to buy into the lifestyles promoted by influencers—going so far as to spend thousands of dollars on an event that showed little evidence, aside from a social media campaign, of actually happening—was a powerful signal of how severely fractured the connection between reality and socially mediated "authenticity" was becoming.

Fake Followers

In January 2018, the *New York Times* released an in-depth report about the rise of "fake followers" on social media.[35] While bloggers and influencers had for years discussed unsavory practices related to boosting follower count,[36] the *Times* report exposed the extensive ecosystem, or what they called a "black market," that had developed to provide digital content creators, as well as journalists, politicians, and actors, with the "real" followers needed to become a bona fide influencer. The report focused on a company called Devumi, a Twitter bot supplier that promised, "Our followers look like any other followers and are always delivered naturally. The only way anyone will know is if you tell them."[37] But it revealed trends that pervaded social media.

The most obvious of these was the basic logic of the influencer economy: that being visible on social media, cultivating a following, and leveraging that into financial and social opportunities was necessary for professional success in the digital age. "You see a higher follower count, or a higher retweet count, and you assume this person is important, or this tweet was well received," a founder of a search engine optimization company told the *Times*.[38] "Everyone does it," an actress said.[39] It also revealed the lengths to which people would go to effectively participate in this system, sometimes spending thousands of dollars to boost their follower count. Caving to the influencer economy logic was not limited to aspiring influencers or struggling wannabes; the report exposed that established professionals such as the actor John Leguizamo, billionaire Dell Computer founder Michael Dell, and member of British Parliament Martha Lane Fox had purchased Devumi followers.

Most disturbingly, the *Times* report described how this underbelly of the influencer system threatened the privacy and well-being of countless people. Many of Devumi's accounts for sale were actually facsimiles of unsuspecting users' real online identities. Among others, the *Times* highlighted the case of a seventeen-year-old high school student whose name and likeness were stolen to create an account, available for sale by Devumi, that retweeted controversial and harmful content, including graphic pornography. Further, bot retailers like Devumi did not make the fake accounts themselves, but often purchased them from a "thriving global market" of wholesalers.[40] In providing detailed analyses and graphics illustrating the rise of the fake follower marketplace and the means of detecting them, the *Times* showed how complicated, and often obfuscatory, this corner of the influencer industry had become.

Just a few months later, in May 2018, Unilever chief marketing officer Keith Weed, who oversees the $8 billion-plus marketing budget for one of the world's biggest advertisers,[41] announced that the company would no longer work with influencers who bought followers. Further, he called on social media companies to "help eradicate bad practices throughout the whole ecosystem."[42] "There are lots of great influencers out there, but there are a few bad apples spoiling the barrel, and the trouble is, everyone goes down once the trust is undermined," Weed told Reuters.[43] Weed's announcement made waves at Cannes Lions, the annual global marketing conference where he spoke, and beyond. Econsultancy argued that it was "a wake-up call for other brands that have applied less scrutiny to the influencers and influencer agencies they work with."[44] And indeed, many brands voiced support for Unilever's decision and echoed the call to "clean up" influencer marketing.[45] Yet monitoring the legitimacy of influencers' followers would be an enormous task, since—among other issues—at any moment an influencer who was previously free of fake followers could purchase them. While Weed's announcement was a powerful indictment of fraud in the influencer space just months after the *Times* report spurred it into public consciousness, the practical hurdles his call entailed showed how difficult it would be to restore authenticity anchored in real world evidence to the influencer industry. "The reckoning," Racked observed, "comes in fits and starts."[46]

Strategic Repositioning

Marketers

To restore credibility to their own practices and to the influencers they backed in the wake of these controversies, marketers intensified their focus on data collection and analysis and also expanded their definition of what an influencer could be. Throughout all these adjustments, marketers were agreeable and often enthusiastic about adhering to new FTC guidelines and requiring obvious and clear disclosure in social media posts. "It's hard," Hennessy, the director of influencer strategy, admitted. "It's a lot of keep up with . . . Are we using #ad or is this sponsored or what's the FTC doing this day, oh, they just put out another two-hundred-page guideline, let me go read that." But, "the fact is that the consumers are listening to influencers," said Martin of the 360i agency. "The demographic range of people that are listening to influencers are not deterred by the fact that someone is paid by a brand that often. The great thing about influencers is that the people that follow them put the same kind of credibility on a relationship . . . as they do with friends. So even though there's not an actual personal relationship, there is a digital relationship that equates to—that delivers credibility."

Berger of HYPR confirmed in 2018 that clearly disclosing sponsorship turned out to often benefit influencers and brands. "I think people really understand how it all works and how it all goes down," he said. "If you're doing it the right way, you're gonna put #ad or #spon on any of the social posts, right? But these posts . . . actually provide better ROI when it says #ad or #spon . . . So here are all these companies scared to put it on there because of what it means, but it doesn't seem to take away anything. In fact, in everything I've seen, it actually increases the engagement."

Beyond the general repositioning to be on the side of disclosure and regulation, marketers developed more specific strategies for ensuring their continued success. In order to ferret out influencers who misrepresented their followings, marketers shifted deal structures to hold influencers individually accountable for the audiences they promised to deliver. Instead of flat-rate or per-post pricing, where, as one cofounder of an influencer marketing platform wrote in *Forbes*, "you can't guarantee quality or if the content is even seen," industry professionals recommended goal-based pricing based on impressions, engagement, clicks, or acquisition. "When influencers are compensated on their performance, not only do they return higher quality content that is proven to perform, but they also deliver an engaged audience that is inspired to take action," she continued.[47]

Marketers also took steps toward more sophisticated data-driven products for influencer selection and identification. As a means of evaluating influencer effectiveness and potentially circumventing follower fraud, marketers looked to tie influencer campaigns to sales of the advertised products in a more granular way. The founder of influencer marketplace TapInfluence told eMarketer, "What I'm really excited about is what we're doing right now. We have partnerships with Datalogix and Nielsen, where we can actually get loyalty card data and use it to tie influencers to offline purchases."[48] Further, he explained, "we can do marketing mix modeling, meaning that we can correlate spikes in influencer marketing to spikes in sales. We can put that model into our software, and it will tell you on a per-influencer basis how many sales each influencer is driving."[49]

Other agencies developed artificial intelligence-driven products to do the work of influencer campaign planning and to send clients the message that influencers would be thoroughly vetted and analyzed, beyond human capabilities, to ensure trustworthiness. Public relations and digital marketing firm Lippe Taylor, for example, debuted its Starling AI product, promising:

As the problem of "fake followers" increasingly plagues the reliability of influencer marketing, Starling AI counters this issue by qualifying influencers according to their connectivity to fellow influencers, thereby ensuring their audience is genuine. Additionally, Starling AI's tracking of "influencer momentum" ensures that identified influencers are likely to continue to rise in influence throughout an engagement, locking in value for clients longterm.[50]

Even as marketers leveraged more sophisticated software for influencer analysis, they also reoriented themselves to more openly recognizing influencers' personhood rather than continually characterizing them with nonhuman metaphors, as explored in chapter 2. Sabina, the marketing agency director, emphasized, "It's really important to view influencers as people, not just marketing devices."

This dual focus on data analysis and personal relationships further pushed forward the trend toward microinfluencers and nano-influencers, as more sophisticated software detected influential users with smaller followings but more intimate and "real" relationships with their followers and with brands. Sabina continued, "I truly feel like [microinfluencers are] just the next step. This generation really isn't watching television. They're not seeing that Neutrogena commercial with Mandy Moore that we saw. Which, how is that any different? Brands have always leveraged celebrity, so why not leverage this new generation of digital celebrities?"

Nano-influencers also offered financial incentives to marketers and brands. Because their followings were so small, they typically did not "influence" for a living—and would therefore make fewer demands related to travel and compensation. One executive called them "the hometown girls,"[51] noting their small but dedicated followings and that they tended to be "based out of smaller pockets . . . not New York or Los Angeles."[52] By embracing social media users with smaller followings, marketers highlighted the greater proportion of truth in their "just like us" positioning.

Ultimately, the changes marketers made during this time served to exert greater control over ethically questionable influencers and to minimize their exposure. This was most clear in the growing phenomenon of nonhuman CGI influencers. "CGI influencers are the future," said Nadia, a trend forecaster for a global firm. "You can control that behavior then. If you're crafting your own celebrity you don't have to worry about the possibility of any controversial behavior or anything like that." It also helped that there were no regulations around synthetic content.[53]

In 2016, for example, a character named Miquela Sousa—also known as Lil Miquela—gained widespread attention for her Instagram presence, which showed her seemingly attending Hollywood events, hanging out with celebrities, and producing branded content. "No one knows who or what @lilmiquela is, but everyone has a theory," wrote Caitlin Dewey in the *Washington Post*.[54] "Since she posted her first Instagram in April, the Internet's latest 'it girl' (or hoax, or art project, or marketing stunt) has become something of a cult mystery. The problem with Miquela, you see, is that she acts like a real person but doesn't look like one. Her skin's a bit too glossy, her shadows slightly too flat—she has the telltale uncanniness of a computer animation." By 2018, Miquela had amassed more than one million Instagram followers. *Dazed* magazine named her a contributing editor, and she had collaborated with brands on multiple campaigns.

Beth, a marketing manager for a brand that collaborated with Lil Miquela, explained their reasoning to me in 2018:

I think that's the biggest thing that really . . . makes the team excited to work with Lil Miquela because she is—obviously she's not real, but at the same time she definitely embodies this idea of thinking outside the box, doing things a little bit differently, which is what our brand is all about. I think we're always about pushing those boundaries of technology and digital . . . so, that's sort of the way the partnership came about, and it was super exciting.

However, she said, the brand believed their decision could be construed as controversial, and they prepared themselves for blowback.

We were super—just cautious about it, and we knew that like, just anything new that gets brought out, that gets shown to people, there's going to be a positive and a negative reaction. And so I think that we were kind of prepared for that. Ultimately, though, we really didn't see the negative reaction that we anticipated. We were really surprised, or not even surprised, but just excited about how open and interested our followers were about, like, learning about this girl, and [also] who knew her and were excited about the partnership. And so, ultimately, it ended up being a good thing for us.

Indeed, the case of Lil Miquela showed that a nonhuman influencer's seeming lack of "authenticity" would not necessarily be a problem. After

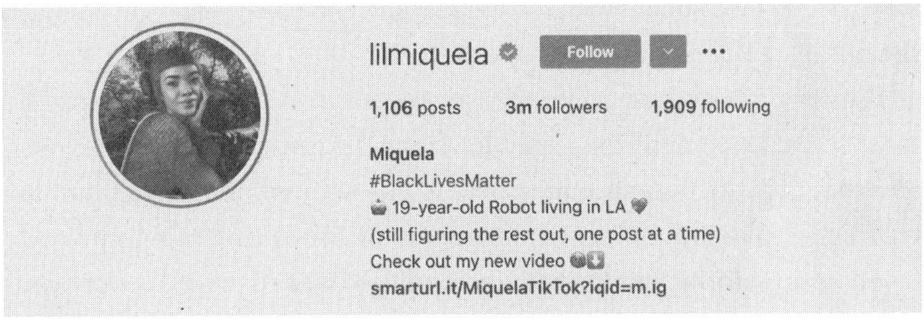

FIGURE 4. The Instagram bio of CGI influencer Miquela Sousa, also known as Lil Miquela.

the unveiling of some of social media's hidden industrial orchestrations, the key to conveying authenticity seemed to be strategic deployment of *honesty*: if something is sponsored, disclose it; if someone or something is not "real," have fun with it. "The effects of social media are multifaceted and hard to quantify, so it feels pointless demanding more authenticity from something that doesn't necessarily require it," observed a writer for Refinery29.[55] "When something is authentic it works best. That said, in today's world it doesn't need to be anywhere near as authentic as it used to be," said Berger.

Brands

In their efforts to maintain appealing brand personae and connections to their customers in an era of increasing distrust, retail brands sought to bring influencers deeper into the fold, cultivating closer and longer-term relationships. Brands saw these relationships as more effective and, ideally, with less room for the kinds of errors of authenticity that could ignite controversy or damage their bottom lines. (According to Media-Post, in the second quarter of 2018, brands spent $211 million on influencer marketing in the United States and Canada—but "$11 million of that was for influencers' fake followers."[56]) This long-term approach meant brands could get to know influencers better on an individual basis and more thoroughly vet them for dodgy practices like buying followers that could more easily remain hidden when engaging with influencers in a transactional way. It also provided brands access to influencers' own social media strategies and expertise—and cachet with the public, when aligned appropriately.

Rather than one-off partnerships, wherein an influencer would be hired to create content for a specific campaign, brands cultivated closer, and ideally more permanent, relationships with influencers. Often this translated to hiring influencers in a sort of consulting role to provide feedback on product and marketing and then also to promote the products later. As Lake, the SVP for Digital Brand Architects, explained:

> I see that influencers are providing brands strategies. We do a lot of meetings with brands and talent where the brand is using the talent as like a consultant when it comes to developing new products or the marketing or the promotion. But then we'll also see brands are now creating product *with* talent—so having the talent actually be part of the brand.

In response to this trend, Lake's company launched a licensing division with the goal of enabling their influencer clients to create and sell product—"not necessarily just through amplification, but using their image and likeness," she said. "Brands are definitely using talent to root campaigns, but also now build products around. I think that we're going to see a lot more products created by talent and influencers." Indeed, in the late 2010s several major retailers worked with influencers to release influencer-branded product lines, including Nordstrom with Chriselle Lim, Atlantic-Pacific, and Something Navy; and Macy's with Natalie Off Duty. "The money is pretty much just rolling in" as a result of these sorts of collaborations, reported Fashionista.[57] Writing about Nordstrom, the journalist noted that influencer brands have "undoubtedly been one of the things that has helped the retailer maintain relevance while its competitors struggle for it."[58]

Part of the appeal of these collaborations is the mutual investment on the part of brands and influencers in the products' success: both have made creative contributions, and the influencer will naturally share information about the product in both the development and launch stages. Further, because an influencer's social media presence is the centerpiece of these brands, retailers are able to reduce financial and public relations risk by garnering input from potential buyers along the way. "Through social sharing and polls on influencers' platforms, we've been able to receive real-time feedback on the design process, inviting them to be a part of the fashion journey in a way that has never been done before," a Nordstrom executive told Fashionista. "For example, Arielle Charnas of Something Navy has been sharing fabric swatches and design elements from her upcoming brand launch with her audience over the past few months. We have been able to consider customers' feedback and edit accordingly."[59]

Even when brands do not go so far as to create product with their influencer partners, they worked to ensure their trusted influencers felt valued as "people, not advertising space"[60] and as respected expertise providers for the brand. Writing for *Adweek*, an agency executive advised brands to have members of their marketing team speak directly with social media influencers rather than transacting through a third party.[61] "It changes the paradigm from rote regurgitation of talking points to integrating the message into one's life," he wrote. Indeed, the writer advised brands to work for total integration into influencers' lives rather than dealing in a transactional manner. If brands could influence the influencers—convincing them of the brand's lifestyle value rather than simply the merits of a single product or campaign—then their efforts could reap rewards for years to come. "You're best off thinking about influencers as scaled-down celebrities who are ready to be turned into a long-lived mouthpiece for your brand . . . To maximize that return, brands ought to have their influencers drinking the Kool-Aid before sending them into the great unknown to rep their products."[62]

Brands continued to build on the strategy of thorough, long-term influencer relationships as they looked for new influencer partners. In 2018, brands were looking ahead to the "next crop of influencers [that] is really going to redefine the business," Nadia, the trend forecaster, told me. These are child influencers, sometimes given the generational nickname "alphas," who are "between the ages of zero to seven," according to Nadia. These young social media stars develop social media personal brands with the help of their parents and can earn tens of thousands of dollars for sponsored content depending on the platform and their metrics. As the *New York Times* pointed out, the Federal Communications Commission has not yet updated their rules for children's content—which are television-focused and explicitly limit product placements and require separation between content and advertisements—to address influencer content.[63] Further, the work of so-called kidfluencers calls into question child labor laws and other regulations. Yet until regulation is enacted, social media's youngest power users offer brands an opportunity that seems too good to miss: "You can essentially have a *really* long-term partnership," Nadia said.

Social Media and Technology Companies

Some social media and technology companies also took steps to respond to the questions raised about the influencer industry. In 2017, both Facebook and Instagram updated their branded content policies to explicitly require users to "comply with all applicable laws and regulations, including by ensuring that you provide all necessary disclosures to people using Facebook or Instagram, such as any disclosures needed to indicate the commercial nature of content posted by you."[64] Instagram launched the aforementioned disclosure tool, which would allow influencers and other content publishers to tag a sponsoring brand and display the partnership at the top of a post. Instagram also announced that they would "begin enforcing branded content that isn't properly tagged"[65] though provided few details on what, in practice, "enforcing" meant. The companies framed these tools as "bring[ing], transparency around Branded Content to the Instagram community," touting transparency as a "value" of "businesses and creators."[66]

Beyond tools for disclosure, the companies creating and managing the technologies upon which the influencer industry relied looked further ahead. "What's next is the shift from social media to social marketplaces," *Forbes* predicted in 2016.[67] And indeed, the idea that influencers could sell *directly* to followers on social media and other platforms seemed to offer a solution to many issues facing the industry, including the need for transparency, the demand for the authenticity of sharing one's whole "lifestyle," and retailers' search for new viable business models. As one marketing journalist wrote, "For influencers . . . moving into e-commerce is a natural next step in their evolution. Digital storefronts provide these content creators with another avenue to monetize their personal brands."[68]

Selling directly through influencers' social media presence worked particularly well for fashion and consumer products. "For certain verticals I could see [sponsorship] being a problem, like if you're promoting software and people paid you to say it. But if it's fashion, and it's a really great-looking dress and you're needing one and it's the right price and some blogger has it and by the way they sponsored it, I'm like, great, I needed this!" said Jung, the founder of influencer platform theShelf. Further, it dovetailed nicely with how "you're always shopping now," as Nadia, the trend forecaster, said. "It's just right there and you're just like, 'This is what I'm going to do to kill time while I'm waiting at the dentist,' or whatever."

Influencers

Before the federal crackdowns, Fyre Festival, and fake follower scandals opened the influencer industry up to widespread backlash, influencers themselves were exposed to negative and sometimes hateful feedback—which perhaps uniquely prepared them to navigate the broader environment of skepticism and distrust in the late 2010s. For years, influencer criticism occurred most publicly on Get Off My Internets (GOMI), an online forum "where participants criticize individual bloggers, picking out and tearing apart examples of all things staged, insincere, unethical, exaggerated—in short, all things inauthentic."[69] Increasingly, critics also appeared on Instagram and blog comment sections—and in rare and the most disconcerting of circumstances, in person.

In an interview, one successful fashion blogger described "a really painful couple of years with being in the public eye." She said, "I've had, like, how can I even explain, attacks on my personal life to the point where I felt unsafe to go out of my own house." But more commonly, she received comments on her posts and was a frequent subject of ridicule on the GOMI forums, which had become an active site for distinctively feminized moralizing, gossip, and cyber abuse that one scholarly analysis characterized as "displaced rage."[70] Followers have posted "malicious, crazy stuff," she said, from conspiracy theories about her personal life to sexist criticism of her appearance.

> I think it's—it's almost like that celebrity culture, which . . . I didn't realize how crazy people get and, like, the rumors that they come up with. Because people really think that they own you, and that's what people will say: It's my right, you put yourself on the internet and I can say whatever I want. And it's like, that's actually not true.
>
> I think it's almost become worse for bloggers because we are real people. And so for [followers], when they see these things like you're getting to go on a free vacation or you're making money from this, it makes them more angry. They see Kim Kardashian doing it; well, whatever; she's untouchable. But they can get a hold of you a lot easier because I don't have that kind of protection. So it's just, it's all become like a bigger issue . . . I'm definitely not special. I'm not the only one that gets this kind of attention; it's kind of everybody.

Similarly, Claudia, a décor and lifestyle blogger, reflected:

> I've definitely gotten my fair share of negative comments and unfollows and things like that. And I think it's just human nature that it hurts. Because the blog for me is such a personal thing, and I'm sharing things that are in my heart and soul and what I spent time creating, so it definitely feels like a personal attack. It's hard not to find your personal worth in the blog because it's you, I mean, so much of it is you. And so those are definitely hard things, but I think I've developed kind of a tough skin.

Indeed, many bloggers and influencers spoke of the need to develop tough or thick skin; as one fashion blogger said, "You can say just about anything to me and I just don't even bat an eye, which is really sad."

Yet the harsh critiques that had previously been limited to a subset of "anti-fans"[71] seeped into public discourse in the late 2010s, with outlets such as *New York* magazine, the *Guardian*, and *GQ* characterizing the influencer industry as a bastion of fakery, superficiality, and other social ills.[72] As public suspicion about their work increased, influencers, too, grew wary of the various systems in place that made their work possible and valuable. Instagram in particular became a frequent subject of debate. Because it was not always clear how the platform's algorithm worked—and therefore, what sort of visibility or engagement their posts might receive—influencers came up with folk theories and collective solutions to the problems they perceived. A common solution was to join a "pod," or a group of typically a few dozen influencers that mutually agree to like and comment on each other's every post to boost "authentic" engagement.[73] Yet platforms worked to shut down pod activities, claiming they were "inauthentic behavior" and casting them as downright immoral.[74] Further, influencers debated the practice among themselves. "I don't really want to be the person that's commenting on everyone's stuff on Instagram. I want to be true and only comment on people's stuff that I love and look up to," Danielle, a microinfluencer, told me. "I'm hoping that in the long run, my honesty will start to pay off. People notice those things. I notice those things."

Some influencers also became critical of their growing roles as drivers of consumerism or models of alleged "perfection" and took steps to remediate it. Lucia, the designer and lifestyle influencer, explained how she had noticed "a shift, in a way, where people who aren't bloggers are feeling the pressure to make their own life look perfect."

> Because for me, I can look at a room in a magazine and I know what work went into making it like that. So I don't look at the [social media] world and think, "My gosh, her life is perfect," but I look and think about how great that styling is . . . when I realized that people didn't have the professional experience that I had on understanding how that works, they look at it and say, "My gosh, this is real"—and only heightened by the fact that normal people are able to produce this on their phone and then share it. I think that . . . I felt sort of a social need to lift the veil.

As such, ahead of a product launch with a major national retailer, Lucia made a strategic decision to share on her social media channels more about her personal struggles with mental illness. "I think I really felt like if I was gonna have that many eyeballs on me, I didn't want to be known for just having perfect images," she said. "I told my story. I'm not gonna dwell on it or tell it over and over again . . . but it was just the time to do it."

While influencers could be self-critical and self-correcting, they were still part of and dependent on an industrial influence system that required them to cultivate authenticity in recognizable ways. With heightened scrutiny on their practices and added financial pressures of shifting deal structures, influencers looked to display even more transparency and "realness" in ways that allowed their continued success. Aside from taking up the "clear and conspicuous" disclosure practices required by the FTC, influencers shared more casual, less staged content, often using new platform affordances like Instagram's Stories feature, which allows users to upload short videos that disappear after twenty-four hours. Stories enabled influencers to share different types of content and to further expand their "lifestyle" personae rather than adhering to a particular genre.

At the same time, influencers spoke of the need to expand their personal brands into businesses beyond social media as a means of regaining control over their income, status, and messaging. "You have to keep finding new ways to keep your business going besides what you have," said Brittiny, the city-focused fashion blogger. Common pursuits include starting marketing agencies, brand consultancies, product lines, or selling online courses on self-branding or influencer marketing.

"I think a lot of creators feel a sense of insecurity," said Jade Kendle-Godbolt, the beauty blogger and content creation business owner, "because you're like, 'Oh, my gosh, did I post them up this week? My engagement's up, my engagement's down, what did I do different? They've got more followers than me, I want that brand deal that they have, why is this brand looking at me?' There's so many forces that will kill your spirit and make you feel like you're not doing good enough in this space, and it's with time and with knowing who you are at your core that you'll learn how to persevere through those seasons because those seasons will never end."

Grossman, the talent manager, observed, "To be able to maximize on the amount of opportunities out there, and to be able to stay authentic and true to what their individual brand is, [influencers] really need to be able to pivot pretty quickly and just be able to be nimble with the technology and the innovations and everything that's changing just as the industry changes as a whole."

Several influencers described efforts to rebuild their blogs or personal websites or start entirely new companies after years of posting content to platforms like Instagram. "At the end of the day, as much as I love Instagram and that's my main platform, I don't own Instagram. I own my blog. So that's what I work really hard toward growing each and every day," said Skylar. Alana explained in detail the financial, industrial, and social realties she and her peers were navigating:

> I am still an influencer, but I am building this amazing social media digital agency and we're doing well, and I like to say it gives me some sort of peace of mind knowing that, let's say tomorrow Instagram shut me down—it's unlikely, but let's say that happens, or maybe influencers fall out of favor, nobody cares anymore, and sponsors don't want to pay us money, I would be fine. And in a way it gives me more authenticity because I can just work with brands that I want instead of like worrying in a way, "Oh gosh, every month I need to secure a certain number of sponsors or X dollar amount." That is pressure. I have friends who have millions of followers and you'd think they're happy, but when I talk to them they feel kind of worried because they know things are changing. I feel that influencers who don't piggyback off their platform and build something more lasting that is not all on social media, they're gonna be in trouble. The writing's on the wall. Every single day there's more influencers or people who want to be influencers coming on board . . . if you're an influencer who has any sort of platform or reach it's time to leverage that and go into something else. Whatever. Go into TV, have a content company, build a fashion line, whatever it is—you need to get something that you have more control on.

The changing pricing and deal structures in the wake of the exposure of fraudulent practices and the growing microinfluencer and nano-influencer trends had material impact on established influencers. Alana continued:

> The benchmark to become an influencer is quite low: you need to get an account, have style, know how to pose. That's not that difficult. Because of that, the money that is being spent for influencers is decreasing. For example, brand X last year would pay me $5,000 for a campaign, this year it's $3,000. Especially with the rise of microinfluencers, brands have been finding they don't even have to pay. Instead of getting that one influencer with all the followers, they'll say, "OK, we'll just go to fifty micro influencers and just give them product and that's it, we don't even have to pay."

For these and other reasons, influencers worked to build out their personal brands on social media as well, continually expanding the lifestyle genre rather than focusing on billing themselves as experts in a particular area as they had in years past. This served the dual purpose of bolstering their authenticity—by sharing more "realness" from their daily lives—as well as offering additional merchandising opportunities. "Most people in the beginning were only in one industry. They were beauty bloggers, fashion bloggers. But then . . . it was like, 'Oh, the more you do, the more money you can make.' So now people who were all beauty are starting to do fashion . . . everyone's doing fitness," said Hennessy, the director of influencer strategy.

Renee, a marketer, confirmed:

> I think that there are definitely a lot of people who are trying to break into more product categories, or just categories in general. Because, one—that gives them the opportunity to work with brands outside of just beauty or just fashion. But, two—it authentically—there's that word again—tells the story of what they're experiencing in their own lives. I think as people try to incorporate content that showcases more of a snapshot of what they're doing on the day to day versus just look at these beauty looks, for example . . . they're able to give an insider look to their audiences of what they are as a real person versus just here I am, full face of makeup, I look perfect all day every day. And so with that comes an evolution in their lifestyle. So as these

influencers start to "grow up," entering new life stages, that brings them into new opportunities to speak about different topics. We were actually just talking about this the other day internally—that, like, an influencer who may have started out on YouTube as a teenager, she grows up and goes to college, you know, you have that whole back to school thing. As she ages out of that, she gets her first job and she's speaking from the point of view of young professionals. She gets engaged, gets married, that's a whole new life stage. Has babies, that's a whole new life stage. Through all that comes new content.

By presenting a seamlessly and thoroughly "shoppable life"—with posts about self-care sponsored by an essential oils brand, an apartment furnished entirely by a big box retailer, and gatherings with friends sponsored by a beverage company, all clearly and conspicuously disclosed—influencers sent the message that yes, the content was sponsored, but only because it was a natural extension of their lives. Further, Renee's recounting of her team's conversation about an influencer's stereotypical life stages reemphasizes *who* has made the most of these opportunities, or at least guides the imagination of industry insiders: educated, white collar women who follow conventional paths of higher education, marriage, and motherhood.

Given the unpredictable nature of public favor, of social media's technological affordances and company policies, and of federal regulation, influencers had grown accustomed to near constant instability as the state of being for their work. "I've always kind of known that was the industry I signed up for. It's like, nobody knows what's going to happen. It's very 'whatever,' so you just have to be kind of prepared for it. I could get thrown some crazy opportunity tomorrow that would just totally change my path, too. So I'm just trying to stay open to whatever," Issa said.

Looking Ahead

In the late 2010s, a series of significant events forced the influencer industry to reexamine its practices and reorient itself for a future where social media users were more suspicious of social media's hidden industrial machinations. Wide-reaching events of global concern, such as

Facebook's leak of user data, led to a fundamental shaking of trust between people and social media companies and pushed concern over the role these companies play in mediating nearly every aspect of the social world into public debate.

The various stakeholders in the influencer industry experienced the influencer backlash in different ways, and they accordingly adjusted their approaches to their work. But what these repositionings shared were an intention to serve as a public repudiation of fakery and endorsement of disclosure—and a private attempt to gain control over a sometimes unruly environment. Through embracing artificial intelligence and data science for influencer selection and campaign matching; exploring the development and use of CGI, rather than human, influencers; and cultivating the commercial potential of microinfluencers and nano-influencers, marketers worked to prove to their clients and the public that they cared deeply about fraud and worked to control it through more thorough vetting and increased control over influencers.

Brands, meanwhile, looked to work more closely and more long-term with influencers to reduce the risk of controversy and loss of control that comes with engaging on a campaign-basis and moving on. By using influencers as marketing consultants *and* marketing channels—and sometimes cultivating deep enough relationships that they launched products in partnership with each other—brands hoped to shield themselves from the errors of authenticity, from fake followers to inadequate disclosure, that contributed to controversy. Social media and other technology companies introduced tools for disclosure to support the growing cultural and regulatory requirement of transparency.

Influencers, accustomed to the precarious work/lifestyle of social media content creation, looked ahead to prepare themselves for any number of potential scenarios. In expanding their businesses *beyond* social media (such as by creating products, starting consulting companies, and countless other ventures) as well as expanding their personal brands *on* social media (by sharing more lifestyle content, often through embracing newer technological affordances such as Instagram Stories), influencers positioned themselves to continue to get by in the current environment and any number of possible futures that could develop.

The influencer space continued to grow, despite the sometimes daunting challenges it faced, including public cynicism and mocking. Perhaps it grew because, given the broader sociopolitical environment, it seemed easier to rebuild one-to-one trust than trust in a larger media outlet or company when they seemed to blend together in a mass of bodies that did not work in the public interest. As the influencer industry repositioned, it moved toward becoming a more thoroughly but casually commercialized sphere, wherein influencers branch out across content forms and genres and present lifestyles that are more "authentic" as they are branded, disclosed, and shoppable. Ultimately, the influencer industry joined—and in some ways, modeled—media industries' broader push toward more casualized integration of buyable products into lifestyle depictions.[75] While these previous forms met stronger resistance (shoppable television, for example, never took off in the way its proponents hoped despite years of efforts)[76] influencers presented themselves as branded personalities whose work had become understandable and acceptable. After all, in a world where so much seems uncertain, as Hennessy said, "wouldn't you take the money?"

Chapter 5

The Industry Becomes Boundaryless

Like many people in 2020, I spent more time on my mobile phone than ever. Under stay-at-home orders with a toddler and an infant, I used my phone as an escape and a lifeline. Every evening, I scanned the day's COVID-19 numbers in my county and region, looked for new guidelines or, really, anything that could help me understand what was happening and what I was supposed to do about it other than Lysol my doorknobs and swallow my fear for the sake of my children. Later that spring, after Minneapolis police murdered George Floyd, I looked for images and information on news sites and Instagram in an effort to understand the horrifying facts of the event and their fallout. As the summer progressed and the U.S. election season heated up, news headlines were full of unforgettable phrases from government officials seeming to condone authoritarian and chauvinistic sentiments or to reject empirical realities. My mind raced daily, filled with both overwhelming gratitude for my safety and a choking fear that my adult life might end up bearing closer resemblance to that of my great-grandparents—who survived a pandemic, depression, and fascist Europe, with trauma that reverberated for generations—than I ever imagined. I felt vulnerable and powerless, and I looked for information as a balm.

While these familial details are mine, we know that this general experience—the sense of helplessness amid chaos and the fervent search for information—was nearly universal during the lockdowns and

social upheaval of 2020. World events and social isolation brought det-
rimental mental health impacts;[1] at the same time, people spent 10 to
20 percent more time on social media,[2] with Instagram and TikTok experiencing huge gains in average monthly visits.[3] But we also know that
where people looked for information and what they found varied
widely, not just in its tone and format but also in its veracity, sourcing,
and agenda. The algorithms governing my personalized social media
experience brought me, most memorably, to two very different Instagram accounts: @KingGutterBaby and @Little.Miss.Patriot.

@KingGutterBaby was run by Laurel Bristow, an infectious disease
researcher at Emory University School of Medicine, who was working
firsthand with COVID-19 patients as her research team studied the virus
and various treatments. Nearly every evening during the pandemic's
first surge in the United States, Bristow would post a series of Instagram
Stories to provide a clearly worded breakdown of some specific topic
related to COVID-19, often translating recent research into layman's
terms or explaining the reasoning behind various public health recommendations. She gained more than 300,000 followers with her accessible, often funny dispatches (she reminded followers that she "needs
the D"—or data—before forming opinions on any rumors or recommendations). While Bristow has stated that she never intended to become an influencer, brands quickly noticed her growing influence. Bristow created sponsored content for clothing company LOFT, which she
says enabled her to afford a down payment on a house.

@Little.Miss.Patriot was run by a young woman named Alexis.[4] Like
Bristow, she also quickly gained more than 300,000 followers that year,
but Alexis's posts centered on ideas associated with the QAnon movement. In July 2020, for example, she shared a theory that had been growing in popularity across Reddit, Instagram, and other platforms that
summer, that online mega retailer Wayfair was trafficking children under
the guise of selling expensive storage cabinets. As online buzz around
the Wayfair conspiracy grew, it morphed into the #SaveTheChildren
campaign. Experts have noted that this campaign, ostensibly about
rescuing children from human trafficking, helped introduce the worldview propagated by "Q" and its followers—anchored in the belief that

President Donald Trump was secretly battling a global cabal of Satan-worshipping Democratic sex traffickers—into countless new homes, especially those of young women and mothers.[5] Alexis also posted about COVID-19, encouraging her followers to flout public mask requirements.[6] According to reporter Stephanie McNeal, Alexis worked with a multilevel marketing company and was trying to sell merchandise before Instagram suspended her account in September 2020.[7] After the suspension, she created multiple new Instagram accounts but largely migrated her online presence to newer platforms like Parler and Telegram.

@KingGutterBaby and @Little.Miss.Patriot obviously differ in their content and credentials. But under the surface, there are worrying similarities. I stumbled upon both through close personal contacts—friends and relatives—who followed them on Instagram. Both accounts were run by women who were "regular people," not already established influencers or celebrities of any kind, who were sharing information that was presumably important to them and that they believed relevant for the current sociopolitical moment. They were both compelling to their followers because of their accessible but passionate tones. They both showed interest in monetizing their followings. And it is reasonable to conclude that they and others like them had material influence on vital matters of immediate public concern—something as simple but significant as whether to wear a mask in public—as well as a more generalized impact in cultivating a worldview for their followers, much as media researchers have long shown television can do.[8]

The difference, of course, is that television programs and advertisements are subject to regulation.[9] And while I don't intend to imply a moral equivalency between their content specialties, Laurel and Alexis were both beneficiaries of an influencer industry whose proverbial barn doors were flapping in the breeze. They chose to cultivate and leverage their digital influence in the way they saw fit, drawing on the communicative norms and commercial and technological incentive structure available to them—a system that had almost no oversight. Instagram may have shut down @Little.Miss.Patriot, but that was *after* she had spread proven misinformation to hundreds of thousands of people for months. While some conspiracy-minded content creators publicly wondered whether the acute social tumult of 2020 was all some sort of social simulation, they were already participating in a more obvious test: Can we, as a people, survive the constant pummeling of information by self-branded specialists granted power by a personality-dominated, commercially-driven media ecosystem that *also* mediates our personal social connections and self-expressions—an industry that is, quite literally, out of control?

In a pattern that in some ways mirrored the perfect storm of events that supercharged the influencer industry's development a decade prior, the social and political tumult of 2020 accelerated the industry's growth in particular directions, drawing on trends and groundwork laid in the years prior. While only time and sustained study will reveal the widespread and varied ramifications of the COVID-19 pandemic, the racial justice movement, and the 2020 U.S. presidential election, there are already clear indicators of potential futures within the influencer industry. In this chapter, I show how the industrial infrastructure that had been developing for more than a decade was, at the start of the 2020s, a cauldron of possibility for good or for ill. In untangling a series of key moments—some encouraging, others deeply worrisome—I explore the industry's present and potential futures. This chapter shows a transformation well underway from an industry centered on what to buy to one concerned with what to think. Just as expectations of "realness" are more heightened than ever, so too are the difficulties in evaluating others' authenticity—and the stakes of getting it wrong.

Internal Resistance and Change

When I interviewed Sarah* in March 2021, she was passionate about her decision to end her career as an influencer.

Sarah is a longtime digital content creator. She started a blog in 2008, like many others in that era, as a creative outlet. She had an intense full-time job in health care and enjoyed having a space to connect with others on lighter topics like cooking, fashion, and travel. Throughout the 2010s, she used Instagram more and began to monetize in earnest, as RewardStyle links and brand partnerships offered her an additional stream of income that she never knew was possible. After 2015, she said, her income doubled every year. She paid down student loan debt and made repairs to her family's home. But over the course of 2020, she told me, she "did a complete 180 in [her] thought process around the influencer space." When we spoke, she detailed her plans to leave all social media platforms in favor of launching a podcast and joining Patreon, a subscription service, unencumbered by obligations to brands. She was done with the business of influencing as she knew it.

Sarah made this decision for a number of reasons, many of them brought into sharp relief by her experiences as a health care provider during the COVID-19 pandemic. She had been pregnant when the pandemic gripped the United States in early 2020, and as she and her husband both took hospital shifts, "we thought we were going to die—literally," she remembered. "It made me really start to rethink." The acute contrast between her experiences as a medical professional in the throes of a public health crisis and an Instagram influencer who earned money by suggesting consumer goods became harder for her to reconcile. Further, when Sarah shared what she was witnessing at the hospital with her half million Instagram followers and was met with disbelief or derision from some who believed the pandemic was fictional or overblown—or that medical experts couldn't be trusted—it felt personal. She felt compelled to respond to every message, comment, or question, which was an impossible task.

"In the beginning, everybody was outside of their houses and ringing bells for the medical personnel, [saying], 'You guys are heroes and you guys are so amazing.' And now a year later, it's 'you guys are with big pharma and you're trying to kill us all with a vaccine.' So it's been really, really, really hard on me, just to be, and to show up on social media," she said. All told, Sarah suspected she was suffering from a form of post-traumatic stress disorder that was exacerbated by her experience as an influencer. By giving it up, "I'm fully aware that I'm probably going to be taking like a 90 percent pay cut. I don't care," she said. She believed that the influencer industry "has gotten out of control . . . just out of touch with reality." Ultimately, the disconnects between her own lived reality and her monetized social media self-expression—and the commercialized digital ecosystem in which it existed, with its clear incentive structure to share, sell, and engage—became too much to bridge. "I just don't see how constantly selling things, like 24/7, and creating photos that are not relatable play into [it]," she said.

Sarah's decision to sunset her income streams might seem extreme, but she is not the only one of my research participants who has done it. Cara, for example, walked away from her thriving fashion blog in 2018 after working on it for nearly a decade. She recounted to me how the work was no longer a good fit for her personally or professionally: "When I realized in order to make it as an influencer, you have to be comfortable sharing a lot more and talking to the camera . . . I tried it and I was like, 'This just doesn't feel right. This doesn't feel like me,'" she said. She added that brand partnerships began to feel "like a chore," and when she sensed mounting pressure to boost her metrics as the field became saturated, she began to "feel like I just have more to offer than that."

Many influencers I interviewed in the late 2010s and early 2020s expressed similar frustrations with what they felt were continually increasing personal demands of working on social media, including heightened visibility and personal sharing, concern over blowback or hostilities from followers, and diminishing returns on their labor. Their experiences highlight a growing internal resistance to some of the industry's established norms and practices, including the curated, aspirational lifestyles depicted by those in the upper echelon and the continual push to shop and to monetize. This resistance strengthened in the public eye in 2020, when a series of highly public influencer-related incidents made it clear that the sense of relatability that so many cultivated had been obfuscating distinct privileges.[10]

In March 2020, for example, Arielle Charnas of Something Navy (one million-plus followers) livestreamed her experience receiving a COVID-19 diagnosis, which included her announcing she had been feeling ill and receiving a drive-up test later that day. At this time, testing was severely limited, and the city where she lived, New York, was experiencing a devastating surge in cases. Health officials had urged people who were young and otherwise healthy to quarantine rather than seek out tests.[11] Days later, she shared that she and her family had left New York City for the Hamptons—one of several high-profile influencers who left cities for "fresh air" and "a little more space" as lockdowns began.[12] Charnas drew ire from followers and mainstream media critics who believed she received preferential access to medical care, potentially endangered others with nonessential travel, and was so ensconced in a world of privilege that she had not anticipated these seemingly obvious criticisms.[13]

In May of that same year, white Minneapolis police officer Derek Chauvin murdered George Floyd, a forty-six-year-old Black man, while arresting him for suspicion of using counterfeit money. Millions of people participated in protests across the country and around the world, calling for police reform and drawing attention to persistent racism in its many forms, particularly within established institutions. Stories of racial bias, pay inequity, and mistreatment by brands had circulated within influencer spaces previously, but rarely received widespread attention. Suddenly, this changed. Adesuwa Ajayi, a talent manager who said she witnessed "Black influencers' experiences, pay, and access to opportunities weren't equal to their white counterparts,"[14] launched an Instagram account called @InfluencerPayGap that chronicled through anonymous submissions the broad disparities in influencers' compensation and the lack of industry transparency about contracts and rates. Submissions described brands who never paid for content produced, brands asking influencers with thousands of followers to produce multiple images and videos for free product, and asking to retain usage rights to the content in exchange for product or a few hundred dollars. One marketer wrote in to say, "[I] just get so frustrated because I'm asked to underpay people all the time."[15]

In another much-publicized incident, former employees accused Leandra Medine, founder of wildly popular blog-turned-media-company The Man Repeller, of leading an "atmosphere of exclusion."[16] Medine's response and its fallout—readers and former employees said her apology lacked evidence of understanding the problems or real plans to change—led to her stepping down from her leadership role in the business, and within months the decade-old company folded.

These events, taking place amid a rapidly changing sociopolitical landscape, were ultimately accelerations to industrial shifts that had been percolating for sometime—long overdue bookends, perhaps, to an era wherein the thin, white, heterosexual, wealthy, and apolitical macroinfluencer set the standards. "We're no longer willing to blindly follow these people who are putting up a life that everyone else should ascribe to," Greg Andersen, CEO of the Omaha-based agency Bailey Lauerman, told *Adweek* in 2019. "Aspiration is about having a good life, defined by stability and the ability to provide for a family and be connected to the community . . . I think there's only a small percentage of people who aspire to the penthouse in Manhattan. I've followed influencers on platforms and the longer I'm there, the more foreign they look to me."[17]

Public industry discourse was shifting a bit, as well. In 2019, a marketing director provided suggestions in *Adweek* for her colleagues in the industry to combat implicit bias in influencer selection[18]; in 2020, in the wake of the George Floyd protests, another admitted in the same venue to not fighting bias and racism because "it was easier than to push back or educate a client . . . to use the excuse that we were making a 'good business decision' than to take a hard look at our actions."[19]

As industry participants engaged in more public conversations about inequality and social justice, many brands, marketers, influencers, and social media companies made strategic decisions in service of addressing inequalities and communicating accountability. Some brands and marketers revised and improved their hiring and influencer compensation practices. Lauren,* a social media manager at a trendy clothing and home goods retailer, described to me how her team standardized their payment structures and decided to always offer payment, rather than free product, to anyone they approached for content. "I don't ever want someone to feel like their work wasn't valued by us," she told me in 2021. Brian Nickerson, founder of monetization company MagicLinks, said that his company implemented "a 30 percent BIPOC casting requirement for all of our strategic brand partnerships." Some influencers overhauled their content strategies with aims toward greater inclusivity. Megan McNamee, a dietician whose family feeding account has more than one million followers, described to me in early 2021 how she and her business partners planned content on topics addressing the intersections of cultures, food, and kids, including a weekly feature wherein a different family "takes over" the account's Instagram Stories to share their daily meal schedule and the factors such as budget, work schedule, and culture, that shape it.

A year later, influencer marketplace IZEA, which serves nearly one million users, released some encouraging data in their annual "State of Influencer Equality" report. The company's founder noted:

> In 2015, Caucasian influencers received 73% of all sponsorship transaction volume. That number has been decreasing over time and now mimics the U.S. population. Thirty-five percent of Americans identify as Non-White, and sponsorship deal flow for those racial minorities has now reached thirty-seven percent.

Further, on their platform, Black Americans out-earned white counterparts, earning an average of 47 percent more per post.[20]

This data does not provide a full picture of the influencer industry, though—just one marketplace—and it covers a year in which marketers and brand managers abandoned their previously tightly held "apolitical" positions to join a highly visible racial justice movement. They were motivated, author and journalist Sarah Frier argued, "by genuine enthusiasm—and the awareness that being tied to a popular civil rights movement would be great marketing."[21] As media scholar Francesca Sobande pointed out, "Brands have responded to galvanizing BLM [Black Lives Matter] organizing in ways that have involved brands opportunistically performing a proximity to Blackness and Black people."[22]

Further, progress has not continued apace. On TikTok, racial pay gaps and appropriation of Black culture is rife[23]—so much so that creators of color on the platform went on strike in 2021. Reflecting on the state of fashion in 2021, The Cut editor-in-chief Lindsay Peoples Wagner wrote, "The fashion industry has made strides in the past few years . . . but fashion has yet to really grapple with its racism. After the murders of George Floyd and Breonna Taylor last year, the industry became obsessed with doing the right thing in the smallest ways, and the complicated conversations barely happened out of concern for the optics."[24]

This sentiment was quite publicly illustrated by "Blackout Tuesday." On June 2, 2020, in the midst of protests over George Floyd's murder, millions of social media users muted their typical content, posted black squares to their Instagram accounts, and some suggested influencers of color to follow. "Blackout Tuesday" almost immediately became an object of criticism, most especially for performative activism. In its wake, many Black influencers experienced a rapid uptick of followers—a "bittersweet" experience[25] because, while huge follower increases can broaden an influencer's reach and open doors to new brand deals and higher pay, it also can mean increased emotional labor dealing with an influx of comments and messages and uncertainty about new followers' motives. As Ayana Lage, a Black woman who runs the lifestyle blog XO Ayana, told Buzzfeed News, "I want to say I feel proud of myself, but it feels strange when I think about what spurred people to action."[26] "You don't ever want to capitalize off of something so tragic," home décor influencer Deena Knight said in the same piece.

Lauren, the social media manager at a popular brand, said that confronting various issues of racial and economic inequality brought to the fore in 2020 "has made our team more malleable, and flexible, and understanding, and also a lot more aware of everything." The permanence and long-term impact of any changes enacted by many in the industry at this moment, of course, will be revealed only with sustained effort and attention over time.

"Genuinfluencers"

In the late 2010s, consumer interest noticeably shifted toward purpose-driven brands and socially conscious influencers. A 2018 study by public relations firm Edelman found that two-thirds of consumers worldwide will buy from—or avoid—a brand based on the brand's stance on social or political issues.[27] *Adweek* in 2019 observed that influencers increasingly wanted to "take a stand" and work with cause-oriented brands.[28] In early 2021, global trend forecasting agency WGSN christened the concurrent increase in purpose-driven influencers as the rise of the "genuinfluencers." They explained: "Focusing on lessons over likes, influencers will continue integrating learnings into everyday content, often partnering with businesses and even governments."[29] The potential for their messages to make real impact is strong: a 2019 U.K. study found that influencer ads generated 277 percent greater emotional intensity and 87 percent higher memory encoding in participants than television, Facebook, or YouTube ads.[30] Plus, that same Edelman study indicated that more than half of people believed that brands are more effective than the government at addressing social problems.

The pandemic, protests, and election season—with its fertile ground for confusion and thus for creating and spreading information and disinformation—allowed some "genuinfluencers" to gain large followings quickly. "Genuinfluencers" cover a range of topics, from parenting to sustainability, and more. But they focused, as WGSN said, on *lessons*, typically delivered in a conversational format on TikTok and Instagram Stories and backed up with feed posts containing easily digestible facts or tips.

One such "genuinfluencer" was Sharon McMahon, a former public school government teacher whose account @SharonSaysSo grew from obscurity to more than 600,000 followers between 2020 and 2021. McMahon gained a following with Instagram-friendly civics lessons, which she emphasized were nonpartisan and fact-based. She created countless Instagram Stories detailing various processes of U.S. government, such as the electoral college and the Supreme Court; highlighted lesser known historical "fun facts," including an elaborate family tree of Alexander Hamilton; and provided accessible explanations of the legal thinking behind hot button legislation related to topics such as abortion and guns. She answered followers' questions daily via Instagram Stories and sold tickets to her live and recorded "deep dive" workshops, which she hosted on Zoom a few times per month. She encouraged followers to think critically about the information they consumed and posted, and she rallied her "#governerd" community to donate money or other resources to causes such as the Red Cross. McMahon also shared "off-topic" content, including photos of animals and videos of her trying on clothing or doing her makeup.

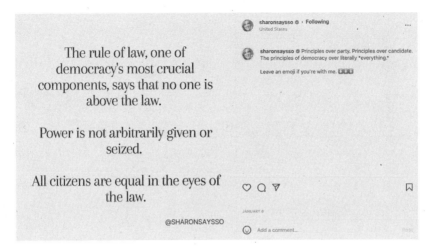

The rule of law, one of democracy's most crucial components, says that no one is above the law.

Power is not arbitrarily given or seized.

All citizens are equal in the eyes of the law.

@SHARONSAYSSO

sharonsaysso ● · Following
United States

sharonsaysso ● Principles over party. Principles over candidate. The principles of democracy over literally "everything."

Leave an emoji if you're with me. 🙌🙌🙌

JANUARY 6

Add a comment...

FIGURE 5. An Instagram feed post by @SharonSaysSo. Reproduced with permission from Sharon McMahon.

In an interview on *The Daily Show with Trevor Noah* shortly after reaching 500,000 Instagram followers, McMahon explained why she believed her account was popular:

> I honestly don't think people believe they can get facts. That is really the crux of the matter; they don't understand where to get facts, they don't know who to trust. They feel like they're getting played every day. It's like a game of *Survivor*: "I don't know what the person's motivation is, I don't know if they're trying to swindle me" . . . and I think when they saw I'm not a politician, I don't work for some big company, I'm literally just a teacher . . . that has just resonated with some people.

In some ways, McMahon's rise is encouraging. It could indicate a growing public interest in history and civics and a potentially effective means of delivering information that is helpful to society. In addition, the millions of dollars she and her followers have raised for charitable causes in such a short time is remarkable. Yet new digital educator-communicators such as McMahon see themselves as battling misinformation spreaders, who, in many ways, do not look all that different from them.

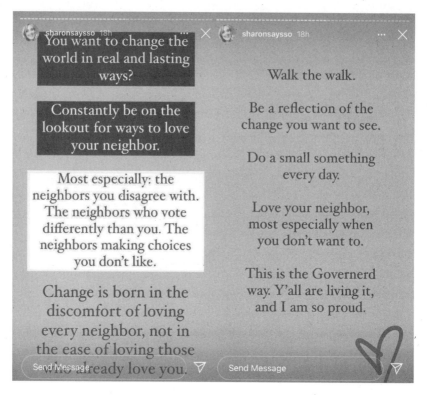

FIGURE 6. An Instagram Story from @SharonSaysSo. Reproduced with permission from Sharon McMahon.

The industrial maneuvers of the influencer space have continually redefined, revalued, and reconstructed authenticity. At this moment, effectively communicating authenticity to the public required personal sharing and transparency and some degree of accountability or self-reflection. Influencers for years had already been dealing with a sense of heightened expectations of personal sharing—"vulnerability porn," as one former influencer described it to the BBC[31]—which years prior had helped usher in the age of "lifestyle" content. By the early 2020s, the trend became more pointed and manifested in a variety of ways: an increase in talking directly and casually to the camera on Instagram Stories; revealing details of current or past actions or controversies, typically via blog posts, Stories, screenshots of statements typed on Apple's

Notes app; and using colorful text slides, often created on the app Canva, to share important "takeaways." Influencers also shared more of what goes on behind the scenes of their own work, including sharing screenshots of hostile direct messages, video Q&As, and updates on their mental health.[32] They worked to remind their followers that "there's another person, a human on the other side," as Megan, the dietician and family nutrition influencer, told me.

While every influencer I have interviewed voiced a desire to present some version of her genuine self online—most people do not go into the work wanting to be dishonest, necessarily—even the most sincere efforts toward "being real" can only provide an illusion of reality. Continual and ephemeral communication tools like Instagram Stories and TikTok, along with easy-access influencer deal marketplaces with little to no human touch, might enable "authentic" and profitable communication, but they also make it possible for anyone who learns to exploit the language of realness to insert almost any message they want into the framework. As author Jo Piazza described it on her podcast *Under the Influence*: "I liked her smoothie recipe, so maybe I should trust her on this as well." Or, as Sarah told me, "We live in a world where everybody gets to share their personal experiences, and so somebody's personal experience is then taken into content without context. And then people are like, 'Oh, well, I can't get the vaccine because Susie Q over here says that her child was injured when he was five, and blah, blah, blah.' It's wild out there. I don't know how else to put it."

Of course, mass media messages have always been ideological, if for nothing more than to encourage viewers to be good consumer-citizens and buy their way to fulfillment and self-actualization, choosing from a set of options that are limited and skewed by necessity. Settled in Los Angeles during their exile from Nazi Germany, cultural theorists Theodor Adorno and Max Horkheimer wrote of the "culture industry"— namely the advertising, radio, and film industries of the era—that kept the common worker in line, providing narratives that reinforced a life rhythm of working so hard that reliance on "mindless entertainment" became a necessity to unwind and then return to work, leaving little opportunity for workers to reflect on their circumstances or resist them.

"The culture industry perpetually cheats its consumers of what it perpetually promises," they argued. "The paradise offered by the culture industry is the same old drudgery . . . pleasure promotes the resignation which it ought to help to forget." Adorno and Horkheimer believed that the culture industry's continual quest for efficiency and profit made its products severely intellectually limited, leaving people only with the "freedom to choose what is always the same" and ultimately "drowning out democracy in pursuit of profit."[33]

While the writings of Adorno and Horkheimer and their colleagues in the Frankfurt School of social theory have, in many ways, turned out to be strikingly prescient for the cultural industries of the twenty-first century,[34] the influencer industry's infrastructure offers potential ideological reach on a level that was perhaps unimaginable in their lifetimes. The industry's norms of communication mean that successfully constructing authenticity happens in ironically insidious ways. The chit-chat, humor, and easily shareable imagery are particularly amenable to propaganda, mis- or disinformation, and the nonstop product pushing that we've come to experience as de rigueur. People enact and experience these norms within a technological system that offers tools that allow nearly anyone to participate with few rules and little oversight, in an industrial media environment that profits from the attention of all engaged in it. "Just being real" is almost never just that.

While there is no evidence that Sharon McMahon specifically has misused her power, the same cannot be said for others. "Genuinfluencers" run the gamut, as does the level of their involvement in selling product. From a parenting influencer who might suggest Montessori-inspired toys, to a lifestyle influencer hawking CBD supplements, to a self-styled "skeptical" wellness influencer who characterizes COVID-19 as a "scamdemic,"[35] the slope between harmless and harmful is slippery—particularly among a population that has always defined itself as *outside* the "establishment," and an industrial structure that has followed suit.

In a 2020 discussion about widespread pandemic misinformation, Professor Philip Howard of the Oxford Internet Institute told British Parliament that he believed "in some ways, influencers are the gateway drug."[36] The opportunities for veering away from established evidence are many, particularly when it comes to complicated topics. "They use scientific language, and then they layer pseudoscience on top of it. It sounds like they know what they're talking about because they use certain expressions that make sense, but then add false things to that," a psychotherapist observed to *Mother Jones.*[37]

These examples make clear how the industrial construction of authenticity can be used in ways that can be both beneficial and severely damaging to other people and society at large. We as a people must consider— are we willing to accept the benefits as well as the damages of the status quo? If not, how can we enable entrepreneurialism, connection, and self-expression online without paying such a high cost of unfettered "authenticity?" And who can—or should—manage it all?

Political Influencers

In November 2019, a curious campaign appeared on AspireIQ, a marketplace that connects influencers and brands for sponsorship deals. It was titled "United We Win: Keep Cory Booker in the Fight." At the time, Senator Cory Booker of New Jersey was a candidate in the U.S. Democratic presidential primary. Through AspireIQ, approved influencers could earn a few hundred dollars by encouraging their followers to "keep Cory in the fight with a small donation."

After Buzzfeed News reported the story, AspireIQ removed the campaign from their site, and a Democratic super PAC called United We Win took responsibility for the posting.[38] In a statement, a spokesperson from the super PAC defended their initial effort: "This is simply another way to engage dedicated grassroots supporters online, and those supporters will be compensated for their time in the same way that more traditional campaign efforts like canvassing are also often compensated."[39] The event prompted some conversations among influencers about the appropriateness of engaging in paid political campaigns but did not receive much further press coverage.

A few months later, though, it happened again. The campaign for Michael Bloomberg, a candidate in the same race, quietly posted on Tribe, another marketplace. "Are you sick of the chaos [and] infighting overshadowing the issues that matter most to us? Please express your thoughts verbally or for still image posts please overlay text about why you support Mike," it read. According to the Daily Beast, the post "encourages submissions to be well lit, mention why the influencer thinks 'we need a change in Government,' and for the creator to 'be honest, passionate and be yourself!'"[40] The pay: $150 per post.

This time, the potential campaign caused a stir, with numerous media outlets reporting or opining on the situation. Some mocked it, suggesting that the candidates just wanted to "seem cool."[41] Others rightfully wondered: Is it ethical to pay people to support political campaigns? If so, how does one determine a rate? How should the transaction be disclosed? The Federal Election Commission had no rules regarding social media influencers, though it required disclosure of funding sources for paid content generally. The Federal Trade Commission, the regulatory body that had paid the most attention to influencers in prior years, had just released in late 2019 an updated guide to disclosures, and even the Library of Congress offered a guide to influencer marketing that highlighted three "areas of concern"—but nothing mentioned political speech or political advertising. An undercurrent of worry understandably coursed through even the most measured analyses of the Booker and Bloomberg events: *Where could this lead?*

Formally leveraging social media personalities to support political messaging wasn't exactly new. For example, the Democratic Congressional Campaign Committee paid influencers in 2018 for "get out the vote" messaging, and the conservative group Turning Point USA maintains a network of both paid and unpaid social media "ambassadors."[42] But something about these influencer marketplace transactions certainly felt *different*. One problem is their potential scale. Tribe and AspireIQ, two of countless influencer marketing platforms, boasted tens of thousands of influencers in their marketplaces who could theoretically be reached and mobilized through one simple post by a sponsor. We have already seen, through examples like the fiasco when Lord & Taylor saturated Instagram with a poorly disclosed dress campaign, or the mid-2010s tyranny of "millennial pink" and other

"Instagrammable" aesthetics, that the mechanisms are in place for sponsors to overwhelm social media feeds with unified messaging, as are the incentives to repeatedly serve the same types of content once something performs well.

Another concern is who these campaigns targeted. Both Bloomberg's and Booker's campaigns looked to utilize nano-influencers or microinfluencers—people with a few thousand followers, not big names. It is a telling strategic move aimed at reaching a wide range of the most "ordinary-seeming" people possible and slipping paid endorsements into their followers' feeds with the smallest chance of being recognized as such. This could set a worrisome standard for groups of all kinds to mobilize more and more people to engage in paid messaging.

Yet another concern is the lack of clarity on who was behind the influencer marketplace postings and whether it violated any sort of rules or norms of the industry. It took days for United We Win to come out as the entity behind the Cory Booker post, for example, and AspireIQ removed the post only after it leaked to the public. And finally, the glaring problem in all of this is that there were no safeguards in place to prevent noncommercial groups from leveraging the influencer industry's dealmaking structure for their own ends.

For much of the industry's existence, influencers and brands were expected—by each other and seemingly by their followers—to be so apolitical as to be anodyne. A post about an election, a political issue, or even an influencer's personal experience with anything that could invite heated debate was off-limits. But the popularization of social impact-oriented brands during the 2010s (epitomized, perhaps, by glasses company Warby Parker's "buy one give one" mantra) and the changing nature of profitable authenticity helped begin a slow shift. By 2019, Business of Fashion proclaimed that it was "riskier *not* to take a stance."[43] Amid the charged social problems of 2020, particularly the U.S. presidential election, "there's more pressure than ever before for influencers and creators to pick a side," one executive told Digiday. "There's no way you can be an influencer today and be on the sidelines . . . your audience just won't let you."[44]

In this changing landscape, then, a political message is less obvious and its motivations even less so. And political campaigns are hopeful about capitalizing on this moment. "This mechanism is the best way for a Democratic or Republican party to load in the fans that are already passionate and rile them up in a coordinated way," a consultant with influencer platform Heartbeat told the *Wall Street Journal*.[45] Of course, sponsoring individuals to stump for political candidates or issues—and supported by technological affordances that allow consumers to immediately "swipe up" to donate or hand over their personal information—seems out of step with the deliberation upon which democracy relies, as well as the rules and expectations around advertising that have applied to our media system for generations. Researchers at the University of Texas at Austin called politically sponsored microinfluencer campaigns "a new and growing form of 'inorganic' information operations—elite-dictated propaganda through trusted social media spokespersons."[46]

While politicians (and groups supporting them) leveraging the influencer marketplace is cause for concern in and of itself, it also points to bigger problems. The influencer industry is unregulated, marketplaces are wide open, and platforms can't follow the money behind posts—or even know whether a post is sponsored at all—because transactions primarily occur off-platform. Marketplaces and social media companies are woefully behind in identifying and solving issues when they need to be anticipating them. Influencers, in a constant hustle for the next paycheck, are incentivized to participate. Do we want to accept politicians or political groups having the ability to pay individuals for endorsements? Is selling access to our personal self-expression a net positive for society?

Everyone's an Influencer

The expanding understanding of "regular" people and their value to the influencer marketplace was helped along by new platforms that specialized in content with an unpolished and spontaneous feel. TikTok, the short-form video app, emerged in the late 2010s and quickly became a global powerhouse boasting a seemingly endless supply of scrollable, typically lighthearted content. TikTok grew its userbase to nearly two billion people within roughly three years of its 2017 global launch and boasted more than a hundred million monthly users in the United States by August 2020.[47] That same month, Instagram, in an effort to compete, launched Reels, a feature that allowed users to make short video clips with a range of visual and audio effects. The ephemeral, seemingly off-the-cuff content helped deepen the growing resistance to aspirational, heavily curated feed content—and provided new formats in which brands could insert their messaging.

Beth, the brand marketer, explained in a 2021 interview: "Influencers and brands are really having to keep up with this, even more so pulling-back-the-curtain-mentality, of keeping things super real, not showing that high-res, glossy brand imagery that you once maybe did on social media. But really shifting back to what is real, what is authentic, and not just *trying* to be." She continued, "[That's] what Instagram was really built on . . . showing that highlight reel. But now, people are really shifting to say, 'No, we don't want to see that. We want to see the real thing.' And TikTok's really made that idea flourish and take hold. So I think audiences are getting keen to that perspective, and it's causing everybody to have to shift their content."

Brands and marketers noted the growing interest in—and availability of—less edited, more accessible content and digested it for their own purposes. Many brands sought to enroll more "regular people" into their influencer programs. Banana Republic, for example, asked people to pose in their favorite Banana Republic outfits on Instagram in exchange for $150 gift cards. Even on @InfluencerPayGap, submissions praised the potential of nano-influencers (those with around one thousand to five thousand followers) and smaller. One budding content creator who identified herself as "a south-Asian Canadian with less than 1k followers" shared that a skincare company offered her four free products of her choice and $100 to review each—a relatively "good deal" in the scope of this marketplace. She wrote, "For all my small pages, keep doing you and don't sell yourself short. Even if you have a small following, brands will notice you."[48]

Other brands looked to feature "regular people" in-house, encouraging their own employees to act as influencers. Walmart, for example, launched their Spotlight program, which asks employees to post day-in-the-life content about their jobs or about particular Walmart features or programs. Spotlight began with five hundred U.S. associates in 2020 with the goal of expanding to 1.5 million within a few years and becoming "the world's largest employee-influencer program," a vice president told Modern Retail. The company presents Spotlight as an effort to "humaniz[e] its brand and giv[e] customers authentic, relatable content that they actually want to see and engage with," but, tellingly, it is not all just chit-chat.

> While personal content makes up the bulk of Spotlight posts, brand sponsorships are on the rise. In November, Walmart introduced a partnership with action figure brand Funko: Spotlight influencers were asked to make posts with Funko products . . . and the top ten posts (based on an algorithm that measures engagement) received $200 each in cash. Other challenges are higher paid. For a new challenge that Walmart posted with the hoverboard brand Hover-1, the top prize is $1,000.[49]

Unsurprisingly, Walmart also frames the Spotlight program as empowering to workers, though an employee advocacy expert raised concerns about setting a "dangerous precedent" wherein employees who boasted "influencer skills" are rewarded with bonuses, raises, or potential promotions.[50] Of course, programs like Spotlight are also potentially powerful tools for combating rogue messaging by current or former employees, whose "potential to influence brand perception on TikTok is limitless"[51]—and for bolstering employee loyalty. If part of a person's job becomes publicly discussing their employer's positive attributes, and the employee's success at the task brings financial and potentially other rewards, how much harder would it be to walk away or fight for changes within the workplace?

As brands shifted their strategies to include more people under the influencer tent, those on the technology side of the influencer industry—platform companies and tech-minded marketing and monetization businesses—found ways to make more things for sale, and developed more tools to make in-app commerce easier. In 2019, Instagram introduced a shopping cart feature as well as "drop notifications" that allowed brands to ping followers' home screens to tease new product releases. In 2020, the affiliate business boomed: RewardStyle reported a 40 percent year-over-year increase in commissions and 30 percent increase in paid campaigns during the first month of pandemic lockdowns, and their competitor ShopStyle reported that their affiliate business had increased between 90 and 100 percent in that same period.[52] As brick-and-mortar stores closed, retailers increasingly relied on influencers to push marketing content and drive sales, a trend that shows no sign of reversing course as pandemic restrictions lifted. Influencer-led campaigns were profitable, efficient, and promising for future growth as more and more people become potential channels for commerce. Fittingly, Instagram in 2021 released their own affiliate tool under the guise of helping creators, but it was also a clear attempt to eat into the enormously profitable affiliate business and bolster influencers' loyalty after years of letdowns and losses to platforms like TikTok.

Live shopping, when influencers livestream themselves using and recommending products that are immediately buyable, also gained real traction amid pandemic-driven changes in lifestyle and screen use. The major tech companies—Amazon, Facebook, and Google—all launched video shopping initiatives in 2020, as did RewardStyle with LTK Shopping Video. Tech industry outlet The Verge dubbed 2020 "the year of live shopping," observing that "on every platform, it ends up looking like a modern twist on QVC—but with influencers instead of celebrities, and those influencers getting a cut of the sales."[53] Indeed, live shopping has long been a sought-after venue for marketers and brands hoping to capitalize on the combination of personality-driven selling and new media technology.

This endeavor was best epitomized by QVC, the home-shopping television channel that since the 1980s has broadcast live product demonstrations and conversations with brand representatives with the impetus to "call now!" to buy. While QVC and its brethren like the Home Shopping Network have been stalwarts of the cable-television era, broadcasting to hundreds of millions of homes around the world, they also long battled a corny reputation. Tech companies adapting the model for the social media era with influencers at the helm, though, found slicker and effective initial results. These tech-enabled, influencer-centered shopping initiatives led *Vogue* to reflect on the state of influencer marketing at the end of 2020: "It isn't editors who should be worried about losing their market share. It's retailers."[54]

The shift to content that seemed more accessible, less staged, and provided by "regular" people whose lifestyles appeared more broadly accessible had been percolating since the late 2010s. But that shift accelerated dramatically as stay-at-home orders meant people's engagement with influencer content increased and brick-and-mortar shopping options were nearly obsolete. In an unsurprising move of adaptation and self-preservation, the influencer industry reshuffled, making more people eligible for the "influencer" role and its self-monetization lifestyle. Yet, billed as democratic, it brings with it many worrisome externalities. When we expand the influencer tent, we also expose more people to its problems.

We know from the growing research community studying influencers, as well as the journalists working on this specific beat, that the work is taxing in a variety of ways. Influencers must continually navigate a porous border between personhood and business.[55] Their livelihoods are tied directly to their daily behavior on apps governed by opaque algorithms and other third-party technological intermediaries.[56] They work in an industry whose structure often reifies social and economic inequalities,[57] wherein the narratives about gaining success—and what success looks like—are often mythic.[58] Formal supports or resources are nearly nonexistent, and so influencers resort to creating their own atomized means of support.[59] The companies for whom they provide immense value seem to listen to them only when they see a direct benefit. There is no customer service line for the social media companies with which influencers do their entire jobs—no "boss" or HR representative to speak with when the system isn't working, technically or culturally. Unsurprisingly, their mental health suffers.[60]

In 2019, a series of studies (some of which I worked on) raised serious concerns about the personal and social costs of the influencer industry. One untangled the myriad ways social media companies publicly frame content creators' efforts to "do well" on the platforms as morally wrong, while at the same time engaging in those same behaviors—an entrenched, uneven power dynamic dubbed "platform paternalism."[61] Another study explored the intersection of gender and algorithms in showing how beauty vloggers, traditionally thought of as outside the realm of "technical experts," had developed productive modes of gossip to help themselves succeed in the face of major platforms' algorithmic opacity.[62] Yet another explored the gendered dynamics of social media's "visibility mandate," wherein women creators found themselves in a particular bind—between needing to portray themselves as "real enough" without going too far and becoming "too real," in either case risking harassment and hate.[63] And two more outlined, in differing ways, the industrial and political economic forces behind life becoming a nonstop, technologically enabled shopping experience.[64] That same year, though, a survey found that a striking 86 percent of Americans ages thirteen to thirty-eight were willing to post sponsored content for money.[65]

The influencer industry's moves in the early 2020s show that its problems and potential are no longer contained to creative industries that have been dealing with influencer-led changes for years, but that there is proven progress and unlimited possibilities for the industry's logics and technologies to take over more and more people's experiences of daily life—from their workplaces, to their leisure time, to their communications with other people. Taylor Lorenz wrote in the *New York Times* of one particularly dystopic future, wherein some influencers moved beyond selling products and tested the idea of selling the power to make decisions about their lives—auctioning off decisions like what to eat or do that day.[66] Whether this specifically develops into a viable or more widely used income stream remains to be seen, but the overarching trend begs the question: When monetizing one's daily life is a growth industry, where does it end?

Professionalization

As the influencer industry continued to grow, the pains of the space became more obvious. The economic and racial issues brought to the fore in 2020 were tangled up in a broader problem—a lack of professional protections and cohesion and the desperate, long overdue need for them. Influencer marketing was a nearly $10 billion business in 2021,[67] but the precarity that has defined it since its inception had taken an obvious toll. The continually increasing need for personal sharing and self-commodification with unclear payout, no unifying code of ethics, and a lack of transparency about why and how things worked, from deal negotiations to algorithmic visibility, were just a few of the issues wrought by the total lack of professional stability. Influencers were clearly a professional class of their own, in terms of both cultural contributions and financial value, and it is fair to say they should be considered a professional field of culture production in the vein of advertising, film, or journalism. Yet there was no Society of Professional Journalists to turn to for ethical guidance; no Screen Actors Guild or Freelancers Union to rely on for benefits and other support; no Association of National Advertisers or 4A's to seek out for community and professional development. There was, however, a profound sense of disrespect for the personally risky, bottom-line-boosting work that influencers performed.

"Creators are American small business owners, and that narrative is not projected," Qianna Smith Bruneteau told me in 2021. A former blogger, editor, and social media marketer, Bruneteau is the founder and executive director of the American Influencer Council (AIC), a nonprofit trade organization that launched in 2020 with the goal of addressing some of these issues. The AIC aims to bolster the careers of young creators, providing education and networking opportunities. It also seeks to develop professional standards and to support regulation that would protect creators' professional interests.

"I think that there is a desire for equitable opportunities and creating a culture that promotes business ethics and standards," Bruneteau said. She believed only the "extreme" ends of influencing got attention with the broader public, whether it was Kim Kardashian's endless stream of product launches and selfies in rarefied surroundings, or a "bad actor" being caught in a scandal. "The majority of our industry is . . . your hard-working American who is putting their everything into being a publisher and producing agency-quality media that's fueling the growth for the global demand of authentic content, but you don't see them; they're not visible," she said. "And so it's that group who suffer, [when those] at the extreme end have defined what influencing looks like. And I think that's why our space desperately needs standards."

Aliza Licht, whose @DKNYPRGIRL account served as proof of concept for the nascent influencer industry in the late 2000s, said another goal is to "define what it means to be a career influencer. What is that criteria? What are those best practices? Really the official stamp of, are you a career influencer, or are you just someone who posts a couple pictures? Because the career influencers are microagencies. They are doing incredible work, the good ones. It's a lot of work . . . I think a lot of creators do feel a little bit frustrated that people think like, 'Oh, they wake up, they take a few selfies, they post it, and that's the day.' And that's not true."

Indeed, common industry practices like white-listing—when a brand runs influencer-created content as an ad in their own feeds, not the influencer's—make it clear that many influencers are operating at a professional level without correlating protections or professional education. Bruneteau pointed out the Michael Bloomberg campaign example: "Why was he tapping creators to make memes for a couple hundred dollars? Well, he doesn't have to pay tax for advertisement . . . You don't necessarily understand that when you're twenty and someone's offering you $1,000 to make a couple of memes, right?"

In February 2021, SAG-AFTRA, the union for film, television, and radio professionals, announced a new contract for influencers after three years of data gathering and deliberation. The contract allows content creators who work alone, are incorporated, and produce video content to join the union and become eligible for benefits including health and pension as well as professional guidance. "I think the biggest thing that I heard from influencers is the exploitation," union president Gabrielle

Carteris told *Teen Vogue*.[68] "They realized they had no control, and that was really frustrating—particularly as they started to grow in the business. These are big corporations, and it's really difficult to feel empowered when you feel like you're a lone voice."

Part of what the AIC and SAG-AFTRA contracts aim to do is bolster the security and resources available to "good actors" in the influencer industry in hopes of edging out "bad actors." However, they are only at the beginning of defining these parameters in practice. Where can one draw a professional boundary, and who will have the authority to do it? Whose interests will be protected?

Assessing the Circumstances

In the early 2020s, the era-defining COVID-19 pandemic, racial justice movement, and American political turmoil broadly revealed what researchers and many industry participants, especially those from underrepresented economic and ethnic backgrounds, had long known: the industry that trades on aspirational "realness" is not free of the more loathsome parts of reality. They are interconnected. With a spotlight upon them, influencers and brands shifted their strategies to try to meet the moment.

Some of these shifts signaled promising progress in service of accountability, equity, inclusion, and professional support, and the success of some influencers tackling issues of public concern is certainly a reason for some cautious optimism. To be sure, digital content creation can be a positive thing, enabling personal connections, self-expression, and businesses to flourish. But the influencer industry as it stands also offers frightening opportunities for exploitation—both *by and of* social media companies, brands, influencers, marketers, governments, and other groups. When we judge others' authenticity by how well they perform within an industrially constructed version of reality, worrisome outcomes are possible. These concerns are no longer limited to sites of formalized cultural production like fashion, journalism, or music. We are all targets, in some way, for the influencer industry—by commercial participants who, in various ways, desire to enroll more "real people," and by ideologically driven entities who want to use the industry's tools and norms to reach us with their messaging.

Ultimately, the events explored in this chapter reveal that the influencer industry, whether its participants realized it or not, was already behind in the need to grapple with some existential questions. While the original, commercially driven industry participants still jostle over their chaotic marketplace, the infrastructure they created for producing, evaluating, and promoting influential social media content—personality-driven and readily monetizable through a large number of platforms and tools—bled beyond their control. Any number of groups, political or otherwise, could utilize the industry's tools and norms to present themselves and their ideas as another innocuous product to consider like the latest bespoke hair care line. At the same time that the industry is trying to separate influencers from non-, we are also becoming more similar. There are few safeguards in place to prevent it, just individuals and companies patching their immediate domains. All of this is happening right under our noses, on the primary platforms for digital sociality, self-expression, and information sharing. The industry and the public would be right to wonder: Who is really in charge? Do we consent to this?

Chapter 6

The Cost of Being Real

In July 2021, teenage singer Olivia Rodrigo visited the White House as part of a strategic campaign to encourage young people to get vaccinated. The visit consisted of a series of meticulously planned photo ops and social media-friendly content creation, including meeting with Vice President Kamala Harris while wearing coordinating light pink suits and President Joe Biden in matching aviator sunglasses. Rodrigo and Dr. Anthony Fauci, director of the U.S. National Institute of Allergy and Infectious Diseases and the chief medical adviser to the president, made a video in which they read positive tweets about vaccines, drawing on a popular late-night television trope wherein celebrities read tweets about themselves. The whole visit was a meticulously planned, openly acknowledged attempt to leverage Rodrigo's status as a "Gen Z influencer" to deliver a message to a targeted population. These sorts of public relations stunts—pseudo-events, as historian Daniel Boorstin called them—have happened for generations. The interesting thing about this one was who orchestrated it: not the usual squad of PR flacks and managers but a man named Landon Morgado, whom the White House had recently hired for the job of "directing creator partnerships." That the White House created this role—and filled it with a person from Instagram's fashion team, no less—illustrates how far the influencer industry had come from the days when it struck people, including me, as profoundly odd that a historic magazine would hire a preteen blogger.

People and organizations at every corner of society have embraced the influencer logic, to a wide variety of ends.[1] The next logical question seems to be, *what now?* First, an assessment: The influencer industry as it exists today is a complex and far-reaching informational-commercial-personal communication apparatus whose incentive system is profoundly borked. In what follows, I detail what I see as the primary ways that incentives for social media companies, brands, influencers, and "everyday" media users are misaligned, and who or what might be best positioned to help the situation.

I use this framing to point out ways the industry's technologies, norms, and practices *incentivize* people and businesses to make certain choices over others. The situation is not deterministic. But there is enough evidence of patterned behaviors and outcomes for us to acknowledge both the benefits (typically individual) and the damages (often societal) that have come with the influencer industry developing in the way that it has—and to know that interventions to these issues must happen at every level at which they exist, including the individual, industrial, and regulatory. These interventions are cumulative; a fix in one area will likely benefit another.

Social Media Companies Accumulate Power with Impunity and Must Be Regulated

As the influencer industry has developed, there has been an overarching trend of power shifting *away* from individuals and individual ownership (such as with blogs) and *toward* social media companies (such as the recently restyled Meta), as well as toward companies proffering various technologies of self-commercialization (such as Reward-Style and its peers).

This power shift occurred in part through corporate buyouts or rip-offs of smaller platforms. Some notable buyouts over the last decade include that of HelloSociety, which changed corporate owners several times and ultimately ended up under ownership of the *New York Times*; Twitter's purchase of the Niche agency; and Google acquiring the influencer marketplace FameBit. The biggest "win" for corporate power, of course, went to Meta-owned Instagram, which offered robust analytics to users with business accounts in 2016, introduced the long-denied technology to make Instagram feeds shoppable *without* a third-party app in 2019, and launched in-house monetization tools, including an affiliate marketing tool, in 2021—all implemented under the banner of "helping creators" but primarily serving to strategically derail competitors' prospects and bolster the time users spend on Instagram instead of other apps.

Perhaps the most significant factor in social media companies' ability to accumulate power was industry stakeholders' desire to maximize efficiency and minimize risk: individual participants, particularly influencers, wanted to gain income and visibility; brands wanted consistency and predictability in content; and marketers sought to make these processes efficient and profitable. Social media companies increasingly courted and catered to these stakeholders because of how sizeable and lucrative the space had become. They did this by hiring big-name professionals from various creative industries to lead "partnerships" divisions (for example, former magazine editors Eva Chen of *Lucky* and Derek Blasberg of *Vanity Fair* and *Harper's Bazaar* went to Instagram and YouTube, respectively, to cultivate fashion partnerships), as well as by dedicating resources to studying the influencer space and introducing tools to ease influencers' experiences using the platforms. This, in turn, changed these social media platforms—which are used by billions of other people—providing tools for users to more deeply engage with and follow in the influencer paradigm, from making one's presence shoppable to posting more frequently and "authentically"—in its continually shifting form—in hopes of gaining algorithmic visibility, boosting follower counts, and garnering positive audience feedback.

This macroshift in power toward media and technology companies occurred through several smaller "ping pong matches" of power as experienced by the influencers I interviewed. As they described it, influencers came to exist in their current form, in part, because they lacked power in their planned career paths and repositioned themselves away from them; soon advertisers noticed and wanted to utilize them, and influencers gained considerable negotiating power. Later, marketers and other middlemen got involved in hopes of bolstering and profiting from the situation. Influencers lost a measure of power by signing up for more predictable deal streams and by needing to position themselves to suc-ceed on various platforms (which, as illustrated by the quick rise and fall of Twitter-owned short-form video platform Vine, were precarious in and of themselves) and cede control of their content to these same platforms.

These and other trends, such as the drive toward data-driven identi-fication of smaller and smaller subsets of influencers, led to a growing chasm between "classes" (or "buckets," as described in chapter 3) of influencers—between those who could be paid handsomely for their work of promotion and persuasion and those who were expected to work for free or for gifted products. This is most clearly illustrated in the con-trasting experiences of two women I interviewed: Danielle, a fashion microinfluencer, believed that she was "kind of robbing someone" by asking brands for remuneration for the promotional work she carried out. Meanwhile Alana, the influencer with hundreds of thousands of followers who later started her own agency, felt able and equipped to charge for her work in a manner that afforded a comfortable lifestyle—though she, too, had recently found brands less willing to pay what she believed her efforts to be worth as they looked to smaller influencers like Danielle who would ask for less.

Power has tilted so decidedly toward the influencer industry's tech-nological gatekeepers that it is their agendas that are most clearly observ-able in the industry's continued evolution. The way the influencer indus-try developed—with individuals entwining their self-presentations with commercial brands, marketers helping brands and influencers identify their potential commercial impact, and social media tools enabling users to "buy now" from the content they encounter—empowered and accelerated the creep of commercialization across the web and into people's presentations of self. As far back as 2015, an industry observer wrote in AdExchanger that a crucial part of an influencer campaign is "inspiring UGC [user-generated content]."[2] In other words, brands and marketers see a critical part of influencers' modes of expression—which are increasingly similar and marked by a call to shop—is inspiring "reg-ular" social media users to mimic them. In this way, every social media interaction becomes a potential point of commerce, and the influencer industry advances advertisers' and marketers' long-held aim of separating consumers from their money with less and less friction. Or, as Jezebel more bluntly described it: it is "an extension of big businesses' desire to sell you more shit."[3]

The intimacy between selfhood and commerce is unprecedented on such a widespread scale. When the central tools for digital communication all but require users to reckon with—and often adopt—a marketplace mindset, a reorganization of the way people know and understand themselves and others seems unavoidable (recall Erica's description, in chapter 2, of trying to "capture" other people with content). Further, the commercial sphere's nonserious reputation conceals the larger social and material problems with the influencer space, including potential environmental effects, significant labor issues, and the industry's latest use as a tool for misinformation and propaganda—illustrating what sociologist David Hill referred to as platforms' "moral injury."[4]

Legislative attention must be paid to the gross imbalance of power and lack of transparency between platform companies and their users, as well as to the imbalance of power between the major platform companies and those who attempt to compete with them. Further, government agencies, lawmakers, and company leadership must understand that the market has led us to many antisocial outcomes. As author and Harvard Business School professor Shoshanna Zuboff observed, "Historically, great concentrations of corporate power were associated with economic harms. But when human data are the raw material and predictions of human behavior are the product, then the harms are social rather than economic. The difficulty is that these novel harms are typically understood as separate, even unrelated, problems, which makes them impossible to solve. Instead, each new stage of harm creates the conditions for the next stage."[5] Ensuring security, safety, and integrity on social media is "a public service trapped in private entities."[6] The drive to regulate "Big Tech" is broadly supported by the American people,[7] and lawmakers must keep this at the top of their agendas until people-focused, well-founded solutions are passed.

Influencers Work in Opacity and Need Professional Organization

In the summer of 2021, Instagram released a series of announcements and video content intended to inform and engage the platform's influencers. In one video, when asked how influencers can continue to be successful when they feel "like the algorithm is working against them," Instagram head Adam Mosseri responded:

> One of the most important things is to experiment, to try new things and figure out what's resonating with your audience now because it might be different from what it was a half a year, a year ago. There are other broad things. I think leaning into video is good. Videos need to be catching the first two seconds to get people's attention as they scroll by in the feed. I wish there was a silver bullet. I wish there was just a formula I could hand over to you, but there isn't.[8]

The content and tone of Mosseri's advice is telling. Under the guise of making himself available to answer influencers' questions, he did not tell them much at all. Trying new things has always been the bedrock of influencers' work. Their problem is that the rules seem to have changed again with no transparency, and the person who should be able to explain why and how better than anyone will not be straightforward about it. Further, by the time this video was released, it had become clear that all manners of dishonest, harassing, or otherwise negative content can perform quite well. Suggesting influencers "figure out what's resonating" in a time when mis- and disinformation is flourishing seems inappropriate at best, and reckless at worst. This exchange illustrates what influencers have long understood—that they are ultimately on their own.

Influencers' work creates enormous value for brands and social media companies, but the growth in their cultural and economic importance has not necessarily changed their precarious positions. As this book has shown, the platforms and brands to whom influencers are beholden incentivize them to be always "on," frequently pivoting their skills and continually sharing personal stories but in a monetizable way—when the definition of what is "monetizable" frequently changes. Booking campaigns and getting paid for them typically happens at the mercy of others, and pay discrepancies and discrimination are rife. Influencers' work has become critical to the commercial sphere, but it is not sustainable in its current form.

Influencers must recognize themselves as the cultural laborers they are and organize accordingly, through unionization and other professionalization efforts. Some of this has begun: the SAG-AFTRA contract and the development of the American Influencer Council discussed in chapter 5 are two optimistic developments on this front. But more can be done. The incentive structure needs to change—technologically and culturally—such that content creators are incentivized to adhere to professional standards rather than simply "what resonates." As media and cultural historian Fred Turner observed of the influencer landscape, "The performance of individualism—the revelation of the whole person in the context of public debate that was meant for so long to be a bulwark against totalitarianism—has also allowed today's authoritarians to claim a new legitimacy."[9] As a professional group, influencers must install their own bulwarks against authoritarianism, and hold themselves responsible to each other, their audiences, and empirical realities.

It is worth noting here that the very term influencer carries implicit meanings, with consequences for how, when, and by whom it is used. Recall that in Socrates's and Shakespeare's times, influence had a negative connotation, associated with "a kind of irrational servility."[10] In its more recent history in marketing and quantitative social science, "influencer" was often neutral or positive—a person with an important role to play, sometimes one they couldn't help playing. In the influencer industry, the term has become loaded. Some influencers, for example, don't appreciate the insinuation that their work is nefarious, intended only to get people to behave in certain ways. Others argue that "influencer" is tied up in outmoded marketing discourses and is unevenly applied to women.[11] Still others believe their work has become more sophisticated than the "influencer" term implies. As South Korean beauty influencer Pony told Glossy:

I do think it's time for a new word. There isn't anything wrong with "influencer," but I see myself as a curator and an educator. I work with brands and use their brand story and products to spread makeup artistry around the globe. We have reached a period where we need another term that can encompass everything. The industry is growing, and influencers are changing. Roles and responsibilities are evolving, and it's time we adapt and not limit ourselves.[12]

In an effort to resolve some of these issues, social media companies, brands, and influencers have increasingly adopted the term "creator." And indeed, media scholars Stuart Cunningham and David Craig have argued convincingly for its use as a term to encapsulate the many forms of social media content producers thriving today, from vloggers and livestreamers to Instagrammers and TikTok stars.[13] While I acknowledge these merits and support workers' moves toward self-definition, I also cannot help but notice a key difference. "Influencer," as it evolved in recent years, requires some proof: a certain number of people have done something based on something you posted. Not everyone influences on these terms—but we can all "create." In this way, a shift in language appears quite advantageous for social media companies. If more and more people can view themselves through the influencer paradigm—as "creators" with boundless potential—that could attract more users to social media, more time spent on apps creating content, and more people experiencing the world through the constraints of industrialized authenticity.

Brands and Marketers Must Prioritize Values-Driven Creativity over Ambivalent Efficiency

Brands and marketing agencies, while different in many respects, both act within the influencer industry to contract and promote influencers' work. For years now, brands and marketers have faced a glut of aspiring influencers and content and thus implemented various tools and practices for identifying with whom to work, under what terms, and how to do it all efficiently. Many of their moves toward maximizing efficiency were discussed in chapter 3. Continued internal and external pressures led to a situation where they sense a need to prioritize performance over values. Over time, these changes had a variety of impacts. To understand some of them, I return to where this research began: the fashion industry.

Despite its increasingly fuzzy boundaries, fashion has consistently been one of the more visible and lucrative verticals in the influencer industry.[14] As such, some of the influencer industry's significant impacts on creative industries—which include the speeding up of production and marketing cycles, products increasingly made for short-term use, and minimized creative risk-taking related to the need to "do well" on social media—were acutely observable within this space before they ballooned out to encompass much of our cultural landscape. In 2015, the now-late Lanvin designer Alber Elbaz reflected:

> We designers started as couturiers with dreams, with intuitions and with feelings. We started with, "What do women want? What do women need? What can I do for women to make their lives better and easier? How can I make a woman more beautiful?" That is what we used to do. Then we became creative directors, so we have to create, but mostly direct. And now we have to become image-makers, making sure it looks good in the pictures. The screen has to scream, baby—that's the rule. And loudness is the new thing. Loudness is the new cool, and not only in fashion.[15]

That same year, Li Edelkoort, often referred to as one of the most globally impactful trend forecasters, proclaimed that "the perversion of marketing is killing" fashion. "Marketing has taken over power within the major companies and is manipulating creation, production, presentation and sales," she wrote in a widely circulated manifesto.[16]

The pressure to keep up with trends that are safe bets for gaining likes, comments, and other metrics of influence has led some people to buy clothes "just for the 'gram" and then return them. A U.K. study, for example, found that nearly one in ten British shoppers engage in this behavior.[17] Further, some online-only fast-fashion companies have popped up to explicitly leverage the "churn and burn" ethos of influencer-driven social media commerce. The Los Angeles-based company Fashion Nova, for example, offers around a thousand new styles each week, each "meant to be worn once, maybe twice, photographed, and discarded."[18] This is in addition to older, global fast fashion companies such as Zara and H&M, whose two-week production time has enabled them to continually ship new items in response to trends, many of which are scouted via social media.[19]

It was in this vein that some influencers I interviewed brought up one of the unseen and unglamorous burdens of their jobs: dealing with the high volume of packages they regularly receive from brands. Processing the influx of products they get in the mail on a daily basis takes "so much of my time, and I work super hard," Skylar told me. This issue illustrates the broader environmental impacts of a speeded-up consumer culture, of which the influencer industry is only one—though not insignificant—mechanism. In considering the technology influencers who receive countless plastic-constructed, lithium battery-powered items, the intricately packaged cosmetics sent to beauty influencers, the toys sent to "kidfluencers," and the immense volume of clothing implicated in all this—products that are typically manufactured by underpaid workers in developing countries—one can only imagine the human and environmental costs related to this system (and one must, as there is no comprehensive data available on the subject). While individual influencers, in interviews as well as social media posts, sometimes report their efforts to donate or sell the products they do not use, as of yet there is no real means of tracking the influencer industry's material impacts.

At the same time, the case of fashion offers illustrative examples of the influencer industry's more positive impacts. While the common "democratization" narrative that has surrounded social media since its inception—implying that this technology enables anyone to have a voice in formerly inaccessible halls of power—is severely limited and problematic, there is some evidence that the rise of bloggers, influencers, and other digital content creators changed the fashion industry's approach to representation and helped empower some people looking to develop and share their points of view. As *Bitch* magazine pointed out:

> For a generation of predominantly young women and nonbinary people of color, fashion and beauty blogging mainstreamed the

internet in crucial ways. Young users learned—sometimes without even realizing it—the basics of both coding and writing; equally important, they developed an aesthetic and language outside of fashion's normative standard-bearing magazines and retailers, one that centered more expansive views of beauty and style.[20]

Indeed, many people I interviewed expressed pride in the way they learned new skills and helped build an industry that would allow them to not only get closer to doing the type of work they felt was fulfilling, but also express themselves creatively and connect with like-minded people who may not have otherwise "made it" in the traditional glamour industries.

A robust central professional organization could help resolve the disconnect between brands' desires for creative expression and efficient marketing. Much like how the Council of Fashion Designers of America works to support rising creatives, a strong professional influencer organization can offer support for early career creatives and set best practices for marketing firms and brands, including resources for continued internal assessments and policy changes to identify points of inequity and address them. Embracing influencers as valued professional collaborators, contracted under equitable terms, would not only help correct severe power imbalances but should enable and inspire brands to take bigger creative risks in product development and in marketing. Recognizing that "more" and "faster" as guiding principles often result in diminished quality, brands should embody their expertise in product design and do better, not simply more. The industry must find a way to bolster its benefits—entrepreneurialism, connection, network-building, creative expression, and pushing public conversations about important issues—and reduce the harms.

Users Lack Much-Needed Options and Transparency

While the focus of this book has been the professional participants in the influencer industry, the implications of their work are broad reaching. Social media upended the era of mass media, in many ways with good reason. But we would be foolish to continue running headlong into the era of individuals-as-media businesses without recognizing that despite their messaging to the contrary, influencers, like their predecessors, are beholden to financial, cultural, and personal pressures that audiences do not see. The "unseen mechanisms" that Edward Bernays described in the early twentieth century still exist. Our folly is believing in this era of pervasive, industrialized "authenticity" that we as users can see them all. Even those of us who spend years studying media industries know the limits of our expertise. It takes time to put puzzle pieces together. It is deeply unreasonable to expect users to recognize the various incentives in place for their information providers to do the things they do, every day, with every piece of content.

This can be remedied. A more adequately resourced Federal Trade Commission could shore up its rules and oversight, with more consistent consequences for influencers and brands who obfuscate their relationships, so that consumers can clearly identify paid content. This cannot be as simple as an #ad hashtag, though "clear and conspicuous" disclosure on sponsored content remains necessary. Influencers sell themselves as experts, as "authentic" personalities with an opinion. Increasingly, influencers have identified themselves as "community leaders," indicating more consistent engagement with a particular point of view and the people who subscribe to it. Disclosure in an influencer's bio of the nature of the work they do would help users understand that just because one post is not sponsored does not mean the influencer is "just a regular person." They still must maintain "brand safety" and consistency to continue their work. Until there is widespread understanding of this new field of professional cultural production, we have to flag it.

Further, we must remember how the turn to influencers for information is tied to continued crises in journalism. As this book goes to print, TikTok and Substack are each blossoming in their own ways. Substack, in particular, has attracted a number of established and aspiring writers to its subscription newsletter model. And while these platforms might offer opportunities for new voices to be heard, they also allow content creators to trade on their *performances* of skill and authenticity rather than adherence to professional or public interest values, which invites an array of problems.[21] Journalists and news organizations must work to regain public trust and fix their own broken incentive system. This is a vital piece in creating and maintaining a healthy digital information environment and democracy.[22]

The broader, and trickier, shift comes through mindsets of users. It is profoundly unfair to expect individual users of exploitative platforms to simply stop using them, especially when their livelihoods and/or relationships are tied to these platforms. The issues I detail in this book are structural. But while and until the bodies tasked with solving them do something, I do believe that individuals can take steps, as appropriate for their personal situations, to protect themselves, including their money, time, and mental health. Here I am inspired by the work of artist and author Jenny Odell, who has argued for a form of realistic resistance by increasing our awareness of where we direct our attention, why, and to what ends.[23] Following Odell, my hope is for people to cultivate, as best they can, a mindset of distance and utility—to make our use of social media intentional, however serious or silly the intention may be.

Studying television in the early 2000s, media scholar Mark Andrejevic famously outlined "the work of being watched,"[24] or the way media corporations extract value from consumers by selling their attention.[25] Similar to my advocating for influencers to organize, I believe even nonprofessional social media users should come to recognize the work they do to generate profit for big tech—and vote, advocate for themselves, and use social media with that in mind.

Authenticity Is an Industrial Construction

Through the voices of the influencer industry's participants, this book explores how in the contemporary media environment, social influence is not just a process, but a commodity. It is something assessed and assigned material value by people and technologies. Authenticity is the means by which stakeholders value influence: it is an industrial construction leveraged for the benefit or detriment of different groups at different times. Influencers, brands, marketers, social media companies, and others cultivate authenticity through a range of tactics and continually assess others' authenticity as a means of judging whether they are, or could be, influential. Their rubrics are informed by the complex and constantly renegotiated industrial and sociopolitical dynamics in which they exist, as well as their own prejudices and biases. In this way, influencers' production of authenticity is reminiscent of sociologist Ashley Mears's work on how the modeling industry assigns value to beauty, wherein she observed, "This special quality exists in the social positions and relationships among the producers themselves. It resides in the world of cultural production, composed of vibrant exchanges and ongoing negotiations in the editorial and commercial circuits of the market."[26]

Scholarly conversations around authenticity have evolved such that there exists some agreement that it is a social construct that individuals, groups, organizations, or governments can use for strategic purposes.[27] As author Andrew Potter wrote, "Authenticity is a way of talking about things in the world, a way of making judgments, staking claims, and expressing preferences."[28] There is not, nor has there ever been, one "true" meaning or embodiment of authenticity, as its existence is always dependent on the ideas of the people invested in it at any given time or place.

With this book, I highlight the industrial nature of its production in the contemporary moment. What began as a belief, perhaps naive in retrospect, about the "realness" of early bloggers and digital content creators has, through the influencer industry's development, been transmuted into a particular aesthetic, textual vocabulary, and technological infrastructure leveraged by a wide range of people and groups for financial and ideological gain. Authenticity among influencers is not necessarily spontaneous, if it ever was; it is inextricable from the commercialism that now ensconces digital interactions. As I finished research for this book, the trend away from carefully curated social media feeds and toward unedited, unpolished sharing continued to gain steam. This trend is a direct response to the previously established forms and norms of influencers' self-presentations—yet it was instantly heralded as a new form of authenticity that could signal a change in the prevailing aesthetics of digital influence.[29] In other words, shifts in authenticity in the social media context continue in this same system of cultivation and commodification—just with a different look.

Authenticity means different things to different people. Is it being open about all of your likes and dislikes or being "positive"? Is it about sharing a lifestyle rather than specializing in one content genre? Is it about responding back to your followers and cultivating personal relationships? Is it best indicated by the appearance of rejecting financial gain, or is it better served by radical transparency about sponsorship and pay? Is it most clearly expressed via Instagram Stories, TikTok, or a carefully produced Substack post? Is it about holding yourself publicly accountable for the times in which your content or your behavior has strayed from your values? Is it about maintaining unwavering allegiance to a particular perspective, however pro- or antisocial the details might be? All these criteria are relevant for different people and at different times. As such, what becomes significant is the ecosystem that renders this definitional slipperiness possible.

Because the meaning of authenticity here is always changing with industrial circumstances, its meaning and value lie in how well people perform it within these bounds. This industrial version is still just one out of countless iterations of authenticity in the world, but it has immense technological and economic power behind it. Anyone who reads, watches, or listens to media content today must contend with an industrial version of authenticity.

Rethinking the Damage

One of the more unfortunate externalities of our redefinition of influence as monetizable social power is that the idea of influence has become cynical, when it can be a force for good. As Laurence Scott wrote in the *New Yorker*:

> The relentless commercialization of influence is also a corruption of the more uplifting processes through which we can affect and inspire one another. Our ongoing challenge, then, will be to negotiate the inherent inauthenticity and cynicism of an influence economy while preserving our ability to be occupied, and perhaps changed for the better, by the alien ideas of other people.[30]

To be sure, while there is much to critique about the influencer industry today, we can also remember that it was largely borne of good intentions—and to turn back the clock, if it were even possible, to a time when corporate mass media companies held all the power would be a calamity. The development of the industry enabled people to earn income, explore interests and facets of their identities that they might not have otherwise been able to, learn skills in creative production, and push for more diverse representation across industries. But to simply allow the industry to be led forward by "whatever resonates" in an opaque technical system run by profit-driven companies whose users have little to no recourse has proven capacity for other disastrous results.

The development of the influencer industry was premised on individuals' desires for security and autonomy—with their finances, creativity, and time—that was felt pointedly in the face of professional destabilization and heightened economic insecurity in the 2000s. In redefining social influence as a digital commodity, *theoretically* available to anyone to cultivate and sell,[31] the industry's various participants created and enacted a system of arbitrary value that privileged social media visibility, minimized creative risk-taking, and required that participants entwine their online self-representations with commercialism—all while using the performance of authenticity as a measuring stick. This obsession with authenticity and the drive toward information sources who are perceived as "real" is not new, but it has become more pointed and pervasive in the last decade on account of various technological, economic, and cultural forces. Its relentlessness can at times feel all-consuming, thanks to the social and mobile media technologies that continually connect us to it.

As the top-down structure that characterized the mass media era of the twentieth century became atomized in the twenty-first, personal stories and interactions became vehicles for commercial messages. Digital self-expression, and the degree to which it is considered "real," became tied to the shifting needs of profit-motivated companies. Of course, people are not powerless, but we do exist in societies whose histories, policies, infrastructures, and institutions shape our existence.

Our current regulatory, technological, and cultural environment incentivizes people to participate in the influencer system, constructing brands, cultivating audiences, and chasing visibility—or following others who do it—in patterned ways that are shaping history as we live through it. Despite popular narratives about the influencer industry, most people involved are not participating in it because they are narcissistic children of the social media age. They do it because it seems like a solid opportunity for professional satisfaction in a world that often feels unhinged.

The development of the influencer industry is rooted in a long history of cultural, technological, economic, social, and scholarly evolution, but it was by no means predestined. In practical matters, the story of the industry's growth is ultimately about the enterprising things people do to get by in the face of social rupture and policy failures. The economic and industrial crises outlaid in chapter 1 as part of the perfect storm of events that triggered the industry's blossoming, as well as *who* flocked to the industry and why, are all intimately bound up with policy of the time, as are the ways in which the industry's logics and tools expanded and threatened democratic processes and our very experiences of selfhood when faced with more fundamental social crises in the 2020s. In exploring the development and impacts of the influencer industry, I aim to amplify the voices of the people involved as well as call scholarly and regulatory attention to listen and see what media and technology industries do in moments of social tumult—and the means by which they are able to do it.

Appendix

Background to This Study

The research that grew into this book began in 2014 as a study focused on the changing, mediated dynamics of influence and content creation within the fashion industry. Given my background, and the fact that fashion bloggers were some of the earliest and most visible harbingers of the changes to cultural production that social media would bring, this seemed a logical choice. Yet as the research progressed, it became impossible to maintain this scope. The boundaries between the fashion industry and others blurred as influencers and brands embraced "lifestyle" messaging and aesthetics, with clothing companies sponsoring vacations, influencers sharing advice and personal experiences unrelated to their previously defined area of expertise, marketers embracing the consequently expanded opportunities for brokering sponsorships, and social media companies developing tools and rules to both advance and encumber influencers' work. Indeed, within a year it had become clear to me that it was the burgeoning *influencer industry* that was driving the digital reconfigurations of cultural power that I was interested in examining, and that other industries—not limited to fashion—were being swept along, even as they participated in its development.

Over the next seven years of research, I tracked this phenomenon. I followed the data, starting with bloggers prior to the creation of the recognizable influencer industry. As blogs declined, many bloggers transitioned to Instagram, and thus I followed them there. At time of writing, many of these people are now moving or expanding to TikTok and/or Substack. Tracking bloggers-to-Instagrammers-and-beyond provided a mountain of data. Importantly, it led me early on to the marketing firms, casting agencies, and various other middlemen that are included in the book and that together create the influencer industry. Of course, as with any research project, my data is a portion meant to help illustrate a bigger whole. You may have noticed that other significant platforms of the era such as YouTube and Snapchat were not specifically explored in this book. There is a robust and continually growing literature that explores various cultural and industrial dynamics of platform-specific content creation,[1] and while I did not study YouTube or Snapchat in depth, it is my hope that the dynamics uncovered here apply to them and beyond.

It is important to note again that this book is a U.S.-based study, and as such it is one piece of a global story. Influencer industries exist around the world in forms similar and different to what I have described here, using many of the same social media platforms, including Facebook, Instagram, YouTube, and TikTok. Other platforms, like WeChat in China, have an overwhelming presence in other countries but are not central to the U.S. influencer landscape. Further, third-party intermediaries vary greatly, with some spanning the globe and others focused on particular countries or regions. The stakes by which influencers do their work can shift significantly based on national and local political, regulatory, and infrastructural contexts,[2] and thus the opportunities and constraints experienced by the U.S.-based workers in this research should not be assumed to be globally generalizable.

Method

This book is a structural media industry critique informed by sociological and critical media theories and methods, including the production of culture perspective[3] and critical media industry studies.[4] There are differences and points of debate between these approaches—primarily that the "production of culture" perspective advanced by sociologists does not adequately account for the idiosyncrasies that differentiate cultural industries from other organizations—and in many ways the critical media industries approach was a response and corrective to the production of culture approach. But they are joined by a concern with "how the symbolic elements of culture are shaped by the systems within which they are created, distributed, evaluated, taught, and preserved"[5] and emphasize taking a "helicopter view" of cultural production processes.[6] A "helicopter" view draws on fieldwork and other qualitative analyses, aiming to account for "interactions among cultural and economic forces"[7] and the "complexity and contradiction of power relations."[8] Important, too, is rooting current relationships between culture, society, and commerce in historical context.[9]

Central to this method is drawing on diverse data sources to gain as full a picture as possible of the site of study. As such, I conducted in-depth interviews with influencers, marketers, retail brand executives, and others engaged in influencer marketing; participant observation at industry events; and analyses of industry press and close readings of Instagram. Each of these has strengths and limitations.

In-Depth Interviews

Between 2015 and 2021, I interviewed forty-three professionals working in the influencer industry, including influencers whose followings ranged from 2,500 to more than one million; marketing agency founders, executives, and analysts; people who work for various brands' social media and influencer teams; talent managers; trend forecasters; and others. Some of these people I followed up with over years, conducting multiple interviews to learn how their businesses and lives were changing.

I recruited participants by identifying relevant professionals through readings of industry press, web searches, LinkedIn, and Instagram, through meeting people at industry events, and through snowball sampling. Participants who were not recruited by snowball sampling were cold-contacted via email, in which I introduced myself as a researcher, explained the contours of the project, and asked for a phone call or in-person meeting. Interviews were conducted either in person or, most often, via phone; they varied in length from roughly twenty to ninety minutes. Interviews were recorded with participants' consent and later transcribed by a professional transcription service or me. Participants were given the option to maintain anonymity or grant permission for me to use their real names and/or affiliations in subsequent writing. As such, the book contains a mix of real names and pseudonyms, which are noted by an asterisk on first mention. Starting in 2019, research funds provided by the Annenberg School for Communication allowed me to begin offering interviewees a $20 honorarium per interview.

The different ways in which participants responded to the option to disclose their identities reveals power dynamics and tensions inherent to the influencer industry. Nearly all brand executives and related professionals (such as the trend forecaster who participated) opted for anonymity, noting concerns about their employers disapproving of them speaking about their work and their potential to reveal "hard truths" about the business that might reflect poorly upon themselves or their companies. Most marketers and several influencers elected to reveal their identities, typically mentioning that they would be "happy to get [their] name out there," as one interviewee said. Meanwhile, some influencers (particularly those I interviewed earlier on) were either concerned about publicly critiquing the industry or actively wanted to distance themselves from it, and thus opted for pseudonyms.

Participant Observation

I conducted participant observation and recruited research participants at both in-person and virtual events. These included New York Fashion Week S/S 2015, Philly Tech Week 2015, FashionistaCon 2016, and Social Media Week 2018. At many of these events I sat quietly in observation, but whenever I did participate in discussion or introduce myself to someone, I identified myself as a researcher studying the influencer space.

Readings of Industry Press and Instagram

Using a Google News search for "influencers," I collected more than three thousand press articles on the subject that range in date from January 2006 to December 2020. This trove provided a historical trajectory of the influencer space as it grew and developed, offered relevant statistics, and showed how professionals engaged in the influencer industry publicly discussed its tensions and goals. I also consulted relevant industry reports, such as those from eMarketer, and reports on internet and social media use from sources such as Pew Research, to bolster my understanding of the space. I coded articles manually and using Dedoose, following an inductive, grounded theory approach.[10]

Through regular use of Instagram, I discovered and used new influencer-focused technologies as they were released. For example, my early knowledge of LikeToKnowIt, a plug-in that makes Instagram shoppable and pays influencers a commission of sales made through their content, came from using Instagram. However, my experience as a user of these platforms is shaped and limited by the platforms' personal data collection and algorithms. In other words, I am almost certainly presented more frequently with content from white, feminine women and mothers because I am one. While my own use of social media was not a primary data source, it did clue me in to particular trends to explore, and likely obfuscated others.

The goal with this multipronged approach to data collection was to capture the influencer industry's various levels of activity and articulation as best as possible. Interviews with marketers and retail brands provided insight about the beliefs and practices (for example, about how to measure or select influencers) that guided the economic and technological development of the industry. Interviews with influencers illuminated how those standards set by marketers, retailers, and social media companies were operationalized and experienced. Influencers also explained how they advanced their own agendas by working with and against prevailing norms, how they negotiated their complex public-private identities, and their hopes and goals for the future of digital content creation. All of the interviews helped provide necessary historical context for the trajectory of the industry, and they illuminated how different groups' behavior and strategic decisions were often informed by their perceptions—real and imagined—of what other stakeholders were doing, what the public wanted, and what the world needed.

Reading industry press and attending industry events provided access to knowledge about how the industry talks about and promotes itself, as well as its goals for the future and what it sees as potential hiccups or roadblocks. This, along with my own use (or "reading") of Instagram proved to be deeply informative for identifying significant trends or changes in the industry, which informed both my interview process and my charting of the industry's history.

Notes

Introduction

1. Pooley (2010).
2. Gevinson (2019).
3. See, for example, Frier (2020) and Turow (2017).
4. Enli (2014).
5. See Gillespie (2010).
6. Throughout, their work also exhibits themes linked to classical thinking about industrialization and capitalism (e.g., Marx 2012; Weber 1946), particularly rationalization, dehumanization, automation, and pivots for continued financial growth and cultural relevancy. These themes intertwine and take turns being at the fore throughout the book.

Chapter 1. Groundwork

1. Peiss (Fall 1998).
2. Scott (2019).
3. Weber (1946) focused on the political and economic circumstances out of which influential leaders arise, arguing that "in times of psychic, physical, economic, ethical, religious, [or] political distress" leaders who seem to have exceptional qualities tend to become influential (245). Yet what enables these leaders to thrive is their perceived *authenticity*. According to Weber, charismatic leaders "always reject as undignified any pecuniary gain that is methodical and rational," and they prove themselves not by expertise or training but by their ability to follow through on claims they make about themselves (247). Crucial, too, is an interpersonal relationship between the leader and followers, who tend to create communities with each other around the leader and help to encourage continual reassertions of authenticity.
4. Ewen (1976), 58.
5. Ewen, 43.
6. Ewen, 19.
7. Barton (1925), 151.
8. Barton, 151.
9. Creel (1920), 3–4
10. Creel, 3–4.
11. E.g., Lasswell (1927).
12. Bernays (1928), 9.

13. Maio & Haddock (2010), 3.

14. See, for example, Hovland, Janis & Kelley (1953) and other work of the Yale School.

15. In recent years, reasonable questions have been raised about whether reports of panic in response to this broadcast were overblown. At the time, however, it was broadly accepted that there had been a panic, and the broadcast and its listeners were studied accordingly. For more, see Memmott (2013).

16. See Cantril (1940) and Lazarsfeld, Berelson, Gaudet (1948).

17. Katz (1957), 61.

18. Katz (1957), 62.

19. Katz (1957), 61.

20. Granovetter (1973) was a breakthrough and now widely cited article that pushed the field in this methodological direction.

21. Gitlin (1978).

22. Douglas (2006).

23. Douglas (2006), 42.

24. E.g., Jensen (2009) and Bennett & Manheim (2006).

25. Packard (1957), 4.

26. Taking a slightly more critical view than Berger (2013), Cialdini (2001) also included suggestions for how people can recognize and resist these tactics.

27. Berger (2013).

28. Berger (2013), 18.

29. Keller & Berry (2003), 2.

30. Bernays (1945), 158.

31. Schaefer (2012), xvii.

32. Boorstin (1962) and Currid-Halkett (2010).

33. Turner (2015).

34. Banet-Weiser (2012); Hearn (2010); Marwick (2013a); and Tan (2017).

35. Graeme Turner (2010) referred to this as the media's "demotic turn."

36. Lowenthal (2017 ed.), 219.

37. Goldhaber (1997a).

38. Goldhaber (1997a), 3.

39. Senft (2008).

40. Examples are too many to name, but some books with which to begin: Marwick (2013a), Turner (2014), and Duffy (2017).

41. Marwick & boyd (2010); Senft (2013); Schaefer (2012); and Marwick (2013a).

42. Hearn (2010), 435.

43. Goldhaber (1997b).

44. Scott & Jones (2004).

45. Gard (2004) and Nielsen (2012).

46. Pew Research Center (2018).

47. Baym & boyd (2012).

48. Peters (1997) and Neff (2012).

49. Pink (2001).

50. Hook (2015).

51. Pew Research Center (2014) and Cillizza (2015).

52. Bishop (2009).

53. Shambaugh, Nunn & Bauer (2018).

54. Gill (2010); see also Ticona & Mateescu (2018).

55. Peters (1997).

56. Pope (2018).

57. Hesmondhalgh (2012) and Petre (2015).

58. eMarketer (2016).

59. Turow (2017).

60. Damico (2017).

61. Nichols (2010).

62. The In Cloud (2014).

63. E.g., Serazio (2013).

64. Duffy & Hund (2015).

65. Drolet (2016).

66. E.g., Terranova (2000) and Andrejevic (2002).

67. E.g., Luvaas (2016) and Duffy (2017).

68. E.g., Gill (2010) and Neff (2012).

69. Neff (2012).

70. Duffy (2017).

71. Kuehn & Corrigan (2013).

72. Banet-Weiser (2012); Abidin (2016).

73. Luvaas (2013), 73.

74. Hennessy (2018).

75. Stamarski & Son Hing (2015).

76. Holland (2015).

77. Schulte et al. (2017) and Stone (2007).

78. In this way, the harassment and criticism that many content creators face can also be understood as resentment over some women's abilities to find ways to achieve business success within the bounds of patriarchal restrictions, a phenomenon outlined by Peiss (1998).

79. Duffy & Hund (2015), 9

80. Duffy (2017), 104.

81. Kanai (2018).

82. Brooke Erin Duffy untangles the complicated dynamics of femininity, consumerism, and the promises of technology in her 2017 book, *(Not) Getting Paid to Do What You Love.*

83. Duffy & Hund (2019).

84. Lingel (2017), 24.

85. Lingel (2017), 25.

86. Banet-Weiser (2012), 5.

87. Lingel (2017), 26.

88. Turner (2019).

89. E.g., Petre (2015) and Marwick (2015).

Chapter 2. Setting the Terms for a Transactional Industry

1. Corcoran (2006).
2. Corcoran (2006).
3. Turow (1997).
4. Mediakix (2017).
5. Burns (2014).
6. Blankenheim (2001).
7. Serazio (2013), 16.
8. Peters (1997) and Hearn (2008).
9. Bogost (2018).
10. Talevera (2015)
11. Purinton (2017).
12. Banet-Weiser (2012), 8.
13. Banet-Weiser (2012).
14. Arriagada (2018), 2.
15. Duffy (2017).
16. Clark (2014).
17. Duffy & Wissinger (2018).
18. Duffy & Hund (September 25, 2015).
19. For an overview, see McGuigan & Manzerolle (2014).
20. Ang (1991).
21. Ang (1991), 2.
22. Napoli (2011), 3.
23. Napoli (2011) and Kerani (2013).
24. Napoli (2011).
25. Serazio (2013), 121.
26. Stevenson (2012).
27. Stevenson (2012).
28. Schaefer (2012).
29. Stevenson (2012).
30. Baym (2013).
31. McRae, 2017; addressed further in chapter 4.
32. E.g., Zubernis & Larsen (2011); Maris, 2016.
33. Baym (2013), 8.
34. Duffy (2017).
35. In this way, these firms joined the leading social networking sites of the early 2000s in using claims of authenticity to improve their market position. See Salisbury & Pooley (2017).
36. Ronan (2015).
37. Gaden & Dumitrica (2015), 2.
38. Gaden & Dumitrica (2015), 2.
39. Duffy & Hund (2019).
40. Duffy (2017), 135.
41. Van Dijck (2013).

Chapter 3. Making Influence Efficient

1. Evans (2012).

2. Morrison (2015).

3. Brouwer (2015).

4. Rainey (2015).

5. Talavera (2015).

6. According to the Pew Research Center, in 2011, 35 percent of the U.S. population owned a smartphone; in 2017, 77 percent did—making them "one of the most quickly adopted consumer technologies in recent history" (Perrin, 2017).

7. Pavlika (2015a).

8. Segran (2015).

9. Segran (2015).

10. Kurutz (2011).

11. Lo (2011).

12. Duffy (2017).

13. Duffy & Hund (2015).

14. Leiber (2014).

15. Chen (2016).

16. Pavlika (2015).

17. Maheshwari (2018); addressed further in chapter 4.

18. Bishop (2019), 10.

19. E.g., Duffy (2017) and Marwick (2013b).

20. Trapp (2015).

21. Johnson (2015).

22. E.g., Pham (2013) and Duffy & Hund (2015).

23. Bishop (2021).

24. Duffy & Hund (2019).

25. Lewis (2008), 2.

26. Lewis (2008), 3.

27. Levine (2015).

28. Mari (2014).

29. Mari (2014).

30. See LTK in bibliography.

31. Lorenz (2018).

32. Williams (2018).

33. Johnson (2015).

34. Tietjen (2018).

35. Robles (2015).

36. Wylie (2018).

37. Hund & McGuigan (2019), 20.

38. Lam (2018).

39. Lam (2018).

40. Camintini (2017).

41. Skinner (2018) and McNeal (2020).
42. Robles (2015).
43. Lowrey (2017) and DePillis (2017).
44. Nathanson (2014).
45. E.g., Schonfeld (2010).
46. Leiber (2014).
47. Leiber (2014).
48. Carlson (2015).
49. Gibbs et al. (2015), 257.
50. Shunatona (2015).
51. Alteir (2015).
52. Smith (2018).
53. Hubbard (2016).
54. Tolentino (2019).
55. Coscarelli (2015).
56. Stephens (2017).
57. Avins (2015).
58. Rosman (2014).
59. Rosman (2014).
60. Rosman (2014).
61. Refinery29, "29Rooms."
62. Refinery29, "29Rooms."
63. Weiner (2017).
64. Maheshwari (2018).
65. Gesenhues (2013).
66. Tate (2013).
67. Florendo (2015).
68. Hunt (2015) and O'Neill (2015).
69. O'Neill (2015).
70. Saul (2015).
71. Drolet (2016).
72. Marwick (2013a), 5.

Chapter 4. Revealing and Repositioning the Machinations of Influence

1. The Shorty Awards.
2. Epstein (2018).
3. Wanshel (2018).
4. Epstein (2018).
5. Rife (2018).
6. Smith & Anderson (2018).
7. Perrin (2017).

8. Lorenz (2018).

9. Lowrey (2017).

10. PR Newswire (2016).

11. Moss (2017).

12. Bloom (2019).

13. Contestabile (2018) and InfluencerDB (2018).

14. Pathak (2018).

15. Beck (2015).

16. Federal Trade Commission, "Lord and Taylor Settles FTC Charges."

17. Griner (2015).

18. Federal Trade Commission, "Lord and Taylor Settles FTC Charges."

19. Tadena (2016).

20. Amed (2018).

21. O'Reilly & Snyder (2018).

22. Fair (2017).

23. Daniels (2016).

24. Fyre Festival (2017).

25. Furst & Nason (2019).

26. Karp (2017).

27. Burrough (2017); Ohlheiser (2017); and Baggs (2019).

28. Smith (2019).

29. Smith (2019).

30. Bryant (2017).

31. Gaca (2017).

32. Flanagan (2018).

33. Marine (2019).

34. Furst & Nason, 2019

35. Confessore et al. (2018).

36. E.g., Leiber (2014).

37. Confessore et al. (2018).

38. Confessore et al. (2018).

39. Confessore et al. (2018).

40. Confessore et al. (2018).

41. Geller (2018).

42. Brooke (2018).

43. Geller (2018).

44. Robles (2018).

45. Vranica (2018).

46. Brooke (2018).

47. Sipka (2017).

48. Banks (2015).

49. Banks (2015).

50. Starling AI.

51. McCall (2016).
52. McCall (2016).
53. Webb (2019).
54. Dewey (2016).
55. Jones (2018).
56. Sullivan (2018).
57. Mau (2018).
58. Mau (2018).
59. Mau (2018).
60. Goldberg (2017).
61. Gahan (2017).
62. Gahan (2017).
63. Maheshwari (2019).
64. Facebook, "Branded Content Policies."
65. "Instagram for Business."
66. "Instagram for Business."
67. Agrawal (2016).
68. Angulo (2016).
69. McRae (2017), 14.
70. Duffy, Miltner & Wahlstedt (2020).
71. McRae (2017).
72. E.g., Silman (2018); Noor (2018); and Goodwin (2017).
73. See O'Meara (2019) for a nuanced discussion of engagement pods as worker resistance.
74. Petre, Duffy & Hund (2019).
75. Hund & McGuigan (2019) and McGuigan (2018).
76. McGuigan (2018).

Chapter 5. The Industry Becomes Boundaryless

1. Lush (2020).
2. Williamson (2020) and Statista (2022).
3. Molla (2021).
4. McNeal (2021).
5. North (2020).
6. McNeal (2021).
7. McNeal (2020).
8. Gerbner & Gross (1976).
9. The history and current debates about the television industry's development and regulation are rich, varied, and extensive. Some suggestions: *Stay Tuned* by Christopher Sterling and John Michael Kittross; *Selling the Air* by Thomas Streeter; *The Television Will Be Revolutionized* by Amanda Lotz; *This Program Is Brought to You By . . .* by Joshua Braun.
10. See Kanai (2018) for further analysis of relatability and privilege in digital self-branding.
11. New York City Health Department.

12. Griffith (2020) and Lorenz (2020).
13. Griffith (2020).
14. Carman (2020a).
15. @InfluencerPayGap (2021b).
16. Tashjian (2020).
17. Zanger (2019).
18. Addison (2019).
19. Pomponi (2020).
20. IZEA (2021).
21. Frier (2021).
22. Sobande (2021).
23. Parham (2020).
24. Peoples Wagner (2021).
25. McNeal (2020).
26. McNeal (2020).
27. Edelman (2018).
28. Im (2019).
29. WGSN (2021).
30. Droesch (2019).
31. Blum (2019).
32. Brooke (2019).
33. Horkheimer & Adorno (1944).
34. For a helpful discussion, see Ross (2014).
35. Flora (2020).
36. Reilly (2020).
37. Breland (2020).
38. Chen (2019).
39. Chen (2019).
40. Bixby (2020).
41. Bixby (2020).
42. Culliford (2020).
43. Crump (2019).
44. Monllos (2020).
45. Glazer & Wells (2019).
46. Goodwin, Joseff & Woolley (2020).
47. Sherman (2020).
48. @InfluencerPayGap (2021a).
49. Waters (2020).
50. Waters (2020).
51. Jhaveri (2020).
52. Tietjen (2020a) and Tietjen (2020b).
53. Carman, (2020b).
54. Farra (2020).

55. Wellman, Stoldt, Tully & Ekdale (2020) and Hund & McGuigan (2019).

56. Carah & Angus (2018) and Stoldt, Wellman, Ekdale & Tully (2019).

57. Bishop (2021) and Duffy (2017).

58. Duffy (2015) and Duffy (2017).

59. Bishop (2019) and Petre, Duffy & Hund (2019).

60. Gritters (2019).

61. Petre, Duffy & Hund (2019).

62. Bishop (2019).

63. Duffy & Hund (2019).

64. Stoldt, Wellman, Ekdale & Tully (2019) and Hund & McGuigan (2019).

65. Locke (2019).

66. Lorenz (2021).

67. Influencer Marketing Hub (2021).

68. Germain (2021).

Chapter 6. The Cost of Being Real

1. Indeed, University of Pennsylvania professor Damon Centola has argued that the White House's influencer-led vaccination campaign was not well positioned to deliver results (Centola, 2021).

2. Hercher (2015).

3. Sherman (2019).

4. Hill (2019).

5. Zuboff (2021).

6. Massachi (2021).

7. Brenan (2021).

8. Creators (2021).

9. Turner (2019).

10. Scott (2019).

11. Ellis (2019).

12. Sandler (2020).

13. Cunningham & Craig (2021).

14. HYPR (2016) and Parisi (2019).

15. Chan (2015).

16. Cordero (2016).

17. Kozslowska (2018).

18. Davis (2018).

19. Howland (2017).

20. Afful (2019).

21. See Napoli (2019) for a thorough analysis and recommendations about the role of public interest values in regulating social media.

22. There is a rich literature on the relationship between democracy and journalism. For a recent analysis, see Pickard (2020).

23. Odell (2019).

24. Andrejevic (2002).

25. Andrejevic draws on on a tradition of Marxist scholarship recognizing the value extracted from audiences when commercial media companies sell their attention to advertisers. See, most notably, Dallas Smythe's 1977 theorization of the "audience commodity."

26. Mears (2011), 250.

27. E.g., Banet-Weiser (2012); Marwick (2013a, 2013b); Gaden & Dumitricia (2015); Duffy (2017); and Lingel (2017).

28. Potter (2010), 13.

29. Lorenz (2019).

30. Scott (2019).

31. As the work of Duffy & Hund (2015), Duffy (2017), Hearn (2018), and others makes clear, the popular idea that "anyone can do it" obscures persistent social inequalities.

Appendix

1. For starters, see the work of Sophie Bishop, Jean Burgess, Stuart Cunningham, David Craig, and Zoe Glatt.

2. See Abidin et al. (2020) for a cross-cultural comparison of popular press attention to influencers during the COVID-19 pandemic.

3. Petersen & Anand (2004).

4. Havens, Lotz & Tinic (2009).

5. Petersen & Anand (2004), 311.

6. Havens et al. (2009).

7. Havens et al. (2009), 237.

8. Havens et al. (2009), 239.

9. Hesmondhalgh (2012).

10. Glaser & Strauss (1999).

References

Abidin, C. "Visibility Labour: Engaging with Influencers' Fashion Brands and #OOTD Adver-torial Campaigns on Instagram." *Media International Australia* 161, no. 1 (November 2016): 86–100. https://doi.org/10.1177/1329878X16665177.

Abidin, C., Jin Lee, Barbetta, T., & Miao, W. S. "Influencers and COVID-19: Reviewing Key Issues in Press Coverage across Australia, China, Japan, and South Korea." *Media International Australia* 178, no. 1 (February 2021): 114–135. https://doi.org/10.1177/1329878X20959838.

Addison, L. "Influencer Marketing Has an Implicit Bias Problem." *Adweek*, October 28, 2019. https://www.adweek.com/brand-marketing/influencer-marketing-has-an-implicit-bias -problem/.

Afful, A. "Fashion Blogging Gave Us a Whole New Industry of Aspiration." *Bitch*, March 5, 2019. https://www.bitchmedia.org/article/from-information-superhighway-to-digital-runway /fashion-blogging-and-the-rise-of-a-new-tech-democracy.

Agrawal, A. J. "Why Influencer Marketing Will Explode in 2017." *Forbes*, December 27, 2016. https://www.forbes.com/sites/ajagrawal/2016/12/27/why-influencer-marketing-will -explode-in-2017/.

Ahmed, I. "Kim Kardashian Means Business." Business of Fashion, April 23, 2018. https://www .businessoffashion.com/articles/people/kim-kardashian-means-business.

Alteir, N. "Hipster Barbie's Maker Reveals Herself, Calls It Quits." *The Oregonian*, November 5, 2015. https://www.oregonlive.com/portland/2015/11/hipster_barbies_maker_reveals.html.

Andrejevic, M. "The Work of Being Watched: Interactive Media and the Exploitation of Self-disclosure." *Critical Studies in Media Communication* 19, no. 2 (2002): 230–48. https://doi.org /10.1080/07393180216561.

Ang, I. *Desperately Seeking the Audience.* London: Routledge, 1991.

Angulo, N. "FameBit, Shopify Deal Catapults Influencers into E-commerce." Marketing Dive, February 18, 2016. https://www.marketingdive.com/news/famebit-shopify-deal-catapults -influencers-into-e-commerce/414111/.

Arriagada, A. "Social Media Influencers and Digital Branding: Unpacking the 'Media Kit' as a Market Device." Paper presented at the 19th Annual Conference of the Association of Inter-net Researchers in Montreal, Canada, October 2018. https://www.academia.edu/37606446 /Social_Media_Influencers_and_Digital_Branding_Unpacking_the_Media_Kit_as_a _Market_Device.

Avins, J. "The Hottest Thing in Fashion: Instagrammable Moments." Quartz, March 13, 2015. https://qz.com/361288/how-fashion-manufactures-instagrammable-moments/.

Baggs, M. "Inside the World's Biggest Festival Flop." BBC, January 18, 2019. https://www.bbc .com/news/newsbeat-46904445.

Bakshy, E., Karrer, B., & Adamic, L. A. "Social Influence and the Diffusion of User-Created Content." Proceedings of the 10th ACM Conference on Electronic Commerce. https://doi .org/10.1145/1566374.1566421.

Banet-Weiser, S. AuthenticTM: The Politics of Ambivalence in a Brand Culture. New York: NYU Press, 2012.

Banks, R. "Influencers Have Become Measurable Media Channels." eMarketer, December 15, 2015. https://www.emarketer.com/Interview/Influencers-Have-Become-Measurable-Media -Channels/6001851.

Barton, B. The Man Nobody Knows: A Discovery of Jesus. Chicago: Bobbs-Merrill, 1925.

Baym, N. K. "Data Not Seen: The Uses and Shortcomings of Social Media Metrics." First Monday 18, no. 10 (October 2013). https://doi.org/10.5210/fm.v18i10.4873.

———. Playing to the Crowd: Musicians, Audiences, and the Intimate Work of Connection. New York: NYU Press, 2018.

Baym, N. K., & boyd, danah. "Socially Mediated Publicness: An Introduction." Journal of Broadcasting & Electronic Media 56, no. 3 (2012): 320–29. https://doi.org/10.1080/08838151.2012.705200.

Beck, M. "FTC Puts Social Media Marketers on Notice with Updated Disclosure Guidelines." Marketing Land, June 12, 2015. https://marketingland.com/ftc-puts-social-media-marketers -on-notice-with-updated-disclosure-guidelines-132017.

Bennett W.L., & Manheim, J.B. "The One-Step Flow of Communication." The ANNALS of the American Academy of Political and Social Science 608, no. 1 (2006): 213–32. https://doi.org /10.1177/0002716206292266.

Berger, J. Contagious: Why Things Catch On. New York: Simon & Schuster, 2013.

Bernays, E. L. Propaganda. New York: Routledge, 1928.

———. Public Relations. Norman, OK: University of Oklahoma Press, 1945.

Bishop, K. "Young Job Hunters Seek Work through Twitter." Financial Times, June 21, 2009. https://www.ft.com/content/6ebbc882-5eab-11de-91ad-00144feabdc0.

Bishop, S. "Managing Visibility on YouTube through Algorithmic Gossip." New Media & Society 21, no. 11–12 (Novemer 2019): 2589–2606. https://doi.org/10.1177/1461444819854731.

———. "Influencer Management Tools: Algorithmic Cultures, Brand Safety, and Bias." Social Media + Society 7, no. 1 (January 2021). https://doi.org/10.1177/20563051211003066.

Bixby, S. "Mike Bloomberg Is Paying Influencers to Make Him Seem Cool." Daily Beast, February 7, 2020. https://www.thedailybeast.com/mike-bloomberg-is-paying-influencers-to -make-him-seem-cool-9.

Blankenhorn, D. "Bigger, Richer Ads Go Online." Advertising Age 72, no. 25: (June 2001). https://www.proquest.com/docview/208349299.

Bogost, I. "Brands Are Not Our Friends." The Atlantic, September 7, 2018. https://www .theatlantic.com/magazine/archive/2018/10/brands-on-social-media/568300/.

Boorstin, D. J. The Image: A Guide to Pseudo-Events in America. New York: Vintage Books, 1962.

Braudy, L. The Frenzy of Renown: Fame and Its History. New York: Vintage Books, 1986.

Bray, S. "The Founders of LIKEtoKNOW.it on the Secret to Instagram Success." Gotham Magazine, October 15, 2018.

Breland, A. "Wellness Influencers Are Spreading QAnon Conspiracies about the Coronavirus." *Mother Jones*, April 15, 2020. https://www.motherjones.com/politics/2020/04/wellness-qanon-coronavirus/.

Brenan, M. "Views of Big Tech Worsen: Public Wants More Regulation." Gallup, February 18, 2021. https://news.gallup.com/poll/329666/views-big-tech-worsen-public-wants-regulation.aspx.

Brooke, E. "Unilever Banned Influencers with Fake Followers. Is a Reckoning Next?" Racked, June 18, 2018. https://www.racked.com/2018/6/18/17475152/influencers-buy-followers-unilever.

———. "Why Influencers Are Pivoting to Anxiety." Refinery29, September 3, 2019. https://www.refinery29.com/en-us/2019/09/240780/instagram-influencer-anxiety-mental-health-posts.

Brouwer, B. "Former Apple Exec Dave Dickman Joins Influencer Marketing Platform Reelio as President." Tube Filter, September 11, 2015. https://www.tubefilter.com/2015/09/11/dave-dickman-president-reelio/.

Bryant, K. "The Fyre Festival, Built on Instagram, Dies by Instagram." *Vanity Fair*, April 28, 2017. https://www.vanityfair.com/style/2017/04/fyre-festival-disaster-bahamas.

Burrough, B. " Fyre Festival: Anatomy of a Millennial Marketing Fiasco Waiting to Happen." *Vanity Fair*, June 29, 2017. https://www.vanityfair.com/news/2017/06/fyre-festival-billy-mcfarland-millennial-marketing-fiasco.

Caminiti, S. "A Blogger's Social Media Idea Sparks a Retail Revolution, and $1 billion in Sales." CNBC, September 27, 2017. https://www.cnbc.com/2017/09/27/rewardstyle-liketoknow-it-sparks-1-billion-in-retail-sales.html.

Cantril, H. *The Invasion from Mars.* Princeton, NJ: Princeton University Press, 1940.

Carah, N. and Angus, D. "Algorithmic Brand Culture: Participatory Labour, Machine Learning and Branding on Social Media." *Media, Culture & Society* 40, no. 2 (March 2018): 178–94. https://doi.org/10.1177/0163443718754648.

Carlson, K. "How to Gain More Instagram Advertising ROI." Business 2 Community, September 16, 2015. https://www.business2community.com/instagram/how-to-gain-more-instagram-advertising-roi-01324579.

Carlson, M. "Blogs and Journalistic Authority." *Journalism Studies* 8, no. 2 (2007): 264–79. https://doi.org/10.1080/14616700601148861.

Carman, A. "Black Influencers Are Underpaid, and a New Instagram Account Is Proving It." The Verge, July 14, 2020. https://www.theverge.com/21324116/instagram-influencer-pay-gap-account-expose.

———. "Influencers' Next Frontier: Their Own Live Shopping Channels." The Verge, October 22, 2020. https://www.theverge.com/2020/10/22/21526535/live-shopping-instagram-facebook-amazon-influencers.

Centola, D. "TikTok Stars Shouldn't Hawk Vaccines." *The Philadelphia Inquirer*, August 13, 2021. https://www.inquirer.com/opinion/commentary/vaccine-hesitancy-white-house-tiktok-joe-biden-20210813.html.

Chan, S. "Alber Elbaz Is Leaving Lanvin." *Hollywood Reporter*, October 28, 2015. https://www.hollywoodreporter.com/news/alber-elbaz-is-leaving-lanvin-835070.

Chen, T. "Influencers and Bloggers Are Being Offered Money to Post Sponcon in Support of Cory Booker." Buzzfeed News, November 26, 2019. https://www.buzzfeednews.com/article/tanyachen/cory-booker-paid-social-media-influencer-campaign?origin=web-hf.

Chen, Y. "'Dashboards Are Not Real Technologies': Influencer Marketing Technology Is a Hot Mess." Digiday, August 19, 2016. https://digiday.com/marketing/dashboards-not-real-technologies-influencer-marketing-technology-hot-mess/.

Cialdini, R. B. *Influence: Science and Practice*. Boston: Pearson, 2001.

Cillizza, C. "Millennials Don't Trust Anyone. That's a Big Deal." *Washington Post*, April 30, 2015. https://www.washingtonpost.com/news/the-fix/wp/2015/04/30/millennials-dont-trust-anyone-what-else-is-new/.

Clark, D. "Why You Should Pay Attention to Influencer Marketing." *Forbes*, October 15, 2014. https://www.forbes.com/sites/dorieclark/2014/10/15/why-you-should-pay-attention-to-influencer-marketing/.

Confessore, N., Dance, G. J. X., Harris, R., & Hansen, M. "The Follower Factory." *New York Times*, January 27, 2018. https://www.nytimes.com/interactive/2018/01/27/technology/social-media-bots.html.

Contestabile, G. "Influencer Marketing in 2018: Becoming an Efficient Marketplace." *Adweek*, January 15, 2018. https://www.adweek.com/digital/giordano-contestabile-activate-by-bloglovin-guest-post-influencer-marketing-in-2018/.

Corcoran, C. T. "The Blogs That Took Over the Tents." *Women's Wear Daily*, February 6, 2006. https://wwd.com/fashion-news/fashion-features/the-blogs-that-took-over-the-tents-547153/.

Cordero, R. "Li Edelkoort: 'Fashion is Old Fashioned.'" Business of Fashion, December 5, 2016. https://www.businessoffashion.com/articles/voices/li-edelkoort-anti-fashion-manifesto-fashion-is-old-fashioned.

Coscarelli, A. "The 41 Most Instagrammed It Items of 2015." Refinery29, December 19, 2015. https://www.refinery29.com/en-us/most-popular-instagram-items-2015.

Creators (@Creators). "What does it take to grow on Instagram in 2021?" Instagram Reel, August 18, 2021. https://www.instagram.com/reel/CSuN32YAcmo/.

Creel, G. *How We Advertised America: The First Telling of the Amazing Story of the Committee on Public Information That Carried the Gospel of Americanism to Every Corner of the Globe*. New York: Macmillan, 1920

Crump, H. "The New Rules of Influencer Marketing." Business of Fashion, May 29, 2019. https://www.businessoffashion.com/articles/news-analysis/the-new-rules-of-influencer-marketing.

Cunningham, S., & Craig, D. *Social Media Entertainment: The New Intersection of Hollywood and Silicon Valley*. New York: NYU Press, 2021.

Currid-Halkett, E. *Starstruck: The Business of Celebrity*. New York: Farrar, Straus and Giroux, 2010.

Damico, D. "Social Media and the Democratization of Influence." Adspire, July 29, 2017. http://adspiresocial.com/social-media-democratization-influence/.

Daniels, C. "FTC Takes Aim at Pay for Play." *PRWeek*, September 2, 2016. https://www.prweek.com/article/1407712?utm_source=website&utm_medium=social.

Davis, A. P. " Fashion Nova Is Tailor-Made for Instagram." The Cut, August 2, 2018. https://www
.thecut.com/2018/08/fashion-nova-is-tailor-made-for-instagram.html.

DePillis, L. "Ten years after the recession began, have Americans recovered?" CNN Money,
December 1, 2017. https://money.cnn.com/2017/12/01/news/economy/recession
-anniversary/index.html.

Dewey, C. "I think I Solved Instagram's Biggest Mystery, but You'll Have to Figure It Out for
Yourself." Washington Post, September 22, 2016. https://www.washingtonpost.com/news
/the-intersect/wp/2016/09/22/i-think-i-solved-instagrams-biggest-mystery-but-youll
-have-to-figure-it-out-for-yourself/.

Douglas, S. J. "Personal Influence and the Bracketing of Women's History." The ANNALS of the
American Academy of Political and Social Science 608, no. 1 (November 2006): 41–50. https://
doi.org/10.1177/0002716206292458.

Droesch, B. "What Does Your Brain on Influencer Marketing Look Like?" eMarketer, August 26, 2019. https://www.emarketer.com/content/your-brain-on-influencers
-neuroscience-study-explains-the-effects-of-influencer-marketing.

Drolet, D. "Marketers to Boost Influencer Budgets in 2017." eMarketer, December 13, 2016.
https://www.emarketer.com/Article/Marketers-Boost-Influencer-Budgets-2017/1014845.

Duffy, B. E. "Manufacturing Authenticity: The Rhetoric of 'Real' in Women's Magazines." The
Communication Review 16, no. 3 (2013): 132–154. https://doi.org/10.1080/10714421.2013
.807110.

———. (Not) Getting Paid to Do What You Love: Gender, Social Media, and Aspirational Work.
New Haven: Yale University Press, 2017.

Duffy, B. E., & Hund, E. "'Having it All' on Social Media: Entrepreneurial Femininity and Self-
Branding Among Fashion Bloggers." Social Media + Society 1, no. 2 (2015): https://doi.org
/10.1177/2056305115604337.

———. "The Invisible Labor of Fashion Blogging." The Atlantic, September 25, 2015. https://
www.theatlantic.com/entertainment/archive/2015/09/fashion-blogging-labor-myths
/405817/.

———. "Gendered Visibility on Social Media: Navigating Instagram's Authenticity Bind." International Journal of Communication 13 (2019): 4983–5002.

Duffy, B. E., K. Miltner, and A. Wahlstedt. "Policing 'Fake' Femininity: Anger and Accusation
in Influencer 'Hateblog' Communities." AoIR Selected Papers of Internet Research 2020 (October 2020). https://doi.org/10.5210/spir.v2020i0.11204.

Duffy, B. E., & Pooley, J. "Idols of Promotion: The Triumph of Self-Branding in an Age of Precarity." Journal of Communication 69, no. 1 (February 2019): 26–48, https://doi.org/10.1093/joc
/jqy063.

Duffy, B. E., & Wissinger, E. "Mythologies of Creative Work in the Social Media Age: Fun, Free,
and 'Just Being Me.'" International Journal of Communication 11 (2017): 20.

Edelman. "Two-Thirds of Consumers Worldwide Now Buy on Beliefs." October 2, 2018. https://
www.edelman.com/news-awards/two-thirds-consumers-worldwide-now-buy-beliefs.

eMarketer. "Facebook, Instagram Are Influencers' Favorite Social Platforms." August 16, 2016.
https://www.emarketer.com/Article/Facebook-Instagram-Influencers-Favorite-Social
-Platforms/1014349.

Enli, G. *Mediated Authenticity: How the Media Constructs Reality.* New York: Peter Lang, 2014.

Epstein, A. "For 10 Glorious Minutes, Social Media Influencers Were Mocked at Their Own Awards Show." Quartz, April 17, 2018. https://qz.com/quartzy/1254504/the-2018-shorty -awards-were-hilariously-roasted-by-actor-adam-pally/.

Evans, B. "Why Influencer Marketing Isn't about the 'Influencers.'" *Ad Age*, March 6, 2012. https://adage.com/article/digitalnext/influencer-marketing-influencers/233125.

Ewen, S. *Captains of Consciousness Advertising and the Social Roots of Consumer Culture.* New York: Basic Book, 1976.

Facebook. "Branded Content Policies" from August 20, 2018. Accessed May 29, 2019. https:// www.facebook.com/policies/brandedcontent/.

Fair, L. "Three FTC Actions of Interest to Influencers." Federal Trade Commission, September 7, 2017. https://www.ftc.gov/news-events/blogs/business-blog/2017/09/three-ftc -actions-interest-influencers.

Farra, E. "Influencers Are the Retailers of the 2020s." *Vogue*, October 19, 2020. https://www .vogue.com/article/will-influencers-replace-retailers-2020s.

Federal Trade Commission. "Disclosures 101 for Social Media Influencers." November 2019. https:// www.ftc.gov/system/files/documents/plain-language/1001a-influencer-guide-508_1.pdf.

———. "Lord & Taylor Settles FTC Charges It Deceived Consumers through Paid Article in an Online Fashion Magazine and Paid Instagram Posts by 50 'Fashion Influencers.'" March 15, 2016. https://www.ftc.gov/news-events/press-releases/2016/03/lord-taylor -settles-ftc-charges-it-deceived-consumers-through.

Flanagan, A. "Fyre Festival Co-Founder Billy McFarland Sentenced to 6 Years in Prison." NPR, October 11, 2018. https://www.npr.org/2018/10/11/656480640/fyre-festival-co-founder -billy-mcfarland-sentenced-in-manhattan.

Flora, L. "'I Love You, My Beautiful QAnon!' When Lifestyle Influencers Also Peddle Conspiracy Theories." Glossy, June 24, 2020. https://www.glossy.co/beauty/i-love-you-my -beautiful-qanon-when-lifestyle-influencers-also-peddle-conspiracy-theories.

Florendo, E. "The Blonde Salad Has a Harvard Moment." Bustle, February 12, 2015. https://www .bustle.com/articles/64112-blogger-the-blonde-salad-takes-over-harvards-business-school -by-storm-what-like-its-hard.

Frier, S. *No Filter: The Inside Story of Instagram.* New York: Simon & Schuster, 2020.

Furst, J., & Nason, J. W., dirs. *Fyre Fraud.* United States: Hulu. 2019.

Fyre Festival. "Announcing Fyre Festival." Posted on January 12, 2017. YouTube video. https:// www.youtube.com/watch?v=mz5kY3RsmK0.

Gaca, A. "Fyre Festival: A Timeline of Disaster." *Spin*, May 3, 2017. https://www.spin.com/2017 /05/fyre-festival-disaster-timeline/.

Gaden, G., & Dumitrica, D. "The 'Real Deal': Strategic Authenticity, Politics and Social Media." *First Monday* 20, no. 1 (January 2015). https://doi.org/10.5210/fm.v20i1.4985.

Gahan, B. "Micro-Influencers and the Blind Spot in Your Influencer Marketing." *Adweek*, April 7, 2017. https://www.adweek.com/digital/brendan-gahan-epic-signal-guest-post -micro-influencers/.

Gard, L. "The Business Of Blogging." *Bloomberg BusinessWeek*, December 13, 2004. https://www .bloomberg.com/news/articles/2004-12-12/the-business-of-blogging.

Geller, M. "Unilever Takes Stand against Digital Media's Fake Followers." Reuters, June 18, 2018. https://www.reuters.com/article/us-unilever-media-idUSKBN1JD10M.

Gerbner, G., & Gross, L. "Living with Television: The Violence Profile." Journal of Communication 26, no. 2 (June 1976): 172–99.

Germain, J. "Influencers Are Unionizing with SAG-AFTRA to Gain Protection, Community at Work." Teen Vogue, March 16, 2021. https://www.teenvogue.com/story/influencers-union -sag-aftra.

Gesenhues, A. "Why So Sad? Curalate Study Finds Instagram Images with Blue Hues Win More Likes." Marketing Land, November 8, 2013. https://marketingland.com/why-so-sad-curalate -study-finds-blue-hues-get-more-likes-on-instragram-64622.

Gevinson, T. "Who Would Tavi Gevinson Be without Instagram? An Investigation." New York, September 2019. https://www.thecut.com/2019/09/who-would-tavi-gevinson-be-without -instagram.html.

Gibbs, M., Meese, J., Arnold, M., Nansen, B., & Carter, M. "#Funeral and Instagram: Death, Social media, and Platform Vernacular. Information, Communication & Society 18, no. 3 (2015): 255–268. https://doi.org/10.1080/1369118X.2014.987152.

Gill, R. "Life Is a Pitch: Managing the Self in New Media Work." In Managing Media Work, edited by Mark Deuze, 249–62. Thousand Oaks, CA: SAGE, 2011.

Gill, R., & Pratt, A. "In the Social Factory?: Immaterial Labour, Precariousness and Cultural Work." Theory, Culture & Society 25, no. 7–8 (December 2008): 1–30. https://doi.org/10.1177 /0263276408097794.

Gillespie, T. "The Politics of 'Platforms.'" New Media & Society 12, no. 3 (May 2010): 347–364. https://doi.org/10.1177/1461444809342738.

Gitlin, T. "Media Sociology." Theory and Society 6, no. 2 (1978): 205–253. https://doi.org/10.1007 /BF01681751.

Gladwell, M. The Tipping Point: How Little Things Make a Big Difference. New York: Little, Brown, 2000.

Glaser, B., & Strauss, A. The Discovery of Grounded Theory: Strategies for Qualitative Research. Mill Valley, CA: Sociology Press, 1967.

Glazer, E., & Wells, G. "Political Campaigns Turn to Social Media Influencers to Reach Voters." Wall Street Journal, September 23, 2019. https://www.wsj.com/articles/political-campaigns -turn-to-social-media-influencers-to-reach-voters-11569251450.

Goldberg, J. "How Brands Can Have Better Relationships with Influencers." Forbes, September 11, 2017. https://www.forbes.com/sites/forbesagencycouncil/2017/09/11/how-brands -can-have-better-relationships-with-influencers/.

Goldhaber, M. H. "The Attention Economy and the Net." First Monday 2, no. 4 (1997a). https:// doi.org/10.5210/fm.v2i4.519.

———. "Attention Shoppers!" Wired, December 1, 1997b. https://www.wired.com/1997/12 /es-attention/.

Goodwin, A.M., Joseff, K., & Woolley, S. C. "Social Media Influencers and the 2020 U.S. Election: Paying 'Regular People' for Digital Campaign Communication." Center for Media Engagement, October 2020. https://mediaengagement.org/research/social-media -influencers-and-the-2020-election.

Goodwin, T. "If You're an 'Influencer,' You're Probably Not Influential." *GQ*, November 20, 2017. https://www.gq-magazine.co.uk/article/influencer-marketing.

Granovetter, M. S. "The Strength of Weak Ties." *American Journal of Sociology* 78, no. 6 (1973): 1360–1380.

Griffith, J. "Influencer Arielle Charnas Faces Renewed Backlash for Retreating to Hamptons after COVID-19 Diagnosis." NBC News, April 3, 2020. https://www.nbcnews.com/news/us-news /influencer-arielle-charnas-faces-renewed-backlash-retreating-hamptons-after-covid-n1176066.

Griner, D. "Lord & Taylor Got 50 Instagrammers to Wear the Same Dress, Which Promptly Sold Out." *Adweek*, March 31, 2015. https://www.adweek.com/brand-marketing/lord-taylor -got-50-instagrammers-wear-same-dress-which-promptly-sold-out-163791/.

Harrington, C. "VCs Are Hungry for Fast-Casual 'Food Platforms.'" *Wired*, February 18, 2019. https://www.wired.com/story/vcs-hungry-for-fast-casual-food-platforms/.

Harrington, M. "Survey: People's Trust Has Declined in Business, Media, Government, and NGOs." *Harvard Business Review*, January 16, 2017. https://hbr.org/2017/01/survey-peoples -trust-has-declined-in-business-media-government-and-ngos.

Havens, T., Lotz, A. D., & Tinic, S. "Critical Media Industry Studies: A Research Approach." *Communication, Culture & Critique* 2, no. 2 (2009): 234–253. https://doi.org/10.1111/j.1753 -9137.2009.01037.x.

Hearn, A. "'Meat, Mask, Burden': Probing the Contours of the Branded 'Self.'" *Journal of Consumer Culture* 8, no. 2 (2008): 197–217. https://doi.org/10.1177/1469540508090086.

———. "Structuring Feeling: Web 2.0, Online Ranking and Rating, and the Digital 'Reputation' Economy." *Ephemera* 10, no. 3/4 (2010): 421–38.

Hennessy, B. "Why Women Dominate Influencer Marketing—and Why It May Be the Right Career for You." *Entrepreneur*, August 2, 2018. https://www.entrepreneur.com/article/317450.

Hercher, H. "Influencer Marketing Is Not Flying Under the Radar Any Longer. *AdExchanger*, September 28, 2015. https://adexchanger.com/online-advertising/influencer-marketing-is -not-flying-under-the-radar-any-longer/.

Hesmondhalgh, D. *The Cultural Industries*. 3rd ed. London: SAGE, 2012.

Holland, K. "Working Moms Still Take on Bulk of Household Chores." CNBC, April 28, 2015. https://www.cnbc.com/2015/04/28/me-is-like-leave-it-to-beaver.html.

Hook, L. "Year in a Word: Gig Economy." *The Financial Times*, December 29, 2015. https://www .ft.com/content/b5a2b122-a41b-11e5-8218-6b8ff73aae15.

Horkheimer, M., & Adorno, T. "The Culture Industry: Enlightenment as Mass Deception." In *Cultural Theory: An Anthology*, edited by Imre Szeman and Timothy Kaposky. New York: Wiley, 1944.

Hovland, C. I., Janis, I. L., & Kelley, H. H. *Communication and Persuasion: Psychological Studies of Opinion Change*. New Haven: Yale University Press, 1953.

Howland, D. "Report: 'Ultra-Fast' Fashion Players Gain on Zara, H&M." Retail Dive, May 22, 2017. https://www.retaildive.com/news/report-ultra-fast-fashion-players-gain-on-zara-hm /443250/.

Hubbard, L. "How Social Media Is Impacting Cosmetic Surgery Culture and Disordered Eating." Fashionista, November 15, 2016. https://fashionista.com/2016/11/negative-effects-of -social-media-culture.

Hund, E., & McGuigan, L. "A Shoppable Life: Performance, Selfhood, and Influence in the Social Media Storefront." *Communication, Culture and Critique* 12, no. 1 (2019): 18–35. https://doi.org/10.1093/ccc/tcz004.

Hunt, E. "Essena O'Neill Quits Instagram Claiming Social Media 'Is Not Real Life.'" *Guardian*, November 3, 2015. https://www.theguardian.com/media/2015/nov/03/instagram-star -essena-oneill-quits-2d-life-to-reveal-true-story-behind-images.

Hyland, V. "Fashion Is Moving Too Fast, and It's Killing Creativity." The Cut, October 26, 2015. https://www.thecut.com/2015/10/fashions-moving-too-fast-thats-a-bad-thing.html.

HYPR. "The Role of Influencer Marketing in Key Industries: A Look at the Fashion Industry." October 25, 2016. https://hyprbrands.com/blog/role-influencer-marketing-key-industries -look-fashion-industry/.

Im, K. "Infographic: How Much Influencers Like to Take a Stand." *Adweek*, November 17, 2019. https://www.adweek.com/performance-marketing/infographic-influencers-like-to-take-a -stand/.

InfluencerDB. *How Big Is Influencer Marketing in 2018? State of the Industry Report*. 2018. https:// cdn2.hubspot.net/hubfs/4030790/MARKETING/Resources/Education/Infographic /InfluencerDB-State-of-the-Industry-2018.pdf.

Influencer Marketing Hub. *Influencer Marketing Benchmark Report*. 2021. https://influencer marketinghub.com/ebooks/influencer_marketing_benchmark_report_2021.pdf.

InfluencerPayGap (@InfluencerPayGap). "Love your page! Anon please . . ." Instagram photo- graph, March 26, 2021a. https://www.instagram.com/p/CM5EZ76hD_k/.

——. "ANON please. I'm in influencer marketing . . ." March 26, 2021b, Instagram photo- graph. https://www.instagram.com/p/CM5EouWhNgy/.

Instagram for Business. Accessed May 29, 2019, from Instagram for Business website: https:// business.instagram.com/a/brandedcontentexpansion.

IZEA. *State of Influencer Equality Report*. 2021. https://izea.com/influencer-marketing-statistics /2021-state-of-influencer-equality/.

Jhaveri, D. P. "TikTok Is Full of Sephora and Chipotle Employees Spilling Secrets. That Can Get Complicated." Vox, January 20, 2020. https://www.vox.com/the-goods/2020/1/20 /21059143/tiktok-sephora-chipotle-panera-starbucks.

Jensen, K. B. "Three Step Flow." *Journalism* 10, no. 3 (2009): 335–37.

Johnson, M. "5 Ways to Get More Than Influence from Social Influencers." MediaPost, Septem- ber 8, 2015. https://www.mediapost.com/publications/article/257787/5-ways-to-get-more -than-influence-from-social-infl.html.

Jones, D. "Why We Follow Lil Miquela, the Instagram Model with 900K Followers & No Soul." Refinery29, April 10, 2018. https://www.refinery29.com/en-us/miquela-sousa-fake-instagram.

Kanai, A. *Gender and Relatability in Digital Culture: Managing Affect, Intimacy, and Value*. Bas- ingstoke, UK: Palgrave Macmillan, 2018.

Karp, H. "At Up to $250,000 a Ticket, Island Music Festival Woos Wealthy to Stay Afloat." *Wall Street Journal*, April 2, 2017. https://www.wsj.com/articles/fyre-festival-organizers-push-to -keep-it-from-fizzling-1491130804.

Katz, E. "The Two-Step Flow of Communication: An Up-to-Date Report on an Hypothesis." *Public Opinion Quarterly* 21 (1957): 61–78. https://doi.org/10.1086/266687.

Katz, E., & Lazarsfeld, P. F. *Personal Influence: The Part Played by People in the Flow of Mass Communications*. Glencoe, IL: Free Press, 1955.

Keller, E. "Unleashing the Power of Word of Mouth: Creating Brand Advocacy to Drive Growth." *Journal of Advertising Research* 47, no. 4 (2007): 448–52. https://doi.org/10.2501/S0021849907070468.

Keller, E., & Berry, J. *The Influentials: One American in Ten Tells the Other Nine How to Vote, Where to Eat, and What to Buy*. New York: Free Press, 2003.

Kozlowska, H. "Shoppers Are Buying Clothes Just for the Instagram Pic, and Then Returning Them." Quartz, August 13, 2018. https://qz.com/quartzy/1354651/shoppers-are-buying-clothes-just-for-the-instagram-pic-and-then-return-them/.

Kuehn, K., & Corrigan, T. F. "Hope Labor: The Role of Employment Prospects in Online Social Production." *The Political Economy of Communication* 1, no.1 (2013). http://www.polecom.org/index.php/polecom/article/view/9.

Kurutz, S. "Fashion Bloggers Get Agents." *New York Times*, September 28, 2011. https://www.nytimes.com/2011/09/29/fashion/fashion-bloggers-get-agents.html.

Lam, B. "Generation Sell Out." Refinery29, August 3, 2018. https://www.refinery29.com/en-us/2018/08/205859/selling-out-millennials-why.

Lasswell, H. D. "The Theory of Political Propaganda." *American Political Science Review* 21, no. 3 (1927): 627–31. https://doi.org/10.2307/1945515.

Lazarsfeld, P. F., Berelson, B., & Gaudet, H. *The People's Choice: How the Voter Makes Up His Mind in a Presidential Campaign*. New York: Columbia University Press, 1948.

Lazzarato, M. "Immaterial Labour." In *Radical Thought in Italy: A Potential Politics*, edited by Paolo Virno and Michael Hardt, 133–47. Minneapolis: University of Minnesota Press, 1996.

Leiber, C. "The Dirty Business of Buying Instagram Followers." Racked, September 11, 2014. https://www.vox.com/2014/9/11/7577585/buy-instagram-followers-bloggers.

Levine, B. "TapInfluence Launches a Fully Automated Platform That Could Turn Influencer Marketing into Mass Media." VentureBeat, September 18, 2015. https://venturebeat.com/2015/09/18/tapinfluence-launches-a-fully-automated-platform-that-could-turn-influencer-marketing-into-mass-media/.

Lewis, T. *Smart Living: Lifestyle Media and Popular Expertise*. New York: Peter Lang, 2008.

Lieber, C. "Why Laxative Teas Took Over Instagram." Vox, April 27, 2016. https://www.vox.com/2016/4/27/11502276/teatox-instagram.

Lingel, J. *Digital Countercultures and the Struggle for Community*. Cambridge, MA: MIT Press, 2017.

Lo, D. "Hollywood Agency CAA Is Signing Fashion Folks Left and Right." Racked, September 19, 2011. https://www.racked.com/2011/9/19/7750593/hollywood-agency-caa-is-signing-fashion-folks-left-and-right.

Locke, T. "86% of Young People Say They Want to Post Social Media Content for Money." CNBC, November 8, 2019. https://www.cnbc.com/2019/11/08/study-young-people-want-to-be-paid-influencers.html.

Lorenz, T. "Don't Call Adam Pally a Hero: It's 2018 and Not Cool to Hate on Creators." Daily Beast, April 17, 2018. https://www.thedailybeast.com/dont-call-adam-pally-a-hero-its-2018-and-not-cool-to-hate-on-creators.

———. "The Instagram Aesthetic Is Over." *The Atlantic*, April 23, 2019. https://www.theatlantic
.com/technology/archive/2019/04/influencers-are-abandoning-instagram-look/587803/.

———. "Flight of the Influencers." *New York Times*, April 2, 2020. https://www.nytimes.com
/2020/04/02/style/influencers-leave-new-york-coronavirus.html.

———. "For Creators, Everything Is for Sale." *New York Times*, March 10, 2021. https://www
.nytimes.com/2021/03/10/style/creators-selling-selves.html.

Lowenthal, L. "Biographies in Popular Magazines." In *Radio Research, 1942–43*, edited by Paul
Lazarsfeld and Frank Stanton, 507–48. New York: Duell, Sloan, and Pearce, 1944.

———. *Literature and Mass Culture: Communication in Society*. Vol. 1. United Kingdom: Taylor
& Francis, 2017.

Lowrey, A. "The Great Recession Is Still With Us." *The Atlantic*, December 1, 2017. https://www
.theatlantic.com/business/archive/2017/12/great-recession-still-with-us/547268/.

LTK. "A Brand Built on Creator Innovation." LTK Corporate Website. https://company.shopltk
.com/en/company. Accessed May 17, 2022.

Lush, T. "Poll: Americans Are the Unhappiest They've Been in 50 Years." AP News, June 16,
2020. https://apnews.com/article/virus-outbreak-health-us-news-ap-top-news-racial
-injustice-0f6b9be04fa0d3194401821a72665a50.

Luvaas, B. "Indonesian Fashion Blogs: On the Promotional Subject of Personal Style." *Fashion
Theory* 17, no. 1 (2013): 55–76. https://doi.org/10.2752/175174113X13502904240749.

———. *Street Style: An Ethnography of Fashion Blogging*. New York: Bloomsbury Academic, 2016.

Maheshwari, S. "A Penthouse Made for Instagram." *New York Times*, September 30, 2018. https://
www.nytimes.com/2018/09/30/business/media/instagram-influencers-penthouse.html.

———. "Are You Ready for the Nanoinfluencers?" *New York Times*, November 12, 2018. https://
www.nytimes.com/2018/11/11/business/media/nanoinfluencers-instagram-influencers.html.

———. "Online and Making Thousands, at Age 4: Meet the Kidfluencers." *New York Times*,
March 6, 2019. https://www.nytimes.com/2019/03/01/business/media/social-media
-influencers-kids.html.

Maio, G. R., & Haddock, G. *The Psychology of Attitudes and Attitude Change*, 1st ed. London:
SAGE Publications Ltd., 2010.

Mari, F. "The Click Clique." *Texas Monthly*, August 12, 2014. https://www.texasmonthly.com
/articles/the-click-clique/.

Marine, B. "Kendall Jenner and Fyre Festival's Other Influencers Are Getting Subpoenaed." *W*,
January 28, 2019. https://www.wmagazine.com/story/fyre-festival-bankruptcy-case
-influencers-kendall-jenner-subpoena.

Martineau, P. "Inside the Pricey War to Influence Your Instagram Feed." *Wired*, November 18,
2018. https://www.wired.com/story/pricey-war-influence-your-instagram-feed/.

Marwick, A. E. *Status Update: Celebrity, Publicity, and Branding in the Social Media Age*. New
Haven: Yale University Press, 2013a.

———. "'They're Really Profound Women, They're Entrepreneurs': Conceptions of Authenticity in Fashion Blogging." Paper presented at the Proceedings of the International Conference
on Weblogs and Social Media. 2013b.

———. "Instafame: Luxury Selfies in the Attention Economy." *Public Culture* (2015). https://
scinapse.io/papers/1984733378.

Marwick, A. E., & boyd, danah. "I Tweet Honestly, I Tweet Passionately: Twitter Users, Context Collapse, and the Imagined Audience." *New Media & Society* 13, no. 1 (2011): 114–33. https://doi.org/10.1177/1461444810365313.

Massachi, S. "How to Save Our Social Media by Treating It Like a City." *MIT Technology Review*, December 20, 2021. https://www.technologyreview.com/2021/12/20/1042709/how-to-save-social-media-treat-it-like-a-city/.

Maris, E. "Hacking *Xena*: Technological Innovation and Queer Influence in the Production of Mainstream Television." *Critical Studies in Media Communication* 33, no.1 (2016): 123–37. https://doi.org/10.1080/15295036.2015.1129063.

Marx, K. *Economic and Philosophic Manuscripts of 1844*. Courier Corporation, 2012.

Mau, D. "Are Influencer Brands the Key to Bringing Millennials to Department Stores?" Fashionista, July 20, 2018. https://fashionista.com/2018/07/department-stores-instagram-influencers-brands-marketing.

McCall, T. "What's Next for Influencers in 2017." Fashionista, December 22, 2016. https://fashionista.com/2016/12/influencer-trends-2017.

McGuigan, L. "Selling Jennifer Aniston's Sweater: The Persistence of Shoppability in Framing Television's Future." *Media Industries Journal* 5, no. 1 (2018). http://dx.doi.org/10.3998/mij.15031809.0005.101.

McGuigan, L., & Manzerolle, V. "'All the World's a Shopping Cart': Theorizing the Political Economy of Ubiquitous Media and Markets." *New Media & Society* 17, no. 11 (2014a): 1830–1848. https://doi.org/10.1177/1461444814535191.

McGuigan, L., & Manzerolle, V., eds. *The Audience Commodity in a Digital Age: Revisiting a Critical Theory of Commercial Media*. New York: Peter Lang, 2014b.

McNeal, S. "Influencers Say Their Increase in Followers Since Blackout Tuesday Has Been Bittersweet." Buzzfeed News, July 9, 2020. https://www.buzzfeednews.com/article/stephaniemcneal/black-influencers-demand-change-black-lives-matter.

———. "Gen Z Moms Are Building Their Brands around QAnon." Buzzfeed News, January 22, 2021. https://www.buzzfeednews.com/article/stephaniemcneal/qanon-influencers-little-miss-patriot.

McRae, S. "'Get Off My Internets': How Anti-Fans Deconstruct Lifestyle Bloggers' Authenticity Work." *Persona Studies* 3, no. 1 (2017): 13–27. https://doi.org/10.21153/ps2017vol3no1art640.

Mears, A. *Pricing Beauty*. Oakland, CA: University of California Press, 2009.

Mediakix. "Instagram Influencer Marketing Is Now a $1.7 Billion Industry." March 29, 2017. http://mediakix.com/2017/03/instagram-influencer-marketing-industry-size-how-big/.

Memmott, M. "75 Years Ago, 'War of the Worlds' Started a Panic. Or Did It?" NPR, October 30, 2013. https://www.npr.org/sections/thetwo-way/2013/10/30/241797346/75-years-ago-war-of-the-worlds-started-a-panic-or-did-it.

Molla, R. "Posting Less, Posting More, and Tired of It All: How the Pandemic Has Changed Social Media." Vox, March 1, 2021. https://www.vox.com/recode/22295131/social-media-use-pandemic-covid-19-instagram-tiktok.

Morrison, K. "Report: 75% of Marketers Are Using Influencer Marketing." *Adweek*, October 13, 2015. https://www.adweek.com/digital/report-75-of-marketers-are-using-influencer-marketing/.

Moss, S. "How Your Business Can Benefit from Micro-Influencer Marketing." *Entrepreneur,* May 5, 2017. https://www.entrepreneur.com/article/293824.

Napoli, P. M. *Audience Evolution: New Technologies and the Transformation of Media Audiences.* New York: Columbia University Press, 2011.

———. *Social Media and the Public Interest: Media Regulation in the Disinformation Age.* New York: Columbia University Press, 2019.

Nathanson, J. "Klout Is Basically Dead, but It Finally Matters." Slate, May 1, 2014. https://slate .com/business/2014/05/klout-is-basically-dead-but-it-finally-matters.html.

Neff, G. *Venture Labor: Work and the Burden of Risk in Innovative Industries.* Cambridge, MA: MIT Press, 2012.

New York City Health Department. "COVID-19: Data." Accessed April 22, 2022. https://www1 .nyc.gov/site/doh/covid/covid-19-data-trends.page.

Nichols, M. "Bloggers Carry Growing Fashion Industry Influence." Reuters, September 15, 2010. https://www.reuters.com/article/us-newyork-fashion-internet-idUSTRE68E2 II20100915.

Nielsen. "Buzz in the Blogosphere: Millions More Bloggers and Blog Readers." March 9, 2012. http://www.nielsen.com/us/en/insights/news/2012/buzz-in-the-blogosphere-millions -more-bloggers-and-blog-readers.

Noor, P. "Brands Are Cashing in on Social Media Envy, and Using Influencers to Sell It." *Guardian,* November 5, 2018. https://www.theguardian.com/commentisfree/2018/nov/05/brands -cashing-in-social-media-envy-influencers.

North, A. "How #SaveTheChildren Is Pulling American Moms into QAnon." Vox, September 18, 2020. https://www.vox.com/21436671/save-our-children-hashtag-qanon-pizzagate.

Odell, J. *How to Do Nothing: Resisting the Attention Economy.* New York: Melville House, 2019.

Ohlheiser, A. "The Complete Disaster of Fyre Festival Played Out on Social Media for All to See; 'NOT MY FAULT' Says Organizer Ja Rule." *Washington Post,* April 28, 2017. https:// www.washingtonpost.com/news/the-intersect/wp/2017/04/28/the-complete-and-utter -disaster-that-was-fyre-festival-played-out-on-social-media-for-all-to-see/.

O'Meara, V. "Weapons of the Chic: Instagram Influencer Engagement Pods as Practices of Resistance to Instagram Platform Labor." *Social Media + Society* 5, no. 4 (October 2019): 1–11. https://doi.org/10.1177/2056305119879671.

O'Neill, E. "Why I really am quitting social media." Posted on November 15, 2015. YouTube video. https://www.youtube.com/watch?v=gmAbwTQvWX8&t=214s.

O'Reilly, C., & Snyder, D. "Homeland Security to Compile Database of Journalists, Bloggers." *Bloomberg Law,* April 5, 2018. https://news.bloomberglaw.com/business-and-practice /homeland-security-to-compile-database-of-journalists-bloggers.

Packard, V. *The Hidden Persuaders.* New York: D. McKay Co., 1957.

Pathak, S. "In Cannes, a Marketer Backlash to Influencers Is Growing." Digiday, June 20, 2018. https://digiday.com/marketing/cannes-marketer-backlash-influencers-growing/.

Pavlika, H. "2015 Women's Blogging and Business Report: 'Blogging Is on the Decline.'" Media-Post, September 4, 2015a. https://www.mediapost.com/publications/article/257659/2015 -womens-blogging-and-business-report-bloggi.html.

———. "5 Tips for Running Your First Influencer Marketing Campaign." Mashable, September 24, 2015b. https://mashable.com/2015/09/24/influencer-marketing-tips/.

Peiss, K. L. "American Women and the Making of Modern Consumer Culture." *The Journal for MultiMedia History* 1, no. 1 (Fall 1998). https://www.albany.edu/jmmh/vol1no1/peiss-text .html.

———. "'Vital Industry' and Women's Ventures: Conceptualizing Gender in Twentieth Century Business History." *Business History Review* 72 no. 2 (1998): 219–41.

Peoples Wagner, L. "Is There Room for Fashion Criticism in a Racist Industry?" The Cut, August 30, 2021. https://www.thecut.com/2021/08/is-there-room-for-fashion-criticism-in-a -racist-industry.html.

Perrin, A. "10 Facts about Smartphones." Pew Research Center, June 29, 2017. https://www .pewresearch.org/fact-tank/2017/06/28/10-facts-about-smartphones/.

Peters, T. "The Brand Called You." *Fast Company*, August 31, 1997. https://www.fastcompany .com/28905/brand-called-you.

Peterson, R. A., & Anand, N. "The Production of Culture Perspective." *Annual Review of Sociology* 30 (August 2004): 311–34.

Petre, C. "Managing Metrics: The Containment, Disclosure, and Sanctioning of Audience Data at the New York Times." The Tow Center for Digital Journalism, 2015.

Petre, C., Duffy, B. E., & Hund, E. "'Gaming the System': Platform Paternalism and the Politics of Algorithmic Manipulation in the Digital Culture Industries." *Social Media + Society* 5, no. 4 (October 2019). https://doi.org/10.1177/2056305119879995.

Pew Research Center. "Millennials in Adulthood." March 7, 2014. https://www.pewresearch.org /social-trends/2014/03/07/millennials-in-adulthood/.

———. "The State of American Jobs." October 6, 2016. https://www.pewresearch.org/social -trends/2016/10/06/the-state-of-american-jobs/#:~:text=According%20to%20 experts%2C%209%20the,in%20these%20types%20of%20jobs.

———. "Social Media Fact Sheet." February 5, 2018. https://www.pewinternet.org/fact-sheet /social-media/.

Pham, M. T. "Susie Bubble is a Sign of The Times" The embodiment of success in the Web 2.0 economy. *Feminist Media Studies* 13, no. 2 (2013): 245–67. http://doi.org/10.1080/14680777 .2012.678076.

Pickard, V. *Democracy Without Journalism? Confronting the Misinformation Society.* Oxford: Oxford University Press, 2020.

Pink, D. H. *Free Agent Nation: How Americans New Independent Workers Are Transforming the Way We Live.* Business Plus, 2001.

Pooley, J. "The Consuming Self: From Flappers to Facebook." In *Blowing up the Brand: Critical Perspectives on Promotional Culture*, edited by Melissa Aronczyk and Devon Powers. New York: Peter Lang, 2010.

Pope, K. "So You Wanna Be a Journalist?" *Columbia Journalism Review*, 2018. https://www.cjr .org/special_report/journalism-jobs.php/.

PR Newswire. "Collective Bias Reveals Users View Influencer Content Nearly Seven Times Longer Than Digital Display Ads." February 17, 2016. https://www.prnewswire.com/news -releases/collective-bias-reveals-users-view-influencer-content-nearly-seven-times-longer -than-digital-display-ads-300219746.html.

Purinton, S. "Establishing Your Brand Voice on Social Media." *Adweek*, September 25, 2017. https://www.adweek.com/digital/stephanie-purinton-ignite-social-media-guest-post-establishing-your-brand-voice-on-social-media/.

Rainey, C. "10 Former Viral Sensations on Life after Internet Fame." *New York*, December 2, 2015. http://nymag.com/intelligencer/2015/12/10-viral-sensations-on-life-after-internet-fame.html.

Refinery29. "29Rooms Is Refinery29's Funhouse of Style, Culture, and Creativity." Accessed April 22, 2022. https://www.refinery29.com/en-us/29rooms.

Reilly, J. "Influencers and Celebrities Are the 'Gateway Drug' to Fake Coronavirus News, Experts Warn." *The Sun*, April 30, 2020. https://www.thesun.co.uk/news/11519729/influencers-celebreties-gateway-drug-fake-news/.

Rife, K. "Adam Pally Didn't Even Try to Hide His Despair on Stage at the Shorty Awards." A.V. Club, April 16, 2018. https://news.avclub.com/adam-pally-didnt-even-try-to-hide-his-despair-on-stage-1825293715.

Robles, P. "Has Essena O'Neill Signalled the End of Influencer Marketing?" Econsultancy, November 4, 2015. https://econsultancy.com/has-essena-o-neill-signalled-the-end-of-influencer-marketing/.

———. "Unilever Gets Serious about Influencer Fraud." Econsultancy, June 19, 2018. https://econsultancy.com/unilever-gets-serious-about-influencer-fraud/.

Ronan, A. "Heather 'Dooce' Armstrong Talks Life After Mommy-Blogging." The Cut, May 29, 2015. https://www.thecut.com/2015/05/dooce-talks-life-after-mommy-blogging.html.

Rosman, K. "Your Instagram Picture, Worth a Thousand Ads." *New York Times*, December 21, 2017. https://www.nytimes.com/2014/10/16/fashion/your-instagram-picture-worth-a-thousand-ads.html.

Ross, A. "The Naysayers." *New Yorker*, September 8, 2014. https://www.newyorker.com/magazine/2014/09/15/naysayers.

Sandler, E. "'My role is changing': Mega Influencer Pony on Working with Eastern and Western Beauty Brands." Glossy, January 21, 2020. https://www.glossy.co/beauty/my-role-is-changing-mega-influencer-pony-on-working-with-eastern-and-western-beauty-brands/.

Saul, H. "Yesterday This Woman 'Told the Truth' about Social Media—Today Her Friends Say It's All a Hoax." *Independent*, November 4, 2015. http://www.independent.co.uk/news/people/essena-oneill-quitting-instagram-is-a-hoax-claim-friends-a6720851.html.

Schaefer, K. "How Bloggers Make Money on Instagram." *Harper's Bazaar*, May 20, 2015. https://www.harpersbazaar.com/fashion/trends/a10949/how-bloggers-make-money-on-instagram/.

Schaefer, M. *Return on Influence: The Revolutionary Power of Klout, Social Scoring, and Influence Marketing*. New York: McGraw-Hill Education, 2012.

Schonfeld, E. "On eBay, Twitter Followers Are Worth Less Than A Penny Each." TechCrunch, January 31, 2010. http://social.techcrunch.com/2010/01/31/twitter-followers-ebay-penny/.

Schulte, B., Durana, A., Stout, B., & Moyer, J. "Paid Family Leave: How Much Time Is Enough?" New American Foundation, June 16, 2017. https://www.newamerica.org/better-life-lab/reports/paid-family-leave-how-much-time-enough/.

Scott, E., & Jones, A. "'Big Media' Meets the 'Bloggers': Coverage of Trent Lott's Remarks at Strom Thurmond's Birthday Party (No. Case No. C14-04-1731.0)." Harvard University: John F. Ken-

nedy School of Government, 2004. https://case.hks.harvard.edu/big-media-meets-the
-bloggers-coverage-of-trent-lotts-remarks-at-strom-thurmonds-birthday-party/.

Scott, L. "A History of the Influencer, from Shakespeare to Instagram." *New Yorker*, April 21, 2019.
https://www.newyorker.com/culture/annals-of-inquiry/a-history-of-the-influencer-from
-shakespeare-to-instagram.

Segran, E. "Female Shoppers No Longer Trust Ads or Celebrity Endorsements." *Fast Company*,
September 28, 2015. https://www.fastcompany.com/3051491/female-shoppers-no-longer
-trust-ads-or-celebrity-endorsements.

Senft, T. M. *Camgirls: Celebrity and Community in the Age of Social Networks*. New York: Peter
Lang, 2008.

———. "Microcelebrity and the Branded Self." In *Blackwell Companion to New Media Dynamics*, edited by John Hartley, Jean Burgess, and Axel Bruns, 1–9. Malden, MA: Wiley, 2013.

Serazio, M. *Your Ad Here: The Cool Sell of Guerrilla Marketing*. New York: NYU Press, 2013.

Shambaugh, J., Nunn, R., & Bauer, L. "Independent Workers and the Modern Labor Market."
Brookings, June 7, 2018. https://www.brookings.edu/blog/up-front/2018/06/07
/independent-workers-and-the-modern-labor-market/.

Shunatona, B. "Socality Barbie Is Leaving Instagram." *Cosmopolitan*, November 4, 2015. https://
www.cosmopolitan.com/lifestyle/news/a48813/socality-barbie-leaves-instagram/.

Silman, A. "Influencer Gets Bit by Shark for Sick Instagram and It's Totally Worth It." The Cut,
July 11, 2018. https://www.thecut.com/2018/07/influencer-bit-by-shark-for-sick-instagram
-totally-worth-it.html.

Sipka, M. "Selecting the Right Influencers: Three Ways to Ensure Your Influencers Are Effective." *Forbes*, November 17, 2017. https://www.forbes.com/sites/forbesagencycouncil
/2017/11/17/selecting-the-right-influencers-three-ways-to-ensure-your-influencers-are
-effective/.

Smith, A., & Anderson, M. "Social Media Use 2018: Demographics and Statistics." Pew Research Center, March 1, 2018. https://www.pewinternet.org/2018/03/01/social-media-use
-in-2018/.

Smith, C., dir. *Fyre: The Greatest Party That Never Happened*. United States: Netflix, 2019.

Smith, K. "Saturation Point: Fashion's Latest Color Obsession." EDITED, June 6, 2018. https://
blog.edited.com/blog/resources/fashions-latest-color-obsession.

Smythe, D. "Communications: Blindspot of Western Marxism." *Canadian Journal of Political
and Social Theory* 1, no. 3 (1977): 1–27.

Sobande, F. "Spectacularized and Branded Digital (Re)presentations of Black People and Blackness." *Television & New Media* 22, no. 2 (February 2021): 131–46. https://doi.org/10.1177
/1527476420983745.

Stamarski, C. S., & Son Hing, L. S. "Gender Inequalities in the Workplace: The Effects of Organizational Structures, Processes, Practices, and Decision Makers' Sexism." *Frontiers in Psychology* 6 (September 2015): https://doi.org/10.3389/fpsyg.2015.01400.

Starling AI: Advanced Network Analytics for Influencer Marketing. Accessed May 29, 2019.
https://lippetaylor.com/starling-ai.

Statista. "Social Media Use During COVID-19 Worldwide: Statistics and Facts." Statista, February 8, 2022. https://www.statista.com/topics/7863/social-media-use-during-coronavirus
-covid-19-worldwide/#topicHeader__wrapper.

Stephens, D. "To Save Retail, Let It Die." Business of Fashion, September 5, 2017. https://www
.businessoffashion.com/articles/opinion/to-save-retail-let-it-die.

Stevenson, S. "What Your Klout Score Really Means." *Wired*, April 24, 2012. https://www.wired
.com/2012/04/ff-klout/.

Stoldt, R., Wellman, M., Ekdale, B., & Tully, M. "Professionalizing and Profiting: The Rise of
Intermediaries in the Social Media Influencer Industry." *Social Media + Society* 5, no. 1 (January 2019). https://doi.org/10.1177/2056305119832587.

Stone, P. *Opting Out?* Oakland, CA: University of California Press, 2007.

Sullivan, L. "Amazon—Once Again-—Fights Fake Reviews, Click Fraud." MediaPost, July 30,
2018. https://www.mediapost.com/publications/article/322881/amazon-once-again-fights
-fake-reviews-click.html.

Tadena, N. "Lord & Taylor Reaches Settlement with FTC over Native Ad Disclosures." *Wall
Street Journal*, March 15, 2016. https://www.wsj.com/articles/lord-taylor-reaches-settlement
-with-ftc-over-native-ad-disclosures-1458061427.

Talavera, M. "10 Reasons Why Influencer Marketing Is the Next Big Thing." *Adweek*, July 14, 2015.
https://www.adweek.com/digital/10-reasons-why-influencer-marketing-is-the-next-big-thing/.

Tan, Y. (2017, June 20). "Want to Become a Social Media Celeb? There's a College Degree for
That." Mashable, June 20, 2017. https://mashable.com/2017/06/20/wanghong-china-social
-media-star/.

Tashjian, R. "What Happened to Man Repeller?" *GQ*, December 4, 2020. https://www.gq.com
/story/what-happened-to-man-repeller.

Tate, R. "This Is the Perfect Pinterest Picture, According to Science." *Wired*, June 4, 2013. https://
www.wired.com/2013/06/this-is-the-perfect-pinterest-picture/.

Tepper, F. "LIKEtoKNOW.it's App Helps You Buy the Products in Your Screenshots." Tech-
Crunch, March 6, 2017. http://social.techcrunch.com/2017/03/06/liketoknow-it-app
-launch-screenshots/.

Terranova, T. "Free Labor: Producing Culture for the Digital Economy." *Social Text* 18, no. 2 (63)
(Summer 2000): 33–58. https://doi.org/10.1215/01642472-18-2_63-33.

The In Cloud. Data visualization of fashion industry workers, 2014. Accessed on Style.com
website: http://incloud.style.com/.

The Shorty Awards. "Honoring the Best of Social Media and Digital." The Shorty Awards Website. https://shortyawards.com/. Accessed May 17, 2022.

Ticona, J., & Mateescu, A. "Trusted Strangers: Carework Platforms' Cultural Entrepreneurship
in the On-Demand Economy." *New Media & Society* 20, no. 11 (2018): 4384–4404. https://
doi.org/10.1177/1461444818773727.

Tietjen, A. "How RewardStyle Is Using Data to Create Successful Influencer Partnerships."
Women's Wear Daily, July 31, 2018. https://wwd.com/beauty-industry-news/beauty-features
/rewardstyle-data-influencer-partnership-campaigns-1202766954/.

———. "Are Influencers the Escape Social Media Wants during Coronavirus?" *Women's Wear
Daily*, April 2, 2020. https://wwd.com/business-news/media/influencers-coronavirus
-escape-social-media-1203550224/.

———. "Holiday Shopping: ShopStyle Predicts Influencer Sales Will Double." *Women's Wear
Daily,* November 16, 2020. https://wwd.com/fashion-news/fashion-features/shopstyle
-influencer-sales-double-holiday-shopping-1234657179/.

Tokumitsu, M. *Do What You Love: And Other Lies about Success and Happiness.* New York: Regan Arts, 2015.

Tolentino, J. "The Age of Instagram Face." *New Yorker*, December 12, 2019. https://www .newyorker.com/culture/decade-in-review/the-age-of-instagram-face.

Traackr. "Fashion and Beauty Brands Are Studying Influencers' Social Consciousness Sincerity before Choosing Partners." Glossy, March 23, 2020. https://www.glossy.co/sponsored /socially-conscious-brands-are-winning-big-with-influencer-marketing.

Trapp, F. "What Brands Can Learn from Essena O'Neill's Case against Social Media." Alley-Watch, December 2, 2015. https://www.alleywatch.com/2015/12/brands-can-learn-essena -oneills-case-social-media/.

Turner, F. "Machine Politics." *Harper's*, January 2019. https://harpers.org/archive/2019/01 /machine-politics-facebook-political-polarization/.

Turner, G. *Ordinary People and the Media: The Demotic Turn.* London: SAGE, 2010.

——. *Re-Inventing the Media.* London: Routledge, 2015.

Turow, J. *Media Systems in Society: Understanding Industries, Strategies, and Power.* London: Longman, 1997.

——. *The Aisles Have Eyes: How Retailers Track Your Shopping, Strip Your Privacy, and Define Your Power.* New Haven: Yale University Press, 2017.

Van Dijck, J. *Culture of Connectivity.* Oxford: Oxford University Press, 2013.

Vranica, S. "Unilever Demands Influencer Marketing Business Clean Up Its Act." *Wall Street Journal*, June 17, 2018. https://www.wsj.com/articles/unilever-demands-influencer -marketing-business-clean-up-its-act-1529272861.

Wanshel, E. "Adam Pally Hated Presenting at the Shorty Awards and Let Everyone Know It." Huffington Post, 2018. https://www.huffpost.com/entry/adam-pally-shorty-awards_n _5ad62c9de4b077c89ced441f.

Waters, M. "'A True Influencer Program': Inside Walmart's Growing Army of Employee TikTokers." Modern Retail, December 14, 2020. https://www.modernretail.co/retailers/a-true -influencer-program-inside-walmarts-growing-army-of-employee-tiktokers/.

Weber, M. *From Max Weber: Essays in Sociology.* Translated by T. Parsons, 1946. https://archive .org/details/frommaxweberessa00webe.

Wellman, M., Stoldt, R., Tully, M., & Ekdale, B. "Ethics of Authenticity: Social Media Influencers and the Production of Sponsored Content." *Journal of Media Ethics* 35, no. 2 (March 2020): 68–82. https://doi.org/10.1080/23736992.2020.1736078.

WGSN (@WGSN). "More #info than #ad, influencers will continue to use their platform to spread truth and knowledge." Instagram photograph, February 1, 2021. https://www .instagram.com/p/CKwD1EQFGVx/.

Wiener, A. "The Millennial Walt Disney Wants to Turn Empty Stores into Instagram Play-grounds." *New York*, October 4, 2017. http://nymag.com/intelligencer/2017/10/museum -of-ice-cream-maryellis-bunn.html.

Williams, R. "Study: Instagram Leads as Influencer Marketing Platform." Mobile Marketer, July 18, 2018. https://www.mobilemarketer.com/news/study-instagram-leads-as-influencer -marketing-platform/528030/.

Williamson, D.A. "U.S. Social Media Usage: How the Coronavirus Is Changing Consumer Behavior." eMarketer, June 2, 2020. https://www.emarketer.com/content/us-social-media-usage.

Wylie, M. "InstaBrand, SheKnows Media Help Companies Cash in on Social Media Influencers." Bizwomen, September 17, 2015. https://www.bizjournals.com/bizwomen/news/profiles-strategies/2015/09/the-business-of-influence-risks-and-rewards-of.html.

Zubernis, L., & Larsen, K. *Fandom at the Crossroads: Celebration, Shame and Fan/Producer Relationships.* Unabridged edition. Newcastle upon Tyne, UK: Cambridge Scholars Publishing, 2012.

Zuboff, S. "You Are the Object of a Secret Extraction Operation." *New York Times*, November 12, 2021. https://www.nytimes.com/2021/11/12/opinion/facebook-privacy.html.

Index

academia. *See* research; scholarship

ad-blocking, 102

Adorno, Theodor, 141–42

advertising: and American culture, 13, 15–16; banner, 55; and content, 47; deceptive, 103–9; guidelines, 103–5, 111; as inescapable, 102; and influencers, 38, 42, 44–45, 49, 110; niche, 26; retail, 27–29; and social media, 2, 12, 26–27; strategies, 39–40, 111–13. *See also* branding; marketing firms

aesthetics, 88–96, 169

affiliate links, 55, 77–83, 149, 158. *See also* sponsorships

Ajayi, Adesuwa, 134

algorithms, 54, 121, 129, 150–51, 158, 161

Amazon, 149

American Influencer Council (AIC), 152–54, 162

American literature. *See* literature

analytics. *See* data; metrics; quantification

Andrejevic, Mark, 168, 189n25

Ang, Ien, 46

anti-fans, 53, 120

appropriation, 136

Arriagada, Arturo, 42

artificial intelligence, 112, 126

AspireIQ, 143–45

attention economy, 22–23, 168, 189n25

attention spans, 78

audience. *See* engagement; followers

authenticity: and American culture, 2, 16, 179n3; and the audience, 5, 7, 109; definitions of, 7, 56–57, 70, 168–70; digital, 33–34; the downside of, 142–43, 154; evaluating, 131; the evolution of, 103, 122–23, 127, 140, 145, 147, 169; industrial constructions of, 7–9, 168–70; and inequality, 32; and the influencer industry, 6–7, 9, 14, 56, 96–98, 110, 122, 171; and influencers, 57–60, 69–70, 86, 88–90, 114–15, 124, 147, 169; and marketing, 38–39, 55–56, 59, 80, 102; monetizing, 5, 7–8, 13, 28, 32, 55–56; and pods, 121. *See also* realness

authoritarianism, 17, 35, 128, 162

authority, 15, 20, 27, 33, 36

backlash. *See* criticism

Banana Republic, 147

Banet-Weiser, Sarah, 34, 40

banner ads, 55

Barton, Bruce, 15

Baym, Nancy, 51, 54

beauty vloggers, 151

behavior, 14, 20, 160. *See also* social norms

Berger, Jonah, 20

Berger, Ryan, 40, 51, 65, 111, 115

Bernays, Edward, 16, 21, 167

Berry, Jon, 20

Biden, Joe, 156

Bishop, Sophie, 68, 71

Black Lives Matter (BLM), 136

black markets, 87, 109–10

Blackout Tuesday, 137

Blogger, 24

blogging: decline of, 64; and employment, 4, 25–26; fashion, 1–2, 5, 27–28, 30–32, 36–37, 43; mommy, 24, 83; political, 24; and professional standards, 26–27; the rise of, 5; tensions, 37–38. *See also* digital influence

The Blonde Salad, 96–97

Bloomberg, Michael, 143–45, 153

Booker, Cory, 143–45

Boorstin, Daniel, 22, 156

Box, Amber Venz, 77, 79

Box, Baxter, 77

brand ambassadors, 71–72

branding: commercial, 1, 28, 38, 45, 50; humanizing, 39–41, 113, 117, 148; and inequality, 134–35; and licensing, 116–17; personal, 39, 41–45, 50, 68–69, 74, 76, 102, 122, 124; purpose-driven, 137–38, 145; and safety, 71, 92, 116–17, 167; self, 1, 8, 23, 26, 34, 50, 57–58, 64, 98; and technology, 24, 28–29, 68; values, 40–41. *See also* advertising; retail

Braudy, Leo, 22

Bristow, Laurel, 129

Bruneteau, Qianna Smith, 152–53

Bryanboy, 65

bucket system, 71–72, 159

Buy Instagram Followers, 85–86

Campaigns, 79

Cannes Lions, 110

Carteris, Gabrielle, 153–54

celebrity, 21–23, 72–73, 75, 102, 113, 120

Centola, Damon, 188n1

CGI influencers, 113–14, *115*, 126

Chanel, 93

charismatic authority, 15, 179n3

charity, 139

Charnas, Arielle, 133–34

children. *See* youth

"Chocolate Rain," 63

churn and burn, 164–65

Cialdini, Robert, 19–20

civics, 138–39. *See also* government

collaborations, 116–17, 158

Collective Bias, 102

Columbia School, 17

commercialization, 5–10, 14, 27, 30, 76–87, 98–99, 102–3, 159–60, 170–71. *See also* technologies of self-commercialization

commissions, 76–77, 82–83

Committee on Public Information, 15–16

communication norms, 5–7, 130, 142

community leadership, 167

connectivity, 61

conscious commercialization, 30

conspiracy theories, 129–31. *See also* misinformation; propaganda

consulting, 116, 126

content: and advertising, 47, 73–74; and audiences, 46, 48, 66; and authenticity, 88; and branding, 29, 73–74; children's, 117–18; creators, 48; and lessons, 138–41; lifestyle, 75–76, 140; and metrics, 48–50, 54; niche, 63, 67; organic, 69, 74; and public demand, 5; and relatability, 58; social media, 1; sponsored, 27, 55, 58–59, 65, 69–70, 125, 129, 151, 167, 170; and trust, 70, 81, 108, 111–12; user-generated, 159–60. *See also* strategy

contracts, 73, 134, 153

controversy, 100–108, 114. *See also* scandals

conversion, 79

corporate buyouts, 157

Council of Fashion Designers of America, 166

COVID-19, 128–34, 142, 154, 156, 188n1. *See also* vaccination

Craig, David, 163

Creative Artists Agency, 65

creativity, 47–49, 52, 55, 61, 64, 73, 84, 100–102, 116, 164. *See also* risk taking

creator, 163

Creel, George, 15–16

criticism, 13, 53, 63, 97–103, 119–22, 126, 137, 181n78

cult of personality, 22

culture industry, 141–42